Blest Are We®
Faith in Action

Thus faith comes from what is heard,
and what is heard comes through the word of Christ.
Romans 10:17

Peter M. Esposito
President

Anne P. Battes
Publisher

Mary Sellars Malloy
Project Manager

Mary Wessel
Graphic Designer

GRADE SIX
SCHOOL EDITION

RCL Benziger®
a Kendall Hunt Company

"The Subcommittee on the Catechism, United States Conference of Catholic Bishops, has found this catechetical series, copyright 2018 to be in conformity with the *Catechism of the Catholic Church*."

Nihil Obstat Imprimatur

† Most Reverend Joseph R. Binzer
Auxiliary Bishop
Vicar General
Archdiocese of Cincinnati
March 31, 2016

The *nihil obstat* and *imprimatur* are official declarations that a book or pamphlet is free of doctrinal and moral error. No implication is contained therein that those who have granted the *nihil obstat* and *imprimatur* agree with the contents, opinions, or statements expressed.

***Blest Are We* Faith in Action Team**

Contributing Writers
Christina De Camp, Kate Sweeney Ristow, Gloria Shahin, Susan Stark
Resources: Marilyn Miller
Revelation: Scripture and Tradition: Rev. Robert J. Hater, PhD
Special Needs: Ann Sherzer
Take Home: Donna N. Glaser
Feasts and Seasons: Ron Lamping, Jo Rotunno

Theological Consultant
Rev. Robert J. Hater, PhD

Editorial Staff
Karen Cain, Project Editor
James Spurgin, Editorial Manager
Jo Rotunno, Publisher Emerita

Production Staff
Lori Gray, Graphic Designer
Bob Ishee, Production Manager

***Blest Are We* Faith & Word Team**

Series Authors
Rev. Richard N. Fragomeni, Ph.D.; Maureen Gallagher, Ph.D.; Jeannine Goggin, M.P.S.; Michael P. Horan, Ph.D.

Scripture Co-editor and Consultant
Maria Pascuzzi, S.S.L., S.T.D.

Multicultural Consultant
Angela Erevia, M.C.D.P., M.R.E.

Contributing Writers
Dolores Ready, Paul Sansone, Janie Gustafson, Ph.D.
Catholic Schools in America: Robert Kealey, Ph.D.
Feasts and Seasons: Marianne K. Lenihan
Our Catholic Heritage: Joyce A. Crider, Pat Enright

Advisory Board
William C. Allegri, M.A.; Patricia M. Feeley, S.S.J., M.A.; Edmund F. Gordon; Patricia A. Hoffmann; Cris V. Villapando, D.Min.

Consultants
Margaret J. Borders, M.R.S.; Kelly O'Lague Dulka, M.S.W.; Angela Erevia, M.C.D.P., M.R.E.; Diane Hardick, M.A.; Debra Schurko; Linda S. Tonelli, M.Ed.; Joy Vilotti-Biedrzycki

Music Advisors
Alec Harris (GIA Publications)
Kathryn M. Lewis
Robert W. Piercy, Jr. (GIA Publications)

Acknowledgments
Excerpts from the English translation of the *Roman Missal* © 2010, ICEL. All rights reserved.

Excerpts from *Catholic Household Blessings and Prayers* (revised edition) © 2007, United States Conference of Catholic Bishops, Washington, D.C.

Excerpts from *The New American Bible, Revised Edition* © 2010, 1991, 1986, 1970 Confraternity of Christian Doctrine, Inc., Washington, D.C. Used with permission. All rights reserved. All adaptations of Scripture are based on the *New American Bible, Revised Edition.*

Excerpts from the English translation of the *Catechism of the Catholic Church* © 1994, 1997, United States Conference of Catholic Bishops. Libereria Editrice Vaticana. Used with permission. All rights reserved.

601738

ISBN: 978-0-7829-1738-3

2nd Printing

02/2019

Contents

Unit 2

Unit 5 God Promises Us Everlasting Life

Feasts and Seasons

Our Catholic Heritage

Organized according to the four pillars of the Catechism

Let Us Pray

The Sign of the Cross

In the name of the Father,
and of the Son,
and of the Holy Spirit.
Amen.

Signum Crucis

In nómine Patris,
et Fílii,
et Spíritus Sancti.
Amen.

The Lord's Prayer

Our Father, who art in heaven,
hallowed be thy name;
thy kingdom come,
thy will be done
on earth as it is in heaven.
Give us this day our daily bread,
and forgive us our trespasses,
as we forgive those who trespass
against us;
and lead us not into temptation,
but deliver us from evil.
Amen.

Pater Noster

Pater noster, qui es in cælis:
sanctificétur nomen tuum;
advéniat regnum tuum;
fiat volúntas tua,
sicut in cælo, et in terra.
Panem nostrum cotidiánum da
nobis hódie;
et dimítte nobis débita nostra,
sicut et nos dimíttimus
debitóribus nostris;
et ne nos indúcas in tentatiónem;
sed líbera nos a malo.
Amen.

GO TO BlestAreWe.com for Latin and Spanish texts and a Latin pronunciation guide for the Sign of the Cross, the Lord's Prayer, the Hail Mary, and the Glory Be.

Glory Be

Glory be to the Father
and to the Son
and to the Holy Spirit,
as it was in the beginning
is now, and ever shall be
world without end.
Amen.

Gloria Patri

Glória Patri
et Fílio
et Spirítui Sancto.
Sicut erat in princípio,
et nunc et semper
et in sæcula sæculórum.
Amen.

The Hail Mary

Hail, Mary, full of grace,
the Lord is with thee.
Blessed art thou among women
and blessed is the fruit of thy
womb, Jesus.
Holy Mary, Mother of God,
pray for us sinners,
now and at the hour of our death.
Amen.

Ave, Maria

Ave, María, grátia plena,
Dóminus tecum.
Benedícta tu in muliéribus,
et benedíctus fructus ventris
tui, Iesus.
Sancta María, Mater Dei,
ora pro nobis peccatóribus,
nunc et in hora mortis nostræ.
Amen.

GO TO BlestAreWe.com for Latin and Spanish texts and a Latin pronunciation guide for the Sign of the Cross, the Lord's Prayer, the Hail Mary, and the Glory Be.

The Apostles' Creed

I believe in God,
the Father almighty,
Creator of heaven and earth,
and in Jesus Christ, his only Son,
our Lord,
who was conceived by the Holy Spirit,
born of the Virgin Mary,
suffered under Pontius Pilate,
was crucified, died and was buried;
he descended into hell;
on the third day he rose again from
the dead;
he ascended into heaven,
and is seated at the right hand of God
the Father almighty;
from there he will come to judge the
living and the dead.

I believe in the Holy Spirit,
the holy catholic Church,
the communion of saints,
the forgiveness of sins,
the resurrection of the body,
and life everlasting.
Amen.

Roman Missal

(The Nicene Creed may be found
on page 104.)

Hail, Holy Queen

Hail, holy Queen, Mother of mercy: Hail, our life, our sweetness and our hope. To you do we cry, poor banished children of Eve. To you do we send up our sighs, mourning and weeping in this valley of tears. Turn then, most gracious advocate, your eyes of mercy toward us; and after this our exile show unto us the blessed fruit of your womb, Jesus. O clement, O loving, O sweet Virgin Mary. Amen.

Act of Contrition

O my God,
I am sorry and repent with all my heart
for the wrong I have done
and the good I have failed to do,
because by sinning I have offended you,
who are all good and worthy to be loved
above all things.
I firmly resolve, with the help of your grace,
to do penance,
to sin no more,
and to avoid the occasions of sin.
Through the merits of the Passion of
our Savior Jesus Christ,
Lord, have mercy.

Order of Penance

Grace Before Meals

Bless us, O Lord, and these thy gifts,
which we are about to receive from
thy bounty,
through Christ our Lord.
Amen.

Grace After Meals

We give thee thanks, for all thy benefits,
almighty God, who lives and reigns forever.
Amen.

The Rosary

The Rosary is a prayer that honors Mary, the Mother of Jesus, and helps us meditate on the life of Christ. We pray the Rosary using a set of beads. A group of ten beads is called a decade. Before each decade, recall one of the mysteries, or important times in the lives of Mary and Jesus. There are twenty mysteries, shown at right. The prayers for the beads are shown below.

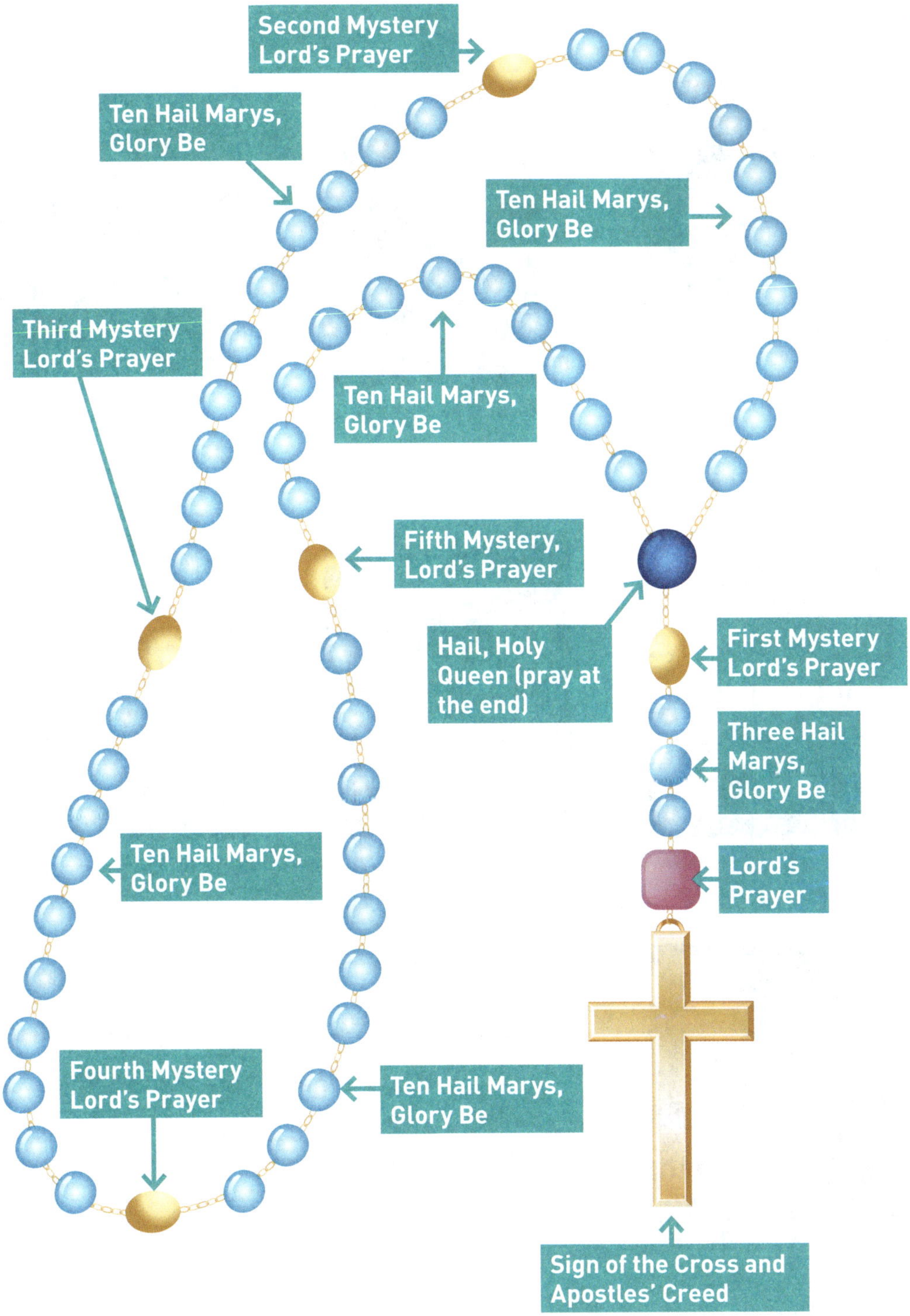

The Mysteries of the Rosary

The Joyful Mysteries

1. The Annunciation
2. The Visitation
3. The Nativity
4. The Presentation in the Temple
5. The Finding of the Child Jesus After Three Days in the Temple

The Luminous Mysteries

1. The Baptism at the Jordan
2. The Miracle at Cana
3. The Proclamation of the Kingdom of God and the Call to Conversion
4. The Transfiguration
5. The Institution of the Eucharist

The Sorrowful Mysteries

1. The Agony in the Garden
2. The Scourging at the Pillar
3. The Crowning with Thorns
4. The Carrying of the Cross
5. The Crucifixion and Death

The Glorious Mysteries

1. The Resurrection
2. The Ascension
3. The Descent of the Holy Spirit at Pentecost
4. The Assumption of Mary
5. The Crowning of the Blessed Virgin as Queen of Heaven and Earth

The Stations of the Cross

1. Jesus is condemned to death.

2. Jesus accepts his cross.

3. Jesus falls the first time.

4. Jesus meets his mother.

5. Simon helps Jesus carry the cross.

6. Veronica wipes the face of Jesus.

7. Jesus falls the second time.

8. Jesus meets the women of Jerusalem.

9. Jesus falls the third time.

10. Jesus is stripped of his clothes.

11. Jesus is nailed to the cross.

12. Jesus dies on the cross.

13. Jesus is taken down from the cross.

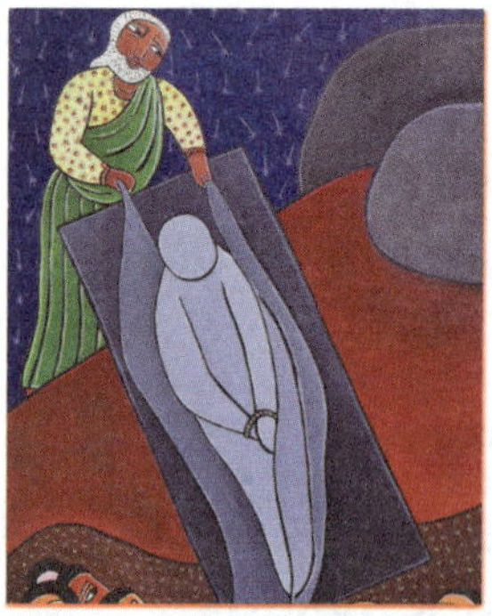
14. Jesus is buried in the tomb.

Some parishes conclude the Stations by reflecting on the Resurrection of Jesus.

A Great Bible Expedition

A Look Inside the Bible

If you were to look at the last page number in the Bible, you would see that the Bible is more than 1,000 pages long! What's inside? There are stories, songs, poems, family histories, letters, wise sayings, parables, prophecies, and many other kinds of writing. Some of the writings date back to about 3,000 years ago. Even the most recently written parts of the Bible are about 2,000 years old. But the Bible is one of the best-selling books of all time, because everything in the Bible has something to reveal about God, human life, and the world.

The Bible is a collection of 73 books. The word Bible comes from the Greek word *biblia*, meaning "books." The Bible is also known as *Scripture*, a word that means "word of God" or "sacred writings." This year you will take a great expedition through Scripture.

You will explore the writings in the first part of the Bible, which is called the Old Testament. These writings describe how God revealed to the Hebrews, or Jewish people, knowledge about himself and his ways. As Catholics, we seek to learn about God with an understanding of our link to the Hebrews. They were the first to hear the Word of God and to form a special relationship with God. That is why we sometimes refer to them as our ancestors in faith. The Old Testament is a collection of 46 books that tell us about the experiences of our ancestors in faith.

You will also study the New Testament, a collection of 27 books that are very important to Catholics and all Christians. These books tell us about the life and teachings of Jesus Christ. He fulfilled the promises God made to our ancestors in faith in the Old Testament.

What Is Your Bible IQ?

How much do you know about the Bible?

Take this fun quiz to find out!

1. The writers of the Bible
- **A** were all disciples of Jesus.
- **B** were inspired by the Holy Spirit.
- **C** wrote what other people told them.
- **D** were all priests.

2. The first part of the Bible is the
- **A** New Testament.
- **B** Old Testament.

3. What body of water parted so the Israelites could escape Egypt?
- **A** Jordan River
- **B** Red Sea
- **C** Dead Sea
- **D** Mediterranean Sea

4. What animal told Eve to eat the fruit of the tree of knowledge?
- **A** a serpent
- **B** a wolf
- **C** a bird
- **D** a mouse

5. What sign did God send to tell Noah there would not be another Great Flood?
- **A** a dove
- **B** a burning bush
- **C** sunshine
- **D** a rainbow

6. According to the Bible, how long did it take God to create the world?
- **A** six days
- **B** five years
- **C** one day
- **D** seven days

7. The man who received the Ten Commandments from God was
- **A** Abraham.
- **B** Jesus.
- **C** Peter.
- **D** Moses.

8. Which angel appeared to Mary to announce to her that she had been chosen to be the mother of the Savior?
- **A** Michael
- **B** Raphael
- **C** Gabriel
- **D** James

9. Who are the four Gospel writers?
- **A** Mark, Luke, John, James
- **B** Mark, Luke, Matthew, John
- **C** Matthew, Mark, Luke, James
- **D** Mark, Paul, John, Peter

10. When Mary and Joseph lost the boy Jesus, they found him
- **A** talking to John the Baptist.
- **B** fishing with the Twelve Apostles.
- **C** changing water into wine at Cana.
- **D** talking to teachers in the Temple.

ANSWER KEY

1. B **2.** B **3.** B **4.** A **5.** D
6. A **7.** D **8.** C **9.** B **10.** D

SCORING

Give yourself one point for each correct answer.

8–11 points	You are a Bible Brainiac!
5–7 points	You get a B in the Bible business!
3–4 points	Brush up on the Bible just a bit!
1–2 points	Don't worry. You will improve your Bible IQ this year!

Important People in the Bible

1. **The Patriarchs**
   Many scholars believed that around 1800 BC the patriarch Abraham, a nomadic shepherd, left Mesopotamia for a land called Canaan, following the call of God. His son Isaac and grandson Jacob also followed the guidance of God. They are known as the patriarchs, or fathers of the faith. At this time, the patriarchs' experiences of God were passed down through the generations by word of mouth.

2. **The Exodus**
   Jacob's son Joseph was taken to Egypt as a slave, but he became a great ruler. His father and brothers moved to Egypt. Their descendants thrived there until Pharaoh, the king of Egypt, made them slaves. God, working through Moses, helped them escape Egypt. They journeyed through the desert, where God gave them the Ten Commandments. Joshua eventually led them to the land God had promised them. It is believed that they conquered Palestine around 1200 BC. The writings that later became part of the Bible were not yet written down.

3. **The Kingdom**
   The Israelites (descendants of Jacob's family) settled in Canaan, the land God had given them. Leaders called Judges helped rule the Israelites, possibly around 1200 to 1000 BC. Eventually, David became king of the southern part of the land. Jerusalem was in its capital. David's son Solomon was king of most of Canaan and built the great Temple. Scribes began to record the ways that God saved the people of Israel.

A Timeline of Bible Events

In the Bible

1200–1000 Judges rule

1800 BC Abraham journeys to Canaan

1700 Joseph and family live in Egypt

1300 Moses and Hebrews leave Egypt

1200 Israelites conquer Palestine

1000 BC King David captures Jerusalem

THE PATRIARCHS | **THE EXODUS** | **THE KINGDOM**

In the World

2000 BC Stonehenge is built in England

1600 First Chinese civilizations develop

1350 Mediterranean peoples migrate to Canaan and Egypt

1200 Iron Age begins in Middle East

1150 BC Olmec civilization in Central America develops

4. The Prophets and the Exile

After Solomon's son became king, the empire divided into Judah in the south and Israel in the north. Prophets such as Isaiah and Micah were called by God to remind the people of their covenant with him. Hezekiah and Josiah were Israel's kings. Each of them worked to eliminate pagan worship and to inspire those they ruled to repent and return to the ways of the Lord. During this time, it is believed that the Babylonians destroyed Jerusalem and the Temple around 587 BC. Many scholars believe that also during this time, many of the ancient writings were being recorded.

5. Greek and Roman Rule

Scholars believed that the Jews had peace during the Persian rule. Alexander the Great conquered the Persian Empire in 332 BC. The Greeks ruled the Jews until about 164 BC. A group of Jews called Maccabees defeated the Greeks. Many scholars believe that by this time, all of the books of the Old Testament had been written. According to historians, Romans began to rule in 63 BC. During the Roman rule, Jesus was born and died. Without knowing the exact time frames, scholars think that the Gospels may have been written in AD 70-100 and the Letters of Paul in AD 50-60. It is believed that the New Testament may have been completed by AD 120.

965-928
Solomon rules and builds temples

928
Kingdom divides

776
First Greek Olympics are held

753
Rome is founded

722
Assyrians conquer Israel

587-537
Jewish exiles live in Babylon

587
Babylonians destroy Jerusalem

539
Jewish exiles allowed to return

THE PROPHETS AND THE EXILE

332
Greeks rule Jews

164
Jews regain independence

110
Trade opens between Far East, Middle East, and Europe

63
Roman rule begins

55
Julius Caesar attacks Britain

6 BC
Jesus is born

AD 30
Jesus dies and rises

GREEK AND ROMAN RULE

The Parts of the Bible

God inspired the Bible. This means that the Holy Spirit guided the writers of the Bible. Because the Bible is the inspired Word of God, it should be treated with respect and care.

Jesus Christ entrusted the interpretation of God's Word to the leaders of the Church. Through the Holy Spirit, the bishops and the pope lead us to a better understanding of the Bible, and Jesus Christ—the eternal Word of God—opens our minds to understand the Bible.

The Bible read by Catholics contains the books that the Church reveres as inspired by God. About AD 400, Saint Jerome, a brilliant priest and scholar, helped the Church decide which books would form the *canon*, or official list, of books of the Bible. He also translated the books of the Bible into Latin for the Latin-speaking Christians. (The books were originally in Greek and Hebrew.) Centuries later, the Bible was divided into chapters and verses. The first translation of the Bible into English was completed in 1384.

Not all religious denominations share the same collections of books. The Protestant Bible contains only 66 books. The Jewish Bible, or Hebrew Scriptures, contains books from the section we call the Old Testament. Here are the books of the Catholic Bible.

OLD TESTAMENT

Pentateuch

(first five books of the Bible, about Israel's covenant with God)

Genesis
Exodus
Leviticus
Numbers
Deuteronomy

(more of the Israelites' story)

Joshua
Judges
Ruth

Historical Books

(Israel's religious history)

1 Samuel
2 Samuel
1 Kings
2 Kings
1 Chronicles
2 Chronicles
Ezra
Nehemiah
Tobit
Judith
Esther
1 Maccabees
2 Maccabees

Wisdom Books

(poetry and instruction)

Job
Psalms
Proverbs
Ecclesiastes
Song of Songs
Wisdom
Sirach

Prophetic Books

(God's Word through the prophets)

Isaiah
Jeremiah
Lamentations
Baruch
Ezekiel
Daniel
Hosea
Joel
Amos
Obadiah
Jonah
Micah
Nahum
Habakkuk
Zephaniah
Haggai
Zechariah
Malachi

NEW TESTAMENT

The Gospels

(life and teachings of Jesus)

Matthew
Mark
Luke
John

Acts of the Apostles

(works of the early Church)

Letters

(letters to early Christians)

Romans
1 Corinthians
2 Corinthians
Galatians
Ephesians
Philippians
Colossians
1 Thessalonians
2 Thessalonians
1 Timothy
2 Timothy
Titus
Philemon
Hebrews
James
1 Peter
2 Peter
1 John
2 John
3 John
Jude

Book of Revelation

(apocalyptic writing)

How to Find Scripture Passages

The Bible is divided into books. The books are divided into chapters. The chapters are divided into verses. For example, Exodus 19:8-9 means:

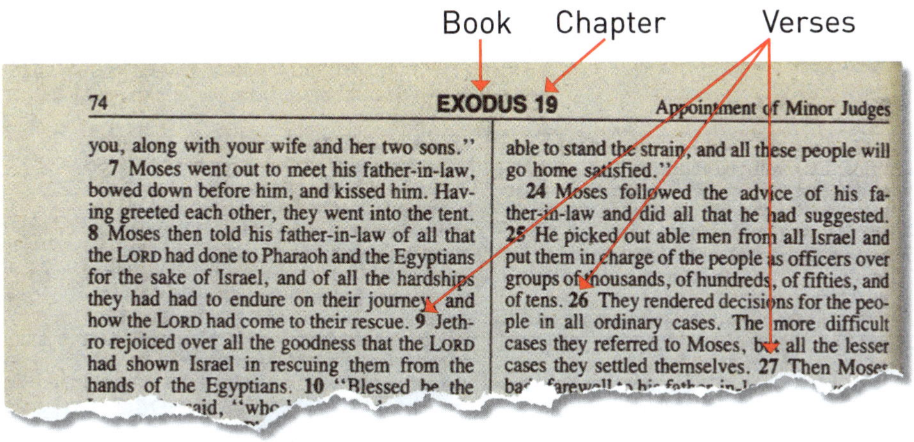

74 **EXODUS 19** Appointment of Minor Judges

you, along with your wife and her two sons."
7 Moses went out to meet his father-in-law,
bowed down before him, and kissed him. Hav-
ing greeted each other, they went into the tent.
8 Moses then told his father-in-law of all that
the LORD had done to Pharaoh and the Egyptians
for the sake of Israel, and of all the hardships
they had had to endure on their journey and
how the LORD had come to their rescue. 9 Jeth-
ro rejoiced over all the goodness that the LORD
had shown Israel in rescuing them from the
hands of the Egyptians. 10 "Blessed be the

able to stand the strain, and all these people will
go home satisfied."
24 Moses followed the advice of his fa-
ther-in-law and did all that he had suggested.
25 He picked out able men from all Israel and
put them in charge of the people as officers over
groups of thousands, of hundreds, of fifties, and
of tens. 26 They rendered decisions for the peo-
ple in all ordinary cases. The more difficult
cases they referred to Moses, but all the lesser
cases they settled themselves. 27 Then Moses

To find a Scripture passage, follow these three simple steps. Try to use the steps to find Matthew 5:1-12.

1. Find the name of the book you need in the Table of Contents at the front of your Bible. The book of Matthew is in the New Testament.
2. In the same list, find the page number of the book you need. This will tell you the page on which the book begins. Turn to that page within your Bible.
3. Now turn the pages until you find the chapter you need. The chapter number is shown either next to the name of the book at the very top of the page or as a large number within paragraphs on the page. When you find the chapter, locate the verses using the small numbers within the paragraphs.

The Types of Writing in the Bible

The following are some of the types of writing found in the Bible.

Songs: *Poems or hymns that are often prayers. Example: The Book of Psalms*

Laws: *Instructions on how to behave. Example: Deuteronomy*

Parables: *Tales that teach a moral lesson. Example: The parable of the Persistent Widow*

Letters: *Written messages from one person or group to another. Example: Paul's letter to the Romans*

Prophecies: *Messages from God told through the words of prophets Example: Ezekiel*

Blest Are We

Words and Music by David Haas
Spanish translation by Ronald F. Krisman

2. For the poor, the meek and the lowly:
We are called, called to serve!
For the weak, the sick and the hungry:
We are called, called to serve!

3. For all those who yearn for freedom:
We are called, called to serve!
For the world, to be God's kingdom:
We are called, called to serve!

2. Por los pobres, los mansos y humildes:
¡Somos llamados para servir!
Por los enfermos, hambrientos, y débiles:
¡Somos llamados para servir!

3. Por los que sufren y quieren ser librados:
¡Somos llamados para servir!
Venga a nosotros el Reino de los Cielos:
¡Somos llamados para servir!

We Answer God's Call

Unit 1

Abraham and Sarah are our ancestors in faith because they responded to God's call to holiness and fidelity. God calls each of us to be faithful to his word and to lead others in holiness.

> The LORD said to Abram: Go forth from your land, your relatives, and from your father's house to a land that I will show you.
>
> Genesis 12:1

Abraham and Sarah traveled across the desert, just as these nomads are doing. The map shows their journey.

I Say "Yes," Lord/ Digo "Sí," Señor

Words and Music by Donna Peña

Getting ready for Chapter 1

Take Home

Revelation and Response

This chapter introduces the story of our ancestors in faith with the Old Testament figures Abraham and Sarah, who accepted God's plan even though they were unsure of what God had in store for them. Like Abraham and Sarah, we often experience challenges that make us wonder about God's plan for us and how he expects us to respond.

ACTIVITY **Faithful Followers Tree**

Create a colorful tree showing people of faith you know. Include a photo and what you know about major events in each person's life, as well as the dates of his or her Baptism, First Communion, Confirmation, and so on.

THROUGH THE WEEK

A Prayer for the Week Lord, may we learn from the example of your faithful servants Abraham, Sarah, and Saint Joseph, to trust in your love and surrender to your will. Amen.

ON SUNDAY
At Mass, listen to the readings and the homily. Did you hear stories about people whose faith helped them through major changes? Discuss the homily with your family or friends.

ON THE WEB
BlestAreWe.com
RCLBLectionary.com
SaintsResource.com

Saint Joseph, Husband of Mary

Saint Joseph was chosen by God to be the protector of Jesus and Mary. He carried out this calling with fidelity and humility. He is an example for us of trust in God and obedience to his will.

Patron Saint of: the universal Church

Feast Day: March 19

Take Home

Scripture Background
Before the Time of Jesus

ABRAHAM A link that binds Christians, Jews, and Muslims is a reverence for Abraham, our common ancestor in faith. Although each religion honors Abraham differently, both Jews and Christians consider Abraham an essential patriarch of faith because of the covenant God established with him. Muslims honor Abraham as one among many who exhibit *islam*, or unconditional surrender to God's will. Learn more about Abraham's faith in God and obedience to him by reading Genesis 12:1–9 and 22:1–12.

Our Catholic Tradition in the Old Testament

A COMMON ANCESTOR God promised Abraham, "I will bless you abundantly and make your descendants as countless as the stars" (Genesis 22:17). Today, thousands of years later, followers of Christianity, Islam, and Judaism consider Abraham part of their religious heritage. Christianity has about 2.2 billion followers, including Catholics, Protestants, and members of the Eastern Orthodox Church. (An Eastern Orthodox cathedral is shown at left.) Islam is the religion of more than 1.5 billion people. Followers of Judaism number about 14 million people.

Revelation and Response

Chapter 1

How varied are your works, LORD! . . .
[T]he earth is full of your creatures.
All of these look to you
to give them food in due time. Psalm 104:24, 27

Share

Even though we can't see the spirit of God with our eyes, we can experience God's presence in many ways. When was a time when you felt God's presence?

ACTIVITY

Complete the following sentences with words that describe ways that God is with us. Some of the letters in the words are already filled in for you.

1. God speaks to us when we read the

   ___ c r [___] ___ ___ u r ___ s.

2. When we tell God our feelings and thoughts

   in ___ r [___] y ___ r, God responds to us.

3. We can see God's work in the beauty of

   n ___ [___] ___ r e.

4. Sometimes we feel closest to God in

   s ___ l ___ ___ c e, when everything is quiet.

5. God's love is in the [___] ___ n ___ s that reach out to us when we share the Sign of Peace.

6. In the Sacrament of Penance and Reconciliation,

   we celebrate God's [___] ___ r g ___ v ___ n ___ ___ s.

Now unscramble the boxed letters to spell the secret word.

Secret word: ___ ___ ___ ___ ___

How should we respond to God?

Hear and Believe **Scripture**

Abraham and Sarah

Our story of faith began almost 4,000 years ago with Abram, who was a descendant of Noah. Abram and his wife, Sarai, were nomadic shepherds, or shepherds who moved around in search of new pastures. They had been married for a long time but had no children.

When Abram and Sarai were old and living with relatives in a land called Haran, the Lord spoke to Abram.

> **The LORD said to Abram: Go forth from your land, your relatives, and from your father's house to a land that I will show you. I will make of you a great nation, and I will bless you; I will make your name great, so that you will be a blessing. . . . All the families of the earth will find blessing in you.** Genesis 12:1–3

Abram and Sarai did as the Lord said. They set off for the new land. At Shechem, a holy place in the land of Canaan, the Lord spoke to Abram again.

> **The LORD appeared to Abram and said: To your descendants I will give this land. So Abram built an altar there to the LORD who had appeared to him.** Genesis 12:7

Abram and Sarai moved on. They eventually settled in Canaan. Years passed. The Lord again spoke to Abram and said:

> **. . . Look up at the sky and count the stars, if you can. Just so, he added, will your descendants be. Abram put his faith in the LORD, . . .** Genesis 15: 5,6

When Abram was ninety-nine years old, the Lord again appeared to him and said:

> **. . . No longer will you be called Abram; your name will be Abraham, for I am making you the father of a multitude of nations. . . . I will give to you and to your descendants after you . . . the whole land of Canaan, . . . and I will be their God. . . . For your part, you and your descendants after you must keep my covenant throughout the ages.** Genesis 17:1,5,8,9

Then the Lord told Abraham to call his wife, Sarai, by a new name, *Sarah,* which means "princess". As God had promised, Sarah gave birth to a son, Isaac. Abraham and Sara were filled with joy at all that God had done.

To read the complete account in Scripture see Genesis 12:1–7; 13:1–4; 15:1, 5–6; 17:1–9, 15–16; 21:1–7.

Models of Faith

Abraham and Sarah's trust in God and his promises showed their great **faith**. They left for an unknown land. They trusted that God's promises would come true. They lived this definition of faith: "Faith is the realization of what is hoped for and evidence of things not seen" (Hebrews 11:1). Isaac's birth was a gift and a sign of the special relationship God had formed with Abraham and Sarah. They would have many descendants who would become the nation of Israel.

When God asked Abraham to follow him, he was beginning a special relationship with the Hebrews, the ancestors of Jewish people. God called the Hebrews "my people." This relationship eventually embraced all people. God said to Abraham, ". . . All the families of the earth will find blessing in you" (Genesis 12:3). Because of Abraham's great faith, God fulfilled this promise and made Abraham the father of countless descendants. Abraham is the **patriarch**, or father, in faith for both Jews and Christians. He is our own father in faith. Muslims, who trace their religion back to him, also honor him.

Faith Words

faith
Faith is the assurance of things hoped for, the conviction of things not seen.

patriarch
A *patriarch*, a term meaning "father," is a great leader of the Hebrews from early Scripture times. A patriarch is also the male leader of a family or clan.

ACTIVITY

The Lord told Abraham,

"... Walk in my presence and be blameless." Genesis 17:1

Imagine that you have been asked to create music that captures the meaning of God's message. In the space below, write six song titles that express ways to walk in God's presence and be blameless (for example, Pray Every Day). Or design a page for an online music streaming site, using drawings, words, or symbols that capture the meaning of God's words.

What are some of the ways God speaks to us today?

Hear and Believe **Scripture**

Mary Says Yes

All Jews descended from Abraham. In the New Testament, the Gospel writer Matthew lists the ancestors of Jesus' family, beginning with Abraham. This helps us understand how God's promise to Abraham, ". . . All the families of the earth will find blessing in you" (Genesis 12:3) came true. In the Gospel of Luke, we read that God's promise to Abraham could not have come true without a certain woman's faith.

The angel Gabriel was sent to a town in Galilee called Nazareth, to a virgin named Mary, who was to marry Joseph. Gabriel appeared to Mary and said:

> **"Behold, you will conceive in your womb and bear a son, and you shall name him Jesus. He will be great and will be called the Son of the Most High, . . ."** Luke 1:31,32

Gabriel then told Mary that Jesus would rule over Abraham's house and that his kingdom would never end. Like her ancestors Abraham and Sarah, Mary trusted God. She believed that nothing was impossible for God and that what God promised her would come true.

> **Mary said, "Behold, I am the handmaid of the Lord. May it be done to me according to your word."** Luke 1:38

To read the complete account in Scripture see Luke 1:26–38.

Our Church Teaches

Catholics believe in **Revelation**, or God's act of revealing himself in words and in deeds. We can know God by reading and learning the Scriptures, and by living our faith according to the Tradition of the Church passed down by the Apostles. We can speak with God in prayer. We can know about God through his works, such as creation. We also know his presence through the grace of the Sacraments, especially in the Eucharist. God's love for us is so great that he reveals himself to us through his Son, Jesus Christ.

Abraham and Sarah responded to God's Revelation with open hearts. They sought to know God's will, and they obeyed it completely. Saint Paul called this type of response to God "the obedience of faith" (see Romans 16:26). In the same way, Mary, the Mother of Jesus, trusted God's promise. When the angel told her she was going to be the mother of God's Son, Mary did not understand how this could be, yet she answered, ". . . May it be done to me according to your word" (Luke 1:38). Catholics are devoted to Mary. She is a perfect model of faith.

GO TO page 370 to learn more about Mary's great faith.

We Believe

People with faith in God welcome God's Revelation. They accept God's will and obey it completely.

Faith Words

Revelation
Revelation is God's act of revealing himself and inviting us to respond with faith.

ACTIVITIES

1. Describe someone you know personally or someone from the news or from history who shows faith in God. List some qualities of this person that you admire.

____

____

____

2. In the New Testament we read:

"What good is it, my brothers, if someone says he has faith but does not have works?" (James 2:14)

Using each of the letters of the word *faith*, create new words that describe some works performed by faithful people (for example: Feeding the hungry).

In what ways does God reveal himself to us today?

Respond

Complete Trust

God invites ordinary people to do his work. We might react to this with doubt and confusion. Even Abraham, Sarah, and Mary had questions about what God expected of them. Yet they trusted in him completely.

ACTIVITIES

1. Read the three stories. Complete the third story by writing on the lines how Rosa can respond with faith.

Abraham

Abraham believed in God's promise to make him the father of nations. In the beginning, he showed his devotion to God without words. He built altars to worship God at each stage of his journey to Canaan. Later, Abraham gave the Lord a gentle reminder that he was still waiting for his promise to be fulfilled.

[Abraham] said,

"... Lord GOD, what can you give me, if I die childless ... ?" (Genesis 15:2)

God told Abraham he did not forget his promise, and Abraham believed. Then God blessed Abraham and Sarah with a baby boy.

Mary

An angel told the Blessed Virgin Mary that she would be the mother of the Son of God. [Mary asked] the angel, "How can this be, since I have no [husband]?" (Luke 1:34) In reply, the angel assured her that nothing is impossible for God. Mary accepted what the angel told her, saying, "... May it be done to me according to your word." (Luke 1:38).

Rosa

Rosa and her religion class were working hard to organize a sixth-grade prayer service. They chose Scripture readings, rehearsed songs, and practiced a candle-lighting ceremony.

Rosa was busy gluing letters onto a banner for the service. Being in the background was fine with Rosa. She stuttered when she was nervous, so she was happy that she didn't have a visible role in the service. Then her teacher approached her.

"Rosa," said her teacher, "you are an excellent reader. Will you read the First Reading at the prayer service?"

Rosa couldn't believe what her teacher was asking. Rosa thought for a moment before she responded. How could she stand up and read in front of everyone?

2. **Describe a time when God helped you face a challenging situation. Tell how your trust in God helped you overcome your fears. Then tell what this experience taught you about trusting in God.**

How might we pray when we are not sure of God's plan for us?

A Prayer of Trust

Abraham's faithful offerings and prayers to God are important examples of prayer from the Old Testament. Thomas Merton, a well-known monk and writer who lived from 1915 to 1968, wrote the following prayer of trust in God. After each part, repeat:

I trust you always, though I may seem to be lost.

My Lord God,
I have no idea where I am going.
I do not see the road ahead of me.
I cannot know for certain where it will end.
Nor do I really know myself,
and the fact that I think I am following
your will does not mean that I am
actually doing so.

But I believe that the desire to please you
does in fact please you.
And I hope I have that desire in all that I am doing.
I hope that I will never do anything apart
from that desire.

And I know that if I do this
you will lead me by the right road, though I
may know nothing about it.
Therefore I will trust you always though I
may seem to be lost and in the shadow
of death.

I will not fear, for you are ever with me,
and you will never leave me to face my
perils alone. Amen.

Chapter Review 1

A **Write** a brief summary of what you learned in this chapter, using the words in the box.

Abraham	ancestors	God	Isaac	Mary	Sarah	trust

____

____

____

____

____

B **Match** Column A with Column B by writing the correct number in the space provided.

A	B
1. faith	_____ a great leader of the Hebrews from early Scripture times, or the male leader of a family or clan
2. Revelation	_____ the assurance of things hoped for, the conviction of things not seen
3. patriarch	_____ God's act of revealing who he is and inviting us to respond with faith

C **Write** the name of the person or people described by each clue.

1. We are the ancestors of the Jews; God called us "my people."

____

2. I am the patriarch of faith for both Jews and Christians, and a person honored by Muslims. _____________________

3. I am the son of Abraham and Sarah. _____________________

4. Catholics are devoted to me and view me as a perfect model of faith. _____________________

1 Chapter Review

D **Complete** the following sentences.

1. People with faith in God long to understand and obey his

   ____________________.

2. The patriarch ____________________ and his wife ____________________ are models of faith because they responded to God with open hearts.

3. "____" is what Saint Paul called the act of seeking God's will and then obeying it completely.

4. Because of Abraham's great ____________________, God fulfilled his promise and made him the father of countless descendants.

5. Our story of faith began almost 4,000 years ago with Abraham,

   who was a descendant of ____________________.

E **Respond** to the following.

1. How did Mary show her trust in God's promise?

   ____

   ____

   ____

2. What are some ways in which you show your trust in God?

   ____

   ____

   ____

3. Write a prayer that expresses your trust in God.

   ____

   ____

   ____

   ____

Take Home

Sacrifice and Promise

Abraham was committed to following God's plan even when God told him to sacrifice his son Isaac. Although Abraham did not understand God's will, he had such strong faith that he was willing to do what God asked. Jesus too showed complete obedience to God the Father, even to the point of sacrificing his own life, so that we might have life everlasting.

Sacrifice for Others Week

Day	Name	Sacrifice	✓
Monday	Judith	Cook meal for neighbor.	
Tuesday	Danielle	Check on Mrs. Sisto's cat.	
Wednesday	Jennifer	Take Joe fishing.	
Thursday	Joe	Mow Grandpa's lawn.	
Friday	Paul	Drive Judith's mom to the airport	

ACTIVITY **Weekly Sacrifices**

Make this "Sacrifice for Others Week." Create a chart listing each family member's name next to a different day of the week. Have each person fill in something he or she will do or has done that day to help another person or another family.

THROUGH THE WEEK

A Prayer for the Week Heavenly Father, in your great love for us you sacrificed your only Son. Teach us to respond to your love with the zeal and conviction of Saint Andrew Kim Taegŏn. Amen.

ON SUNDAY
The Mass celebrates Jesus' sacrifice of his life and the promise of our salvation. Listen for the words *sacrifice* and *promise* at Mass.

ON THE WEB
BlestAreWe.com
RCLBLectionary.com
SaintsResource.com

Saint Andrew Kim Taegŏn (1821–1846)

Saint Andrew Kim Taegŏn lived in Korea during a time when Christians who lived there were persecuted. In spite of great risk, Andrew Kim lived out his faith. He traveled to Macao, China, to study for the priesthood. When he returned to Korea, he was arrested and executed.

Feast Day: September 20

Take Home

Scripture Background
Before the Time of Jesus

THE TESTING OF ABRAHAM In the Old Testament, we read of Abraham and his near-sacrifice of his son Isaac. It is hard for us to understand Abraham's willingness to sacrifice his own child, and even harder to understand why God would call upon Abraham to make such a sacrifice. This story shows that Abraham truly believes in God and his plan. Fittingly, the story of Abraham's willingness to sacrifice his son is read at the Easter Vigil liturgy, when we celebrate Jesus' acceptance of his Father's will, and his great sacrifice and Resurrection. Read about the testing of Abraham in Genesis 22.

Our Catholic Tradition in Art

THE SACRIFICE OF ISAAC
The story of Abraham and Isaac represents a profound test of a human's faith in and obedience to God. The Bible account of this story also affords a very dramatic subject for a religious painting. In his masterpiece, *The Sacrifice of Isaac* (1603), the Italian painter Caravaggio emphasized the contrast between light and dark to heighten dramatic impact. This painting can now be seen in the Uffizi Gallery in Florence, Italy.

Sacrifice and Promise

Chapter 2

... [O]ffer spiritual sacrifices acceptable to God through Jesus Christ. 1 Peter 2:5

Share

A dictionary definition of the word *sacrifice* is "giving up one thing for another thing thought to be more valuable." As Christians, we make sacrifices when we put God and the care of others first. In your own life you make sacrifices when you do good things that might help other people instead of more self-centered things. Each day, you can make trade-offs between things you really want and things that are better for other people or yourself.

ACTIVITY

Write the letter of each Column B item next to the Column A item for which you could trade it. Number 5 has been done for you. What word do the letters spell when you are done?

Column A	Column B
____ **1.** Talk on the phone	**C.** Make friends with kids who seem lonely.
____ **2.** Go out with your friends.	**E.** Clean up your room.
____ **3.** Make friends with only the popular kids at school.	**I.** Donate some money to a good cause.
____ **4.** Use the computer to play games.	**I.** Help set the table for dinner.
_I_ **5.** Watch TV until dinner.	**S.** Talk to God in prayer.
____ **6.** Eat your favorite snack.	**C.** Share your belongings.
____ **7.** Save up money to buy lots of things for yourself.	**R.** Use your computer for homework.
____ **8.** Hide your belongings so that others cannot use them.	**A.** Go to Mass with your family.
____ **9.** Throw your clothes on the floor of your room.	**F.** Give up your favorite snack for Lent.

What great sacrifice was Abraham asked to make?

Easter Vigil Reading

At the Easter Vigil liturgy, we celebrate the great sacrifice and Resurrection of Jesus. The Second Reading, which is from Genesis 22, is about a great **sacrifice** *that proved Abraham's faith in God.*

Some time afterward, God put Abraham to the test and said to him: Abraham! "Here I am!" he replied. Then God said: Take your son Isaac, your only one, whom you love, and go to the land of Moriah. There offer him up as a burnt offering on one of the heights that I will point out to you. . . .

When they came to the place of which God had told him, Abraham built an altar there and arranged the wood on it. . . . Then Abraham reached out and took the knife to slaughter his son. But the angel of the LORD called to him from heaven, "Abraham, Abraham!" "Here I am," he answered. "Do not lay your hand on the boy," said the angel. "Do not do the least thing to him. For now I know that you fear God, since you did not withhold from me your son, your only one." Abraham looked up and saw a single ram caught by its horns in the thicket. So Abraham went and took the ram and offered it up as a burnt offering in place of his son. . . .

A second time the angel of the LORD called to Abraham from heaven and said: "I swear by my very self—oracle of the LORD—that because you acted as you did in not withholding from me your son, your only one, I will bless you and make your descendants as countless as the stars of the sky and the sands of the seashore; your descendants will take possession of the gates of their enemies, and in your descendants all the nations of the earth will find blessing, because you obeyed my command."

Genesis 22:1–2, 9a, 10–13, 15–18

Faith in the Promise

In Abraham's time, people believed that gods controlled their fate. To stay on the gods' good side, or to ask for special favors, they offered sacrifices of animals, food, or firstborn sons to them. But Abraham offered sacrifices to the one, true God. He did not do this in exchange for special favors, but as a way to express his feelings toward the Lord. He offered a holocaust, or burnt offering, as a loving gift to God.

Imagine how confused Abraham felt when the Lord asked him to sacrifice his own child, Isaac! Abraham knew that the Lord's promise depended upon Isaac. God had promised Abraham countless descendants. Isaac needed to grow up and have children of his own. If Abraham tried to understand God's command without having faith, he might have refused to make the sacrifice.

In our own relationship with God, faith is an essential element. Without faith, we could not accept that to have eternal life we must participate in Jesus' sacrifice through the Eucharist. In the Gospels, when Jesus explained this to crowds of people who followed him, they questioned him. How were they going to eat his Body and drink his Blood? Jesus answered, "... [U]nless you eat the flesh of the Son of Man and drink his blood, you do not have life within you" (John 6:53). Jesus Christ invites us to receive his Body and Blood so we can share in everlasting life.

Faith Words

sacrifice
A sacrifice is an act of unselfish giving. It is also a ritual offering made to God by a priest on behalf of the people.

ACTIVITY

In the New Testament, we read that we should offer ourselves as a "living sacrifice" (see Romans 12:1). In this way, we fully join in Jesus' sacrifice of his Body and Blood at Mass. What does it mean to be a living sacrifice? Look at the picture here. How is it an example of a living sacrifice? List three ways you can offer yourself as a living sacrifice.

____

____

____

____

____

What sacrifice can we make?

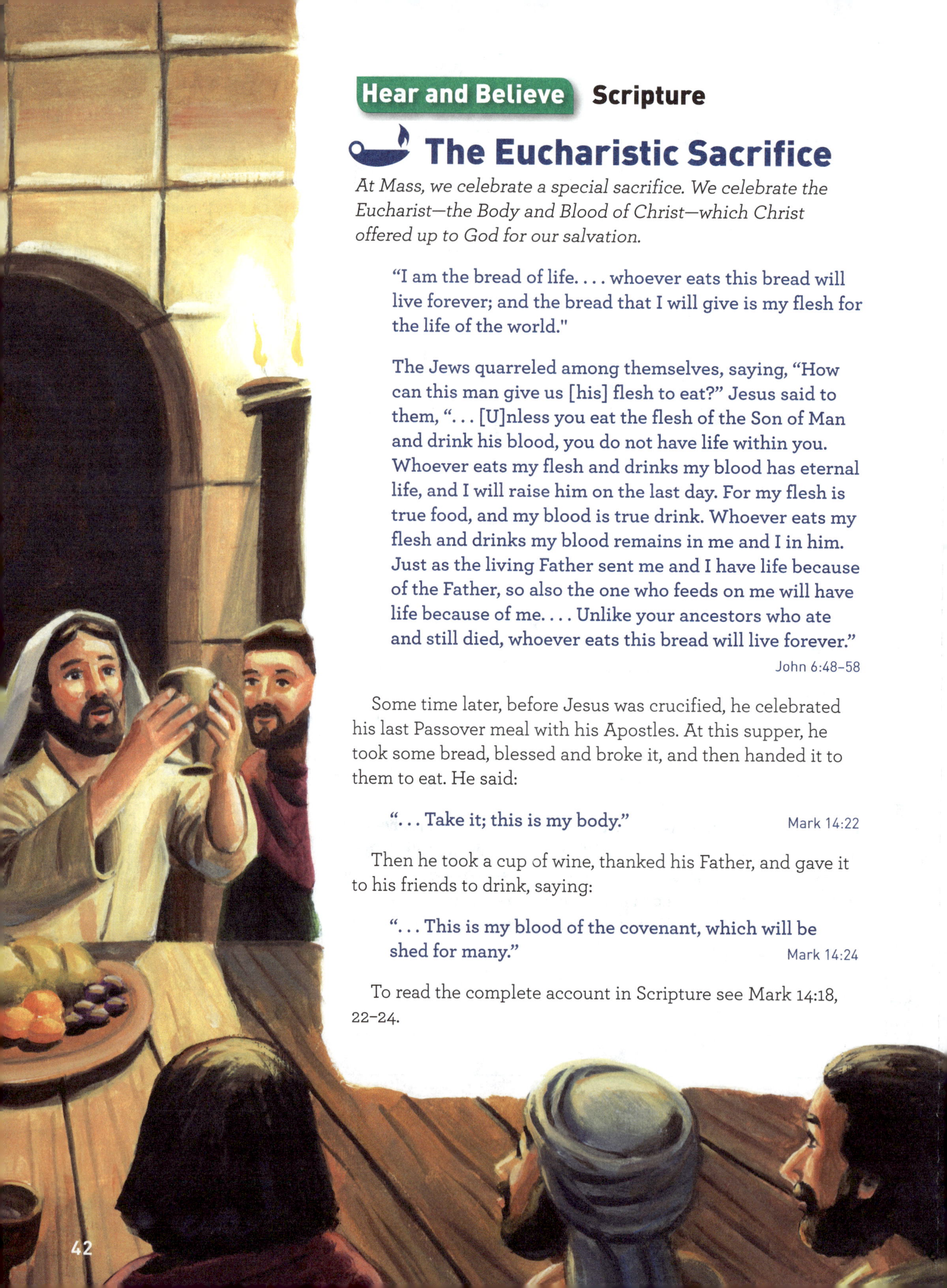

Hear and Believe **Scripture**

The Eucharistic Sacrifice

At Mass, we celebrate a special sacrifice. We celebrate the Eucharist—the Body and Blood of Christ—which Christ offered up to God for our salvation.

> "I am the bread of life. . . . whoever eats this bread will live forever; and the bread that I will give is my flesh for the life of the world."
>
> The Jews quarreled among themselves, saying, "How can this man give us [his] flesh to eat?" Jesus said to them, ". . . [U]nless you eat the flesh of the Son of Man and drink his blood, you do not have life within you. Whoever eats my flesh and drinks my blood has eternal life, and I will raise him on the last day. For my flesh is true food, and my blood is true drink. Whoever eats my flesh and drinks my blood remains in me and I in him. Just as the living Father sent me and I have life because of the Father, so also the one who feeds on me will have life because of me. . . . Unlike your ancestors who ate and still died, whoever eats this bread will live forever."
>
> John 6:48–58

Some time later, before Jesus was crucified, he celebrated his last Passover meal with his Apostles. At this supper, he took some bread, blessed and broke it, and then handed it to them to eat. He said:

> ". . . Take it; this is my body." Mark 14:22

Then he took a cup of wine, thanked his Father, and gave it to his friends to drink, saying:

> ". . . This is my blood of the covenant, which will be shed for many." Mark 14:24

To read the complete account in Scripture see Mark 14:18, 22–24.

Our Church Teaches

An **altar** is a raised place for sacrifice and worship. Abraham built altars for God wherever God spoke to him. At Mass, the changing of bread and wine into Christ's Body and Blood takes place on an altar. This altar is also a table, a place where we gather to share a meal and to celebrate that Jesus sacrificed himself for us. At Mass, we commemorate the Last Supper, when Jesus Christ gave his friends his Body and Blood under the appearances of bread and wine. Faithful to the Lord's command at the Last Supper, we continue to gather to share the Eucharistic meal.

We Believe

The Lord calls us to his table to receive his Body and Blood in the Eucharist. When we receive the Eucharist, we receive new life in Christ, who sacrificed his own life for us.

Faith Words

altar
An altar is a raised place where sacrifices are offered. The altar used for the center of worship during the Mass is also a table, where we gather to share the Eucharistic meal.

ACTIVITY

At the Last Supper, Jesus said, "I will not leave you orphans; I will come to you" (John 14:18). When we receive the Body and Blood of Jesus Christ in the Eucharist, the Holy Spirit comes to us. He remains in us, and we remain in him.

Write a prayer thanking Jesus for the gift of the Eucharist.

____

____

____

____

____

____

____

____

____

____

What types of sacrifices do we make in our families?

Respond

Giving Blood

A girl named Christina suffered from a rare and serious disease. Her only chance for recovery seemed to be a blood transfusion from her five-year-old brother, Vincent. Vincent's blood had special fighting cells that Christina needed to get better. The doctor explained the situation to Vincent and his parents.

Vincent hesitated for a second, then took a deep breath and said, "I'll give my blood if it will save Christina."

The transfusion, or transfer of blood, from Vincent to Christina began. Vincent smiled when the color started to return to Christina's cheeks. Then his smile faded and his face grew pale. He looked up at the doctor and asked with a trembling voice, "Will I start to die right away?" He had misunderstood the doctor—he thought he was going to have to give his sister all of his blood!

What was Vincent's sacrifice? What did he think he was doing?

What does this tell you about Vincent?

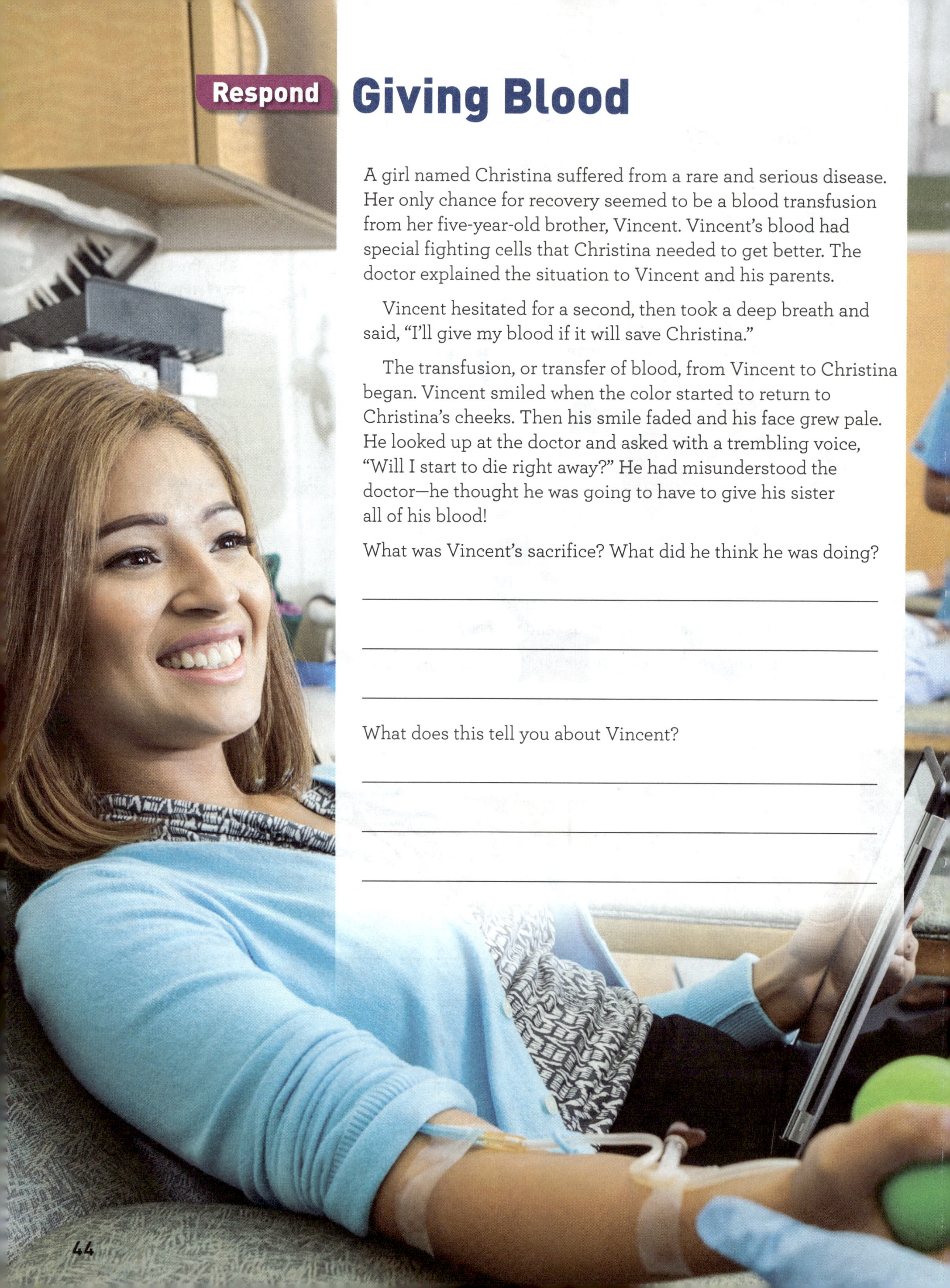

ACTIVITIES

1. God kept his promise to Abraham by sparing Isaac's life. Imagine that you are Isaac living in modern-day times. You want to send an e-mail to a friend about what happened that day in Moriah. In the screen below, describe what God promised your father, your feelings that day, and how God kept his promise.

To

From

Subject

2. Write a journal entry about promises you have made in your own life. At the end of your entry, write one small thing you promise to do this week for someone else.

How can we honor Jesus' sacrifice in our prayers?

A Blessing Prayer

Jewish families celebrate the Sabbath from sundown on Friday to sundown on Saturday. They end the Sabbath with a ritual called Havdalah. With a braided candle, sweet spices, and a cup of wine, they gather and pray this blessing prayer:

Wine Blessing: Blessed are you, Lord, God of all creation;
you have given us the fruit of the vine.

Spice Blessing: Blessed are you, Lord, God of all creation,
Creator of the spices that bring sweetness
and joy to our lives.

Candle Blessing: Blessed are you, Lord, God of all creation,
Creator of the light of fire.

All: **Blessed is the Lord, who separated the**
Sabbath day from the other days.

Based on the Jewish Havdalah prayers

The family then puts the candle out and wishes each other a good week.

Leader: Let us now ask God to bless the food we eat, that it may strengthen us to do his work.

All: **Having received the Bread of heaven**
from your abundance, O Lord,
we pray that it may give us
such hope and strength for our labor,
that we may provide effectively for our own needs
and for those of our brothers and sisters.
Through Christ our Lord. Amen.

Prayer after Communion,
Mass in Time of Famine or for Those Suffering Hunger,
Roman Missal

Chapter Review 2

A **Complete** the sentences, using words from the box. Not all words will be used.

Eucharist	Jesus	sacrifice
Last Supper	Body and Blood	altar

1. A ____________________ is an act of unselfish giving, or a ritual offering made to God by a priest on behalf of the people.

2. A raised place where sacrifices are offered is called an ____________________. It is the center of worship during the Mass.

3. The changing of bread and wine into Christ's

   ____________________________________ takes place on an altar.

4. At Mass we gather to celebrate the fact that ____________________ sacrificed himself for us.

5. At Mass we commemorate what happened at the ____________________________ and give thanksgiving to God for his blessings.

B **Circle** the letter of the best answer.

1. Faithful to the Lord's command at the Last Supper, we continue to gather to share _____.

   a. Penance and Reconciliation **b.** faith
   c. the Passion play **d.** the Eucharistic meal

2. _____ said, ". . . [U]nless you eat the flesh of the Son of Man and drink his blood, you do not have life within you" (John 6:53).

   a. Mary **b.** Isaac **c.** Jesus **d.** Abraham

3. The Lord asked Abraham to sacrifice his own child, _____.

   a. Jesus **b.** Noah **c.** Isaac **d.** Havdalah

4. Abraham took the _____ and offered it up to God in place of his son.

   a. lamb **b.** dove **c.** ram **d.** goat

2 Chapter Review

C **Complete** the following sentences.

1. Abraham built ______________ for God wherever God spoke to him.
2. In the Old Testament, ______________, or burnt offerings, were offered as a loving gift to God.
3. Sunday is the Lord's Day, so we celebrate ______________ on this day.
4. In our relationship with God, ______________ is an essential element.

D **Respond** to the following.

1. What did God promise Abraham for his willingness to obey God's commands and sacrifice his son?

____

____

____

____

____

____

____

2. How do we share in Jesus' sacrifice in our daily lives?

____

____

____

____

____

____

____

Take Home

Covenant and Commitment

A covenant is a kind of agreement that was common in Old Testament times. Covenants were sealed in many different ways, such as with a sacred sacrifice, a special blessing, or a ritual meal. This chapter will explore some signs of the old Covenant, made between God and Israel, and how the old Covenant was renewed in the generations after Abraham.

ACTIVITY **Fidelity Awards**

Make a list of chores and responsibilities for each family member. Use stars to mark the number of times during the month each person has done his or her chore. Reward the most faithful with a chore-free week.

THROUGH THE WEEK

A Prayer for the Week Lord, in unexpected ways you come into our lives and invite us to share in your plan for salvation. Help us to respond to your call faithfully. Amen.

ON SUNDAY
Reflect on the reasons you attend Sunday Mass. How do you honor your commitment to God and to the Church by doing so?

ON THE WEB
BlestAreWe.com
RCLBLectionary.com
SaintsResource.com

Saint Paul, Apostle and Martyr

Before Saint Paul was a follower of Christ, he persecuted Christians. His conversion came in a vision he had in which he encountered the Lord. Paul then dedicated his life to teaching people about Jesus. Paul made the ultimate sacrifice for his faith, dying as a martyr.

Feast Day: January 25

Take Home

Scripture Background
Before the Time of Jesus

REBECCA When Rebecca first appears in the Old Testament (see Genesis 24) she is innocent and beautiful. When we meet her as Isaac's wife and the mother of their twin sons, Jacob and Esau, she has become hard and calculating. Of her sons, Rebecca favors the younger, Jacob. She plots with Jacob to deceive Isaac so he will receive Isaac's inheritance, which rightfully belongs to Esau. The plot succeeded, but Esau's anger at being cheated out of his birthright grew into a murderous fury. Rebecca sent away her favorite son to save his life, and she never saw him again. Read Genesis 27 to find out more about Jacob's deception.

Our Catholic Tradition in Legends

THE HOLY GRAIL Since Bible times, Jewish family meals have often begun with blessing wine, the day, and family members. The wine is held in a special cup called a kiddush cup, or blessing cup. The cup Jesus raised at the Last Supper was probably such a cup. Tradition says the Apostles saved this cup and Peter used it to celebrate the Eucharist. The cup was handed down through the centuries, and its whereabouts were the subject of many legends. It became known as the Holy Grail. The only cup in existence that might be the true cup is a small agate one, shown in the photograph, located in a cathedral in Valencia, Spain.

Covenant and Commitment

Chapter 3

May God give to you
of the dew of the heavens
And of the fertility of the earth . . . Genesis 27:28

Share

In Abraham's time, agreements between people were mostly verbal, or spoken. Written legal contracts were rare. People sealed, or made final, their agreements with symbolic rituals. In a custom we still use today, giving a blessing involved laying hands upon the head of the person being blessed. Gestures such as these seal some of the promises or agreements we make in our everyday lives. What gestures have you used to show that your words are truthful?

ACTIVITY

Draw a line from the gesture to the promise or thought it expresses.

Hand over one's heart •	• "I respect your authority."
First two fingers raised in a "V" shape •	• "In the name of the Father, and of the Son, and of the Holy Spirit."
Three fingers raised •	• "I'm being honest."
Salute •	• "We agree."
Shaking hands •	• "Peace."
Crossing one's heart •	• "I promise to tell the truth."
Right hand raised •	• "I will be faithful to my duties in this group."
Sign of the Cross •	• "I pledge allegiance."

What are some ways God's people show they honor his promise?

Hear and Believe **Scripture**

Jacob and the Covenant

God had promised Abraham that if he kept the **covenant** *God had established with him, he would have countless descendants. Isaac honored the covenant the Lord had made with his father, Abraham. But Isaac's wife, Rebecca, was unable to have children.*

Isaac prayed to the Lord, and Rebecca became pregnant with twin boys. Rebecca could feel the babies wrestling in her womb. She asked the Lord why the babies were fighting. The Lord told her:

> **Two nations are in your womb,**
> **two peoples are separating while still within you;**
> **But one will be stronger than the other,**
> **and the older will serve the younger.**
>
> Genesis 25:23

Esau, Isaac's favorite, was born first. He grew up to be burly and hairy, and enjoyed being outdoors. Jacob, Rebecca's favorite, was the second son. He liked simple things, and would rather stay inside.

According to custom, Esau was entitled to Isaac's birthright, the right to become the family patriarch and receive a large inheritance when Isaac died. One day, Isaac, who was ill and blind in his old age, called for Esau so he could say a special blessing to give Esau his birthright. Rebecca overheard what Isaac said to Esau, but she wanted Jacob to receive Isaac's blessing. She helped Jacob pretend he was Esau. She dressed him in Esau's clothes and hairy animal skins and sent him to see Isaac. Isaac fell for the trick. He gave the blessing to Jacob, saying,

> **". . . May God give to you**
> **of the dew of the heavens**
> **And of the fertility of the earth**
> **abundance of grain and wine.**
> **May peoples serve you,**
> **and nations bow down to you; . . ."**
>
> Genesis 27:28,29

The blessing could not be taken back. Esau was angry with Jacob, so Jacob went away to a safe place. He wandered to a holy place which he later named *Bethel*, meaning "house of God." One night, he fell asleep with his head on a rock. He dreamed that the Lord promised him many descendants, protection, and land. When Jacob awoke, he took the stone he had slept on and blessed it as a memorial to God. He then vowed to be faithful to the Lord.

To read the complete account in Scripture see Genesis 25:19–34; 27; 28:10–22.

Covenant People

It was important for Jacob to receive Isaac's birthright because it meant a special blessing and the right to be the patriarch. Jacob would later have twelve sons whose children would become the Twelve Tribes, or large family groups, of Israel. Jacob's story shows how God renewed his original promise to give Abraham as many descendants as stars in the sky. Rebecca and Jacob's plot to get the birthright was dishonest, but it shows that the fulfillment of God's promises often happens in unexpected ways.

In Jacob's dream at Bethel, God said to him, ". . . I will never leave you until I have done what I promised you" (Genesis 28:15). Jacob trusted God's promises and vowed to be faithful in return. Later on, Jacob would wrestle with a messenger of God. Jacob prevailed against the messenger. Because of this God changed Jacob's name to *Israel*, which means "one who struggled with God."

Faith Words

covenant

A covenant is a sacred agreement or relationship, sometimes sealed by a ritual or ceremony. Isaac honored the covenant the Lord made with his father, Abraham.

ACTIVITY

The Bible has a lot to say about the covenants between God and his people. Each of the following statements from the Bible teaches something about what it means to have a covenant with God. Read each statement, then write in your own words what each statement says about covenants with God.

"Is not my house firm before God?
He has made an eternal covenant with me,
set forth in detail and secured. . . ." (2 Samuel 23:5)

____

I will set my tabernacle in your midst, and will not loathe you. Ever present in your midst, I will be your God, and you will be my people; . . . (Leviticus 26:11–12).

____

Now, if you obey me completely and keep my covenant, you will be my treasured possession among all peoples, though all the earth is mine (Exodus 19:5).

____

What covenant did God make with Noah?

Hear and Believe **Scripture**

Noah and the Covenant

The Old Testament tells this important story to explain what it means to have a covenant with God.

Long before Abraham, Isaac, and Jacob, there lived a man named Noah. He was good and decent and obeyed God. Noah and his family followed God's laws. Other people were so sinful that God had decided to send a flood that would destroy the earth.

To save Noah and his family, however, God instructed Noah to build an ark. It had to be big enough to house his family and a zoo-like variety of birds and beasts. Once the huge boat was finished and Noah and his family and all the animals had gone aboard, God unleashed a flood onto the land. Torrents of water flooded over all life and raised the ark above the mountaintops.

Once the rain ceased and the land had begun to dry out, Noah emerged from the ark.

God said to Noah,

> **When I bring clouds over the earth, and the bow appears in the clouds, I will remember my covenant between me and you and every living creature—every mortal being—so that the waters will never again become a flood to destroy every mortal being.** Genesis 9:14–15

The next time you see a rainbow, remember that God dwells with us and protects us.

To read the complete account in Scripture see Genesis 6:5–8, 11–13; 7:21–23; 8:13; 18; 9:9–17.

Our Church Teaches

God began the everlasting covenant with all living beings when he promised Noah that he would never again destroy the earth by flood. This covenant was a loving and sacred relationship between God and his people. Noah, Abraham, Isaac, and Jacob honored their covenants with God by being faithful to him. We have a part in continuing this relationship. The Bible says, "And if you belong to Christ, then you are Abraham's descendant, heirs according to the promise" (Galatians 3:29). In Jesus Christ, we have forgiveness of sin and hope of everlasting friendship with God. Believing in Jesus, following his teachings, and participating in the Mass strengthen our commitment to live as God's people.

Catholics have many types of covenants. In Confirmation the Holy Spirit strengthens our bond with the Church and our obligation to carry out its mission. Matrimony is a covenant between a baptized man and a baptized woman that requires them to be faithful to each other for their entire lives. We also keep everyday covenants by being loyal to our friends, respecting our parents, and being honest. We strive to keep promises we make and try not to make promises we cannot keep. In the same way, we only take oaths, in which we call on God to be our witness, when absolutely necessary and when the oaths are true.

We Believe

God calls us to bear witness to our faith in our words and through our actions.

ACTIVITY

A covenant is an agreement between two people. Both parties have duties and obligations to fulfill. In the space below, list the duties and obligations you have as:

1. a daughter or son ____________________

____

2. a student in your school ____________________

____

3. a member of your parish ____________________

____

4. a citizen of your country ____________________

____

In what ways does God's love change people?

Respond Saint Paul

The early Christians were often persecuted, and sometimes even killed for their beliefs. Christians put their lives at risk if they identified themselves publicly as Christ's followers.

Before Saint Paul was a follower of Christ, he was one of the people who hated the early Christians. His original name was Saul. His mission was to persecute Christians.

One day, while Saul was on his way to Damascus to hunt for more Christians, a great light shone around him. Suddenly, he fell to the ground and was struck blind.

> **. . . [Saul] heard a voice saying to him, "Saul, Saul, why are you persecuting me?" He said, "Who are you sir?" The reply came, "I am Jesus, whom you are persecuting. Now get up and go into the city and you will be told what you must do."**
>
> Acts 9:4-6

At that moment, through the power of God, Saul received the gift of faith in Jesus. Temporarily blinded, he could see the truth with his heart.

Saul was baptized. He took the name of Paul. After this experience, his mission was to teach people to know and love Jesus. After a life of preaching and being imprisoned for his teachings, Paul made the ultimate sacrifice for his faith. He gave up his life for his beliefs, dying as a martyr in Rome. Martyrs were ordinary people whose extraordinary faith enabled them to give their lives for their belief in Christ. This is the greatest sign of commitment to Jesus and the Church. Paul's story shows just how much believing in the Lord can change someone.

The Feast of the Conversion of Saint Paul, the Apostle, is January 25.

The Conversion of St. Paul
Peter Paul Rubens (1577–1640/Flemish)

A New Life in the Lord

The stories of Abraham and Sarah, Jacob, and Saint Paul show us how God's Revelation can change people so much that they need new names to identify themselves. At Baptism, God calls each of us by name to a new life in Christ Jesus. In the Rite of Baptism for Children, the first question the celebrant asks the parents is, "What name do you give your child?" At Baptism, we take on a new identity.

ACTIVITIES

1. Write your full name on the lines provided. Using the letters in your name, create words that describe something special about you, and write them on the lines below.

first name	middle name	last name
______	______	______

______ ______

______ ______

______ ______

______ ______

2. Acts of faith are not always as dramatic as Abraham's, Jacob's, or Saint Paul's. Draw or write one thing you can do in your everyday life to show you are committed to following Jesus.

What is a prayer of blessing we can pray?

A Family Blessing

Blessings ask God to make someone or something holy. Before their Sabbath meal, Jewish families pray blessings for the day and one another. They hold a candle-lighting ritual and a ceremony called *kiddush*, which involves blessing wine and bread. The prayers that the priest says over the gifts during Mass are similar.

> Blessed are you, Lord, God of all creation, Creator of the fruit of the vine. You have taught us the ways of holiness through your commandments.
>
> Blessed are you, O Lord; you make holy the Sabbath day.

Based on the Jewish kiddush blessings

Share the following Catholic family blessing with your group. Later, share it with your family.

Group 1: May God help you and keep you.

Group 2: May he guide you in life.

Group 1: May he bless you this evening.

Group 2: And keep you from harm.

Group 1: (Make the sign of the cross on the foreheads of those in Group 2.)

Group 2: (Make the sign of the cross on the foreheads of those in Group 1.)

Based on the Parental Blessing of Children,
Canadian Catholic Conference

Chapter Review 3

A **Complete** the following sentences.

1. A ________________ is a sacred agreement or relationship, sometimes sealed by a ceremony.

2. Rebecca helped ________________ trick Isaac into giving him his ________________, which rightfully belonged to Esau.

3. ________________ is a covenant between a baptized man and a baptized woman that requires them to be faithful to each other for their whole lives.

4. A(n) ________________ is a promise that must be truthful and taken only when necessary.

5. In ________________ dream at Bethel, God said to him, "I will never leave you until I have done what I promised you."

6. In the Sacrament of ________________, the Holy Spirit strengthens our bond with the Church.

7. Before ________________ was a follower of Christ, he was one of the people who persecuted the Christians.

8. ________________ were ordinary people with extraordinary faith who gave up their lives for their belief in Christ.

9. Exodus 19:15 tells us: "Now if you obey me completely and keep my ________________, you will be my treasured possession among all peoples, though all the earth is mine."

B **Describe** how God fulfilled his promises to Jacob and Rebecca.

____

____

____

____

____

____

3 Chapter Review

C **Complete** the sentences, using words from the box. Not all words will be used.

Mass
Twelve Tribes
Saul
Esau
faith

1. Paul's original name was ______________.

2. God calls us to bear witness to our ______________, in our words and through our actions.

3. Believing in Jesus, following his teachings, and participating in the ______________ strengthen our commitment to live as God's people.

4. Jacob's sons would become the ______________, or large groups, of Israel.

D **Number** the events from the account of the Old Testament covenant God made with Noah. The first answer is provided.

_____ God told Noah to build an ark.

_____ God promised he would never again flood the earth.

_____ God unleashed a flood over the land.

__1__ Many people sinned and did not follow God's laws.

_____ The water flooded over all life on land.

_____ God decided to send a flood to destroy the earth.

_____ Noah came out of the ark.

E **Respond** to the following.

1. Name some duties and obligations we have as Catholics.

____

____

2. Describe some ways that you can honor your baptismal commitment to live as a follower of Christ.

____

____

Getting ready for Chapter 4

Take Home

Piety and Prayer

Joseph was one of Jacob's sons and a patriarch, or founding father, of the People Israel. As a boy, Joseph's jealous brothers sold him into slavery in Egypt. Through a series of miraculous events Joseph rose from being a servant to being Pharaoh's chief assistant. Throughout all the ups and downs of his life, Joseph was directed by his faith in God. Joseph's trust in God was richly rewarded.

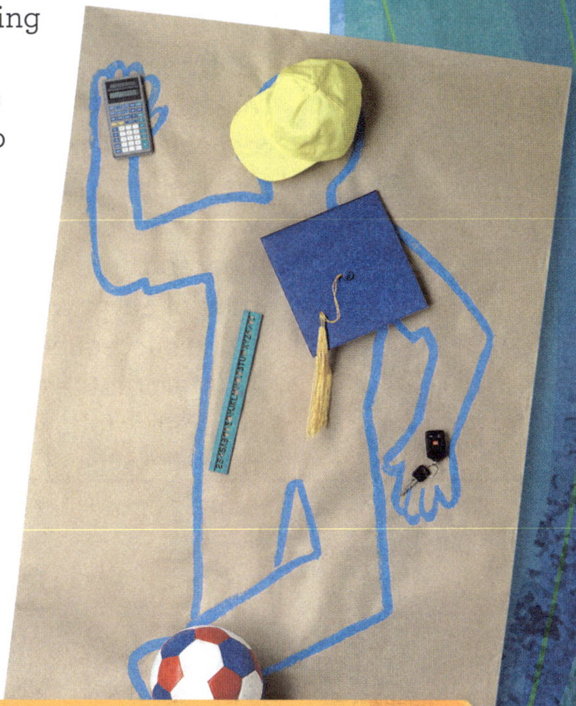

ACTIVITY **Family Callings**

Have family members draw outlines of themselves and fill them in with clothing, tools, or other objects that illustrate what they would like their lives to be like five or ten years from now. Invite each person to talk about the work, cooperation, and trust involved in realizing his or her goals.

THROUGH THE WEEK

A Prayer for the Week God, teach us to hear your voice in our hearts and in the presence of those around us. Like Saint André Bessette, may we live a life of prayer and service. Amen.

ON SUNDAY
When the priest says, "Let us pray," speak to God quietly and listen for God speaking to you.

ON THE WEB
BlestAreWe.com
RCLBLectionary.com
SaintsResource.com

Saint André Bessette (1845–1937)

Saint André Bessette worked as a doorkeeper at Notre Dame College in Montreal for forty years. He had a special ministry to the sick, and many who came to him were healed. Brother André encouraged all who sought intercession to pray to Saint Joseph, to whom he had a special devotion.

Feast Day: January 6 (January 7 in Canada)

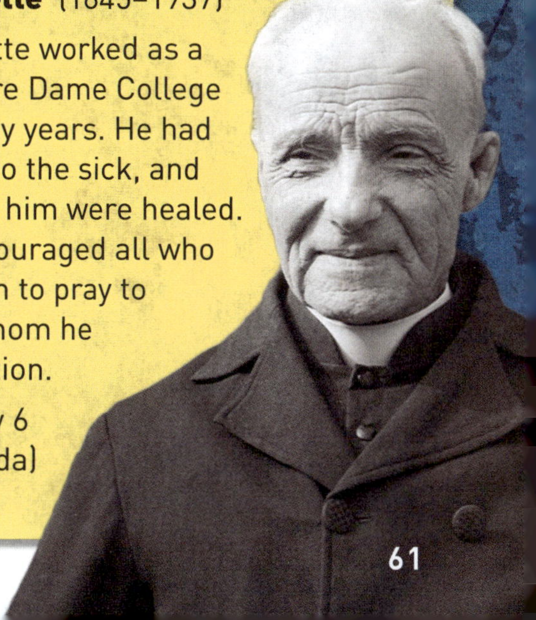

Take Home

Scripture Background
Before the Time of Jesus

INTERPRETING DREAMS For many ancient cultures, dreams were accepted as supernatural messages. The dreams of royalty were considered especially significant, and rulers sought advisers who were able to interpret dreams. Those who succeeded were revered, as is evident in Joseph's story. When Pharaoh dreamed of cattle and crops, all the wise men of Egypt were called upon to interpret his dream. None succeeded. When Joseph, a Hebrew, was able to interpret the dream as a warning of seven years of prosperity followed by seven years of famine, Pharaoh made him his chief assistant. Read Genesis 41 to learn about Pharaoh's dream.

Our Catholic Tradition in Art

MADONNA OF THE MAGNIFICAT
During the Renaissance, European artists created countless paintings of the Blessed Virgin Mary. One of the most famous is Botticelli's *Madonna of the Magnificat,* created in the early 1480s. The painting features nearly life-size figures, and is lavishly covered with gold paint. It depicts Mary being crowned as the Queen of Heaven as she holds the Christ Child and writes the words of the Magnificat.

Today this painting can be seen in the Uffizi Gallery in Florence, Italy.

Piety and Prayer

Chapter 4

The Mighty One has done great things for me,
and holy is his name. Luke 1:49

Share

Finding and being a loyal friend are wonderful blessings. What do you look for in a good friend? You probably want someone with whom you can share your private feelings. You want a friend you can trust not to judge you or betray you. A good friend will also look out for your safety. Most likely, you will do the same things for your close friend, too. This is what loyal friendship is all about. In the same way, God is loyal and true to his people. God is always there when we need him to listen. God will not betray us, and he protects us always.

ACTIVITY

A local newspaper is doing a story on friendships and has chosen you and a good friend as the subjects of the article. Below, write a headline for your article, and draw two pictures about your friendship to go with the story. On the lines under each picture, write a description of what the picture shows.

The Community Herald

LOCAL NEWS | WEATHER | SPORTS | ARTS | TOP STORIES

What are some of the ways that God responds to our loyalty?

Hear and Believe **Scripture**

Joseph, the Loyal Son

After Jacob left Bethel, God kept him safe. He journeyed to Haran and married a woman named Rachel. Rachel was unable to have children. She prayed to have a child and finally gave birth to a son, Joseph. Jacob and his family settled in Canaan.

Jacob had eleven other sons, but his favorite son was Joseph. Joseph's eleven brothers were jealous of him, especially of a colorful tunic that Jacob had given him. They began to hate him even more when he told them about his dreams. They said to each other, "Let us kill Joseph. We can say a wild beast ate him. We shall then see what comes of his dreams!"

The brothers stripped Joseph of his tunic, threw him into a well, and left him out in the desert. Finally, they decided to sell Joseph as a slave, and passing traders took him to Egypt. The brothers dipped Joseph's tunic in goat's blood and gave it to a messenger to bring to their father. "My son's tunic!" Jacob cried. "A wild beast has eaten him!"

But God protected Joseph. Joseph came to live in the home of Potiphar, an assistant of Pharoah, Egypt's ruler. Potiphar liked Joseph and gave him the job of running his household. From then on, the Lord's blessing was upon everything in the home. But then Potiphar's wife began to flirt with Joseph. Joseph ignored her. "How could I commit so great a wrong and offend God?" he said. Potiphar's wife was insulted. To get revenge, she falsely accused Joseph of attacking her, and Joseph was thrown into jail.

Even in jail, the Lord blessed Joseph. The chief jailer put him in charge of the other prisoners. Joseph had a gift for telling other prisoners the meaning of their dreams. Pharaoh was having nightmares, so he sent for Joseph. "In one dream," Pharaoh told Joseph, "I saw seven ears of grain, growing fat and healthy. Behind them sprouted seven ears of grain, shriveled and thin. They swallowed up the seven healthy ears."

Joseph told Pharaoh, "God is telling you that seven years of plentiful food will be followed by seven years of famine." Pharaoh put Joseph in charge of storing food to prepare for the famine. When the famine came, Egypt was ready.

After two years of famine, Jacob and his other sons were running out of food. Jacob sent ten of his sons to Egypt to buy grain. He kept Benjamin, the last child Rachel had before she died, at home with him. Jacob's sons went to see Pharaoh's chief assistant, who was actually Joseph.

Joseph recognized his brothers, but they did not recognize him. Wanting to see his brother Benjamin, Joseph sent his brothers back to get him. The brothers did what Joseph asked. When they returned, Joseph told a servant to hide a silver cup in Benjamin's grain bag. Then Joseph accused the brothers of stealing it, and ordered Benjamin to be jailed. The brothers panicked.

"If Benjamin is not with us when we go back home, our father will die of grief!" pleaded Judah, one of the brothers.

> . . . [Joseph] said: "I am your brother Joseph, whom you sold into Egypt. But now do not be distressed, and do not be angry with yourselves for having sold me here. It was really for the sake of saving lives that God sent me here ahead of you.
>
> "Hurry back, then, to my father and tell him: 'Thus says your son Joseph: God has made me lord of all Egypt; come down to me without delay.'"
>
> Genesis 45:4,5,9

The brothers went home and told Jacob the news, and the whole family moved to Egypt. Pharaoh treated the family well. The twelve sons of Jacob had many children and grandchildren. They all became known as the Twelve Tribes of Israel. Each tribe was named after one of Jacob's sons. They waited patiently for the time when they would return to Canaan.

To read the complete narrative in Scripture see Genesis 29:1–30; 30:1, 22–24; 35:22; 37; 39–47:12; 48:21.

An Example of Piety

Joseph brought joy to his father, and reconciliation to his family. His story shows us the rewards of being loyal and faithful to God. He forgave his brothers instead of seeking revenge. When Potiphar's wife tempted him, he resisted. He was patient even when he was jailed unfairly. God rewarded him for this **fidelity** by making him a great ruler in Egypt. Even as a ruler, Joseph was humble. His only concern was how to serve God. Joseph's **piety** is an example for us.

ACTIVITY

Write about one challenge that Joseph had and how he responded. How was his response an example of piety?

____

____

Faith Words

fidelity
Fidelity is faithfulness and loyalty to something or someone. Joseph is a model of fidelity to God.

piety
Piety is putting God above everything else.

How was another Joseph from the Bible an example of piety?

Hear and Believe **Scripture**

Saint Joseph

The Bible tells the story of another Joseph. This story is found in the New Testament and is about the man who was Mary's husband. This Joseph had many qualities in common with Joseph in the Old Testament. Like his Old Testament namesake, Saint Joseph faced some extremely difficult decisions. Dreams also play an important role in his story.

Joseph was engaged to Mary when she was found to be pregnant through the Holy Spirit. Joseph was considering his difficult situation when an angel appeared to him in a dream. The angel said,

> **". . . Joseph, son of David, do not be afraid to take Mary your wife into your home. For it is through the holy Spirit that this child has been conceived in her."** Matthew 1:20

When Joseph awoke he did as the angel told him.

After Jesus was born, Joseph had another dream. In it an angel told him,

> **". . . Rise, take the child and his mother, flee to Egypt, and stay there until I tell you. Herod is going to search for the child to destroy him."** Matthew 2:13

Joseph immediately left for Egypt with Mary and Jesus, staying there until Herod died and was no longer a threat. In doing this he fulfilled the prophecy:

> **. . . "Out of Egypt I called my son."** Matthew 2:15

Like the Joseph in the Old Testament, Saint Joseph obeyed God. He stood by Mary, believed the astonishing news that Jesus was born of the Holy Spirit, and loved and cared for Jesus as his own. He, too, listened to God.

To read the complete account in Scripture see Matthew 1:18–20, 24; 2:1, 13–15.

Our Church Teaches

As we see from the story of Joseph in the Old Testament, there will always be challenges that can keep us from God. Placed in many difficult situations, Joseph always tried to learn God's will, and he relied on God as his father. The story of Joseph in the New Testament teaches us similar lessons.

Sometimes we face challenges. For example, distractions can interrupt us when we pray. Like both Josephs, we should think of God as our caring Father and turn our hearts back to him.

We Believe

Prayer requires keeping our hearts and minds focused on God. Because we trust God, we pray to God as "Father."

ACTIVITIES

1. From time to time, we face tough decisions. Describe three ways that God helps you with these decisions.

a. ______________________________

b. ______________________________

c. ______________________________

2.

Name moments in your life when you have needed or will need to trust God.

How can your trust in God grow?

How did Hebrew prayers address God?

Respond

The Lord Helps the Lowly

Joseph's own brothers had plotted to kill him. They threw him into a ditch, and he ended up a slave. But the Bible tells us that the Lord was with him and brought success to all he did (see Genesis 39:23). When Joseph became a ruler, he believed that God was responsible for all his blessings. He was a servant of God before anything else.

The Hebrews often prayed to God in hymns and songs that said they were servants of the Lord. They praised God as the protector of all humble servants. Sing or pray this traditional hymn, which praises God for the help he gives to faithful people who are powerless or poor.

Hallelujah!
Praise the LORD, my soul;
  I will praise the LORD all my life;
  sing praise to my God while I live. . . .

Blessed the one whose help is the God of Jacob,
  whose hope is in the LORD, his God,
The maker of heaven and earth,
  the seas and all that is in them,
Who keeps faith forever,
  secures justice for the oppressed,
  who gives bread to the hungry.
The LORD sets prisoners free;
  the LORD gives sight to the blind.
The LORD raises up those who are bowed down;
  the LORD loves the righteous.
The LORD protects the resident alien,
  comes to the aid of the orphan and the widow,
  but thwarts the way of the wicked.
The LORD shall reign forever,
  your God, Zion, through all generations!
Hallelujah!

Psalm 146:1–2, 5–10

ACTIVITIES

1. Reread the lines of the psalm that begin with the words "the Lord." They name things that God does for people who are powerless or in need. Rewrite four of the lines to describe how God helps you.

   The Lord ______________________________

   The Lord ______________________________

   The Lord ______________________________

   The Lord ______________________________

2. Mary, the mother of Jesus, was a Hebrew woman who may have prayed many traditional hymns such as the one you just prayed. When God asked her to be the mother of Jesus, she praised the Lord in a *canticle*, a poem or hymn of praise. Her prayer said that the Lord takes care of the poor and lifts them up.

   The following canticle is based on Mary's prayer. Complete Verse 3 by writing two sentences—one that praises God and one that names something wonderful God has done.

Chorus
Proclaim the greatness of God; rejoice in God, my Savior!
Rejoice in God, my Savior!

Verse 1:
My soul is filled with joy as I sing to God my Savior:
you have looked upon your servant, you have visited your people.

Chorus

Verse 2:
I am lowly as a child, but I know from this day forward
that my name will be remembered, for all will call me blessed.

Chorus

Verse 3:

____

____

Chorus

Chorus: Luke 1:46–55, James Chepponis ©1989 GIA Publications, Inc.
Verses 1 and 2: Luke 1:46–55, David Haas ©1989 GIA Publications, Inc.

What were Mary's own words to God?

Prayer

The Magnificat

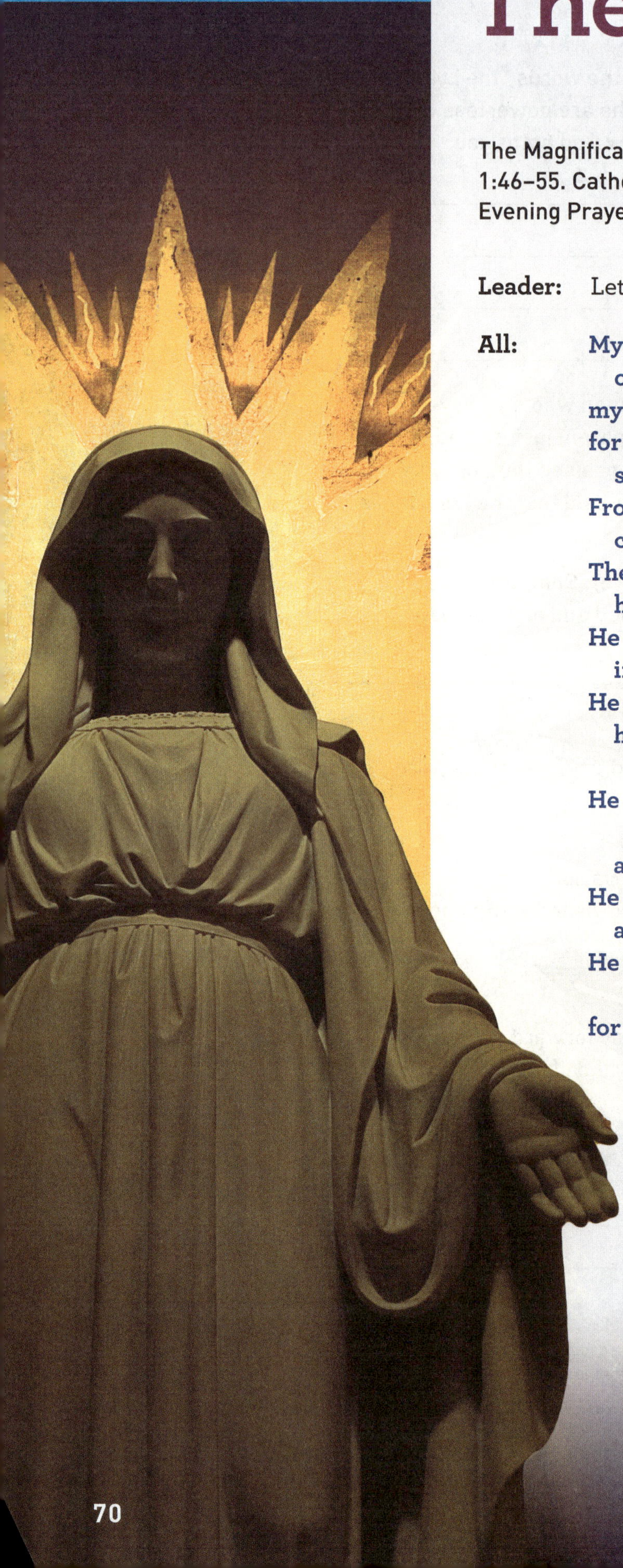

The Magnificat is Mary's canticle of praise. It is from Luke 1:46–55. Catholics traditionally pray the Magnificat at Evening Prayer.

Leader: Let us pray Mary's canticle of praise.

All: **My soul proclaims the greatness**
of the Lord,
my spirit rejoices in God my Savior;
for he has looked with favor on his lowly
servant.
From this day all generations will
call me blessed.
The Almighty has done great things for me,
holy is his name.
He has mercy on those who fear him
in every generation.
He has shown the strength of his arm,
he has scattered the proud in
their conceit.
He has cast down the mighty from
their thrones,
and has lifted up the lowly.
He has filled the hungry with good things,
and the rich he has sent away empty.
He has come to the help of his
servant Israel,
for he has remembered his promise
of mercy,
the promise he made to our fathers,
to Abraham and his children forever.
Amen.

Based on Luke 1:46–55

Chapter Review 4

A **Match** Column A with Column B by writing the correct number in the space provided.

A		B
1.	Rachel	_____ Jacob's favorite son
2.	Pharaoh	_____ Mary's canticle, or song of praise to God
3.	Magnificat	_____ youngest brother of Joseph
4.	fidelity	_____ the title for a ruler of ancient Egypt
5.	Mary	_____ faithfulness and loyalty to something or someone
6.	piety	_____ requires keeping our minds and hearts focused on God
7.	Joseph	_____ putting God above everything else
8.	prayer	_____ wife of Jacob; mother of Joseph
9.	Benjamin	_____ her prayer said that the Lord lifts up the lowly

B **Complete** the sentences, using words from the box. Not all words will be used.

Father
fidelity
Twelve Tribes
Savior
will
First Fathers

1. God rewarded Joseph for his ____________________ by making him a great ruler in Egypt.
2. Like Joseph, we should always remain focused on God's ____________________.
3. Joseph and his brothers became known as the ____________________ of Israel.
4. Because we trust God, we pray to him as "____________________."
5. In the Magnificat, Mary proclaims, "My spirit rejoices in God, my ____________________."

4 Chapter Review

C **Put a checkmark (✓)** next to the actions of the New Testament Joseph that show that he trusted God.

_____ was thinking about his difficult situation

_____ took Mary into his house

_____ had a dream

_____ fled with Mary and Jesus to Egypt

_____ believed the news that the child Jesus was born of God

_____ was engaged to Mary

_____ listened to God

D **Complete** the statements from the Magnificat (based on Luke 1:46–55).

1. My soul proclaims the ________________ of the Lord.
2. From this day all generations will call me ________________.
3. The Almighty has done great things for me, ________________ is his name.
4. He has cast down the ________________ from their thrones, and has lifted up the ________________.
5. He has come to the help of his servant Israel, for he has remembered his promise of ________________.

E **Complete** this prayer of praise to God.

Praise the Lord,

who ________________________________.

Praise the Lord,

who ________________________________.

Praise the Lord,

who ________________________________.

Faith in Action

SCHOOL MAINTENANCE STAFF Working under the guidance of the principal and the pastor, a Catholic school's maintenance staff serves the school community in many important ways, such as cleaning the classrooms, maintaining electrical equipment, and making necessary repairs. By keeping the school environment clean, orderly, and safe, the maintenance staff creates a setting appropriate for learning, and lives the Catholic Social Teaching of **Care for God's Creation.**

In Everyday Life

ACTIVITY Chapter 1 began with a verse from Psalm 104, praising the wonderful works of the Lord. We can find God's presence all around us. It is easy to take for granted the gifts of God's creation which surround us. Spend a quiet moment reflecting on one of these gifts of creation. Then, complete this certificate of appreciation to God for that gift.

Certificate of Appreciation

Presented to God
in gratitude for

____

____

Presented by

____

In Your Parish

ACTIVITY With your classmates, plan a parish-wide Creation Awareness Week on environmental issues. To begin, use the space below to list ideas for how parishioners can reduce, reuse, and recycle. You may also want to research facts about the environment for an Awareness poster, highlighting facts such as: 50 acres of rainforest are destroyed every minute; an aluminum can won't decompose for 500 years; and Americans produce 154 million tons of garbage each year.

____

____

____

____

____

____

____

____

Faith in *Action*

ALTAR SERVERS Altar servers carry the processional cross and candles at Mass. They hold the *Roman Missal* for the priest when he is not at the altar. They also assist in receiving the bread, wine, and water at the Preparation of the Altar and Gifts. They pour water over the hands of the priest as he prepares to consecrate the bread and wine. Altar servers participate with the assembly in prayer responses and songs and are encouraged to be models of grace and reverence. In doing so, they honor the Catholic Social Teaching of **Call to Family, Community, and Participation.**

In Everyday Life

ACTIVITY In this chapter, you learned that Christians make sacrifices when we put God and the service of others first. God calls us to offer ourselves as a living sacrifice. One way we do this is when participate in and build up family life and community life. On the chart below, list three virtues. Then describe how those virtues are practiced by you, within your family, and in the community.

In Your Parish

ACTIVITY Whether you're participating in Mass as an altar server or as a member of the assembly, being calm and attentive is important. Learn to be more quiet and attentive at Mass by spending more time this week in a quiet way. In the space provided, briefly describe two ways you can be more quiet and attentive this week, such as taking a walk or saying a silent prayer.

Faith in Action

THE PASTOR God calls priests to serve the Church in a special way. They preside over the celebration of the Sacraments, they preach the Word of God, and they guide us on our path to holiness as we strive to live as disciples of Jesus in the world today. In addition to these responsibilities, a pastor is entrusted with the pastoral care of the parishioners. He acts as their shepherd under the authority of the diocesan bishop. He sets an example for the parish by living out the Catholic Social Teaching of **Rights and Responsibilities**.

In Everyday Life

ACTIVITY Think about the town you live in and the various people who work to keep it comfortable for the people who live there. List at least three key tasks that these people do. Then describe one thing you, too, can do to be a responsible member of your town.

In Your Parish

ACTIVITY It takes the work of many people to keep a parish running smoothly. Choose one of these people, such as the pastor, the music minister, the deacon, the parish secretary, or the maintenance worker, and write a brief thank-you card or note to this person acknowledging his or her hard work.

Faith in Action

PARISH YOUTH MINISTRY Being involved in parish youth ministry is a great way to meet and to make friends. Young people share good times as well as the challenges of growing up as Catholics in a world that doesn't always respect their values. They may help with parish fundraisers and participate in service projects. Through taking part in parish youth ministry, young people will learn firsthand that Saint Francis was right when he said, "It is in giving that we receive." Parish youth ministry leaders and members honor the Catholic Social Teaching of **Call to Family, Community, and Participation.**

In Everyday Life

ACTIVITY Begin by listing some qualities your friends have that make you like them. Then, list some qualities you have that you think make your friends like you.

What I like about my friends

____

____

____

____

What my friends like about me

____

____

____

____

In Your Parish

ACTIVITY List two or three qualities that you feel are essential for a youth minister to have, and that would make this person a good role model. Explain why these are important. Then name someone you know who would be an ideal candidate for this role.

____

____

____

____

____

____

____

____

____

____

Unit Wrap-up 1

You have learned about the family of Abraham.
Complete Abraham's family tree.

Abraham — S _ _ _ h

I _ _ _ c — R _ _ _ _ _ a

E _ _ _   J _ _ _ b — R _ _ _ _ l

J _ s _ _ _   B _ _ _ _ _ _ n

Zebulun   Issachar   Asher

Naphtali   Gad

Dan   J _ d _ h

Reuben   Simeon   Levi

↓

The _ w _ l _ _ T _ i _ _ s of Israel

1 Unit Review

A **Complete** the sentences, using words from the box.

Abraham	Sabbath	birthright	Paul
Eucharist	sacrifices	Sunday	Jesus
Jacob	Mary	Noah	

1. God's promise to ____________________ could not have come true without Mary's faith.
2. Esau was entitled to Isaac's ____________________, the right to become the family patriarch.
3. As Christians, we make ____________________ when we put God and the care of others above other things in our lives.
4. At Mass, we celebrate the sacrifice that ____________________ made for us.
5. The Lord calls us to receive his Body and Blood in the ____________________.
6. The Jewish weekly day of rest in honor of God is called the ____________________.
7. ____________________ had twelve sons.
8. God began an everlasting covenant with humanity when he made a promise to ____________________.
9. Before ____________________ was a Christian, he hated those who followed Christ.
10. ____________________ is our model of faith because of her response to God's call.

Unit Review 1

B **Complete** the following sentences.

1. Early Christians were ______________, or punished, sometimes even killed, for their beliefs.
2. After the angel told Mary she would be the mother of God's Son, she praised God in a ______________, a sacred song whose words are from Scripture.
3. Mary's canticle is called the ______________. Catholics traditionally pray it at the celebration of ______________ Prayer.
4. In prayer, Christians call God ______________.

C **Circle** the letter of the best answer.

1. Joseph in the New Testament, like Joseph in the Old Testament, faced some difficult ______________.

   a. wars **b.** news **c.** decisions **d.** relatives

2. When Joseph took Mary as his wife, he showed his trust in ______________.

   a. dreams **b.** God **c.** Mary **d.** King Herod

3. If we experience ______________ when we pray, we must try to turn our hearts back to God.

   a. distractions **b.** unity **c.** fidelity **d.** blessings

4. Even though he was a great ruler in Egypt, Joseph's only concern was how to serve ______________.

   a. his brothers **b.** Pharaoh **c.** Egypt **d.** God

D **Write** two ways that we can know God.

____

____

____

1 Unit Review

E **Match** Column A with Column B by writing the correct number in the space provided.

A	B
1. altar	____ an act of unselfish giving, or an offering made to God by a priest on behalf of his people
2. covenant	____ the assurance of things hoped for, the conviction of things not seen
3. faith	____ God's act of revealing himself and inviting us to respond with faith
4. fidelity	____ faithfulness and loyalty to something or someone
5. patriarch	____ putting God above everything else
6. piety	____ a sacred agreement or relationship sometimes sealed by a ritual or ceremony
7. Revelation	____ a raised place where sacrifices are offered; the center of worship during the Mass
8. sacrifice	____ a great leader of the Hebrews from early Scripture times, or the male leader of a family or clan

F **Respond** to the following.

1. In what ways did Abraham and Mary show trust in God and allow the fulfillment of his promises?

____

____

2. What can you learn from Mary and Abraham about trusting God?

____

____

God Saves and Delivers Us

Unit 2

God saved the Hebrew people from slavery in Egypt. Through his life, Death, and Resurrection, Jesus Christ frees us from the slavery of sin to live as the new People of God.

> . . . Sing to the LORD, for he is gloriously triumphant;
> horse and chariot he has cast into the sea.
>
> Exodus 15:21

Hebrew slaves may have helped build this statue of the pharaoh Ramses II. The map shows the Hebrew people's journey out of Egypt to the Promised Land.

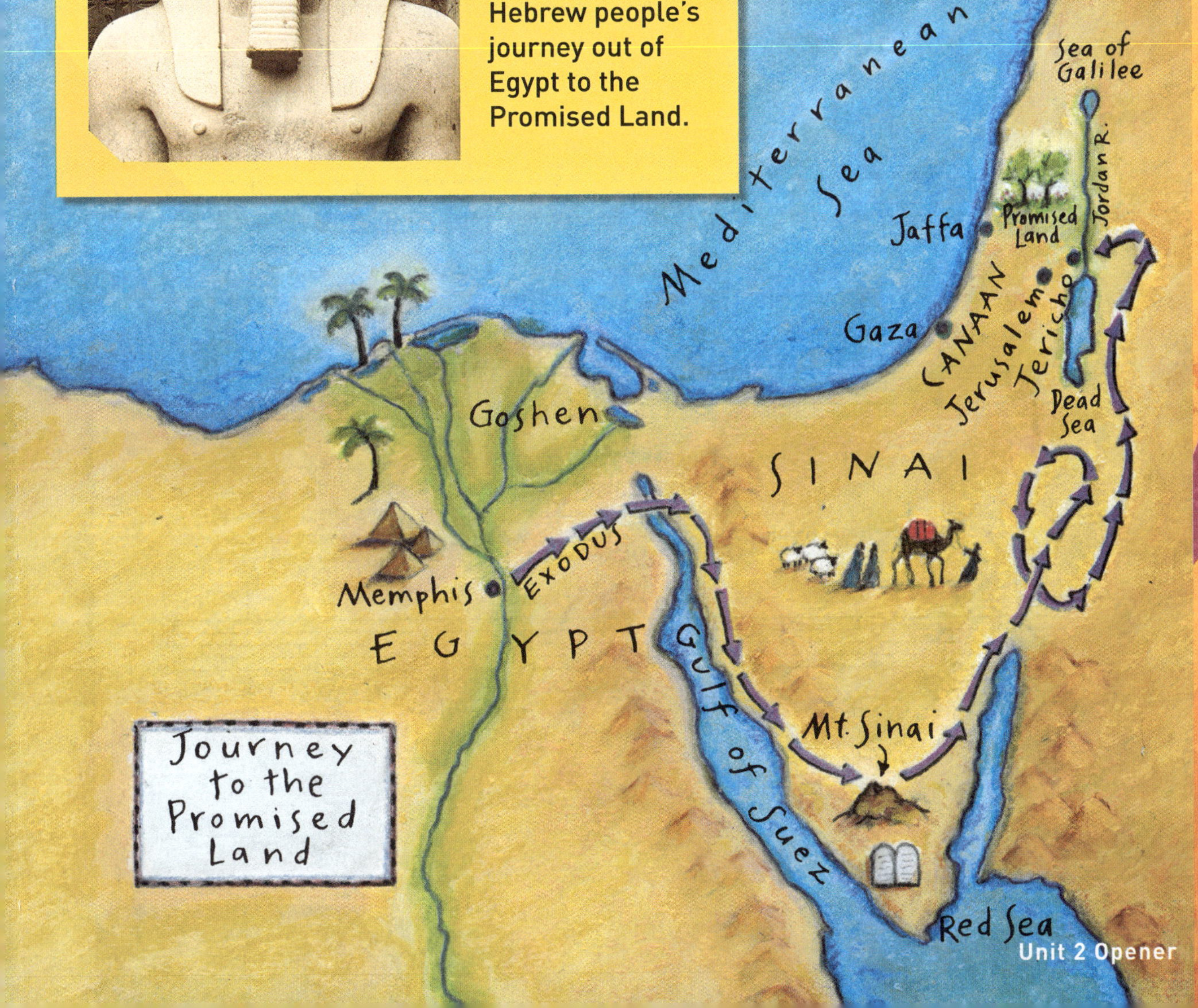

Unit 2 SONG

Wade in the Water

African-American spiritual
Arranged by Diana Kodner

Getting ready for Chapter 5

Take Home

Slavery and Deliverance

The story of Moses and the Exodus is a key part of the salvation story of God's people. God spoke to Moses in a burning bush and asked Moses to lead the Israelites out of slavery to their own land. Through escaping slavery in Egypt, the Israelites learned new lessons about themselves as God's special people. We can learn from their story and from our own family journeys.

ACTIVITY **Family Hieroglyphics**

The ancient Egyptian alphabet, called *hieroglyphics*, consisted of symbols that represented letters. Create an alphabet of symbols that mean something to your family. For instance, a stick figure of a girl could represent the letter H if there is a girl in the family named Hannah.

THROUGH THE WEEK

A Prayer for the Week Thank you, God, for the freedom to be your followers. Give us the courage to stand firm in our beliefs. Amen.

ON SUNDAY
Listen for the themes of journey, slavery, and freedom as you hear the readings proclaimed at Mass.

ON THE WEB
BlestAreWe.com
RCLBLectionary.com
SaintsResource.com

Saint Martin de Porres (1579–1639)

Martin de Porres, a Dominican friar, lived near Lima, Peru, during the time of the slave trade. His days were filled with nursing the sick and caring for slaves and the poor of the city. His love for all people, regardless of their color, race, or status, set an example for others of his time.

Patron Saint of:
racial harmony

Feast Day: November 3

Take Home

Scripture Background

Before the Time of Jesus

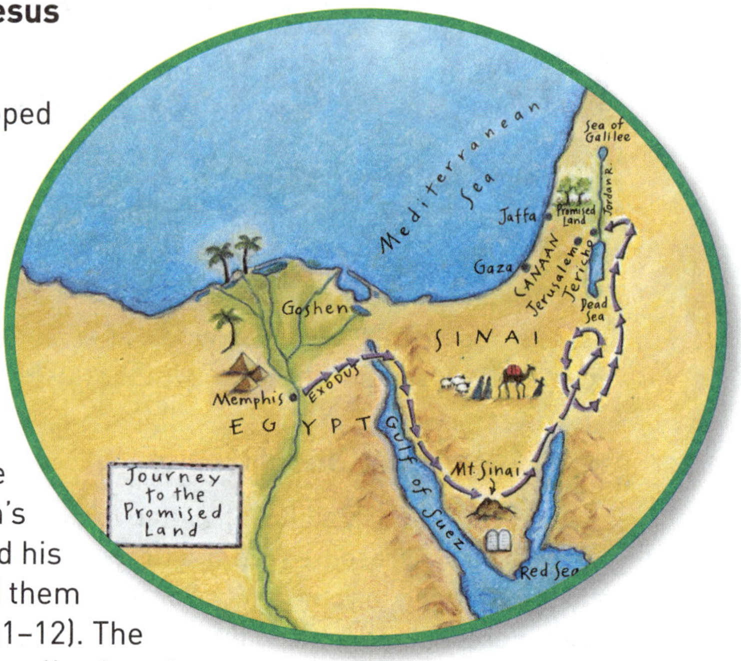

EGYPT AND THE ISRAELITES

The Egyptian civilization developed in the fertile land along the Nile River. From its origins as a distinct state (around 3000 BC) through Roman times, Egypt prospered. The story of the Israelites is often set in Egypt. When famine struck Canaan, Abraham escaped to Egypt (see Genesis 12:10). Later, Abraham's great-grandson Joseph rescued his father and brothers and helped them settle in Egypt (see Genesis 47:1–12). The Book of Exodus recounts the Israelites' enslavement in Egypt and their escape to the Promised Land under Moses' leadership.

Our Catholic Tradition in History

SAINT PETER CLAVER Saint Peter Claver, a Spanish Jesuit missionary, was sent to Cartagena (part of modern Colombia) in 1610. Cartagena was a port of entry for slave-trading ships. Peter soon found himself busy with all the sick and demoralized slaves who had survived the inhumane treatment on the ships. He went into the holds of the ships and gave the slaves food and water. He told them about Jesus and that they were precious in God's eyes. Slave owners believed that slaves only had worth as property, so Saint Peter Claver's message was a subversive one. He called himself "a slave to the Negroes forever." His feast day is September 9.

Slavery and Deliverance

Chapter 5

. . . Sing to the LORD, for he is gloriously triumphant;
horse and chariot he has cast into the sea.
Exodus 15:21

Share

When you hear the word *slave*, you probably think of a person who is completely under the control of another person. But poverty, prejudice, addiction, violence, materialism, and other wrongs in society can also enslave people. Many things can take away a person's freedom to live peacefully and lovingly.

ACTIVITY

Complete the sentences under each photograph.

The people in this picture have become slaves of ______________________.

They do not have the freedom to ______ ______________________.

The people in this picture have become slaves of ______________________.

They do not have the freedom to ______ ______________________.

Pick one photograph and write how the people shown might be delivered, or freed, from slavery. ______________________

____

____

What does Yahweh mean?

Hear and Believe **Scripture**

The Exodus

God had promised Abraham, Isaac, and Jacob that he would give them land that would be home to their descendants, and he fulfilled his promise.

For many years after Joseph's death, the descendants of Joseph's family prospered in Egypt. They were known as the Hebrews, or Israelites.

But then a new Pharoah told the Egyptians, "The Israelites keep growing! Let us stop them before they become powerful." He made the Hebrews slaves, forcing them to build cities and work in fields.

The Hebrew families kept growing. Pharaoh ordered, "Throw every Hebrew baby boy into the river!" Jochebed, a Hebrew woman, gave birth to a son. To keep him from being killed, she hid him. Later, she put him in a basket and placed it in the reeds on the riverbank. Pharaoh's daughter spotted the baby. She adopted him and named him Moses.

A long time passed. The Israelites cried out to God about their slavery. One day, after Moses grew up, he was leading a flock of sheep across the desert. He saw fire coming out of a bush, but not burning it.

> **God called out to him from the bush: Moses! Moses! He answered, "Here I am." God said: Do not come near! Remove your sandals from your feet, for the place where you stand is holy ground. I am the God of your father, he continued, the God of Abraham, the God of Isaac, and the God of Jacob. . . .**
>
> **Now, go! I am sending you to Pharoah to bring my people, the Israelites, out of Egypt. . . .**
>
> **"But," said Moses to God, "if I go to the Israelites and say to them, 'The God of your ancestors has sent me to you,' and they ask me, 'What is his name?' what do I tell them?" God replied to Moses: I am who I am. Then he added: This is what you will tell the Israelites: I AM has sent me to you. . . .**
>
> **Go, tell Pharaoh, king of Egypt, to let the Israelites leave his land.**

Exodus 3:4–6,10,13–14; 6:11

But Pharaoh would not obey. Because of this plagues came upon the land. The Nile River turned into blood. Frogs, gnats, flies, animal disease, boils, hail, locusts, and three days of darkness came. Pharaoh still did not give in. Then the Lord commanded the Hebrew families to prepare a special meal and mark their doorways with lamb's blood so that the next plague would "pass over" their homes. It would be a plague of death! That night, all the firstborns in Egypt died, even Pharaoh's son. Pharaoh sent for Moses. "Leave now, you and the Israelites with you!" he cried.

The Israelites marched out of Egypt. But suddenly Pharaoh wished he had not let the Israelites go. He sent out more than 600 chariots with warriors to catch them.

Pharaoh's armies caught up with the Israelites at the Red Sea. The Israelites called out to the Lord in great fright.

The Lord told Moses, "Stretch your hand out over the sea." When Moses did this, the Lord swept the sea with a strong wind, turning the sea into dry land. The Israelites marched in, with a wall of water on their right and left. When the Egyptians chased after them, the water flowed back, drowning Pharaoh's whole army.

The Israelites sang songs thanking the Lord for leading them safely toward the Promised Land. Moses' sister, Miriam, led the women in dancing and praising the Lord.

To read the complete account in Scripture see Genesis 50:24; Exodus 1—15:21.

God's Love Delivers Us

The **Exodus** is the story about God freeing the Israelites from slavery and leading them out of Egypt. The Book of Exodus is the second book of the Old Testament. The Israelites in Egypt believed in God's promises to their ancestors, so they cried out to God for help. God chose Moses to teach the Israelites his word and to lead them to freedom.

At the burning bush, God revealed an important mystery he had not revealed to the patriarchs Abraham, Isaac, Jacob, and Joseph. God told Moses his sacred name, **Yahweh**, which means "I am who I am." This means God is the only God, who exists forever. No one created God; he created everything and everyone and only he has this power to create. God creates us with the plan to reward us with everlasting life with him. All creation is destined for God's glory. God delivered the Israelites from their suffering in Egypt and led them to the **Promised Land**. In the same way, he delivers us from sin and leads us to everlasting life. This is the greatest deliverance of all.

ACTIVITY

Moses delivered God's people from slavery under the Egyptians. In the space below, describe one form of slavery from which Jesus frees you.

____

____

____

____

Faith Words

Exodus
The Exodus is the Old Testament story of how God freed the Hebrews in Egypt. The Book of Exodus is the second book of the Old Testament.

Yahweh
Yahweh is the most sacred name of God, spoken to Moses. It means "I am who I am."

Promised Land
The Promised Land is Canaan, the sacred place God promised to Abraham, Isaac, Jacob, and the Israelites in Egypt.

What did Jesus say about everlasting life?

Hear and Believe **Scripture**

A Question About Everlasting Life

The Gospel of Luke shares an account about Jesus teaching a crowd of people in the Temple area. Some of the people, called Sadducees, did not believe that there was any kind of everlasting happiness after death. People at that time believed that when a man who had no children died, the man's brother had a duty to marry the widow and have children. In this way, the brother could pass down the family heritage and property. The people in the crowd decided to ask Jesus a trick question about everlasting life.

> . . . "Teacher, Moses wrote for us, 'If someone's brother dies leaving a wife but no child, his brother must take the wife and raise up descendants for his brother.' Now there were seven brothers; the first married a woman but died childless. Then the second and the third married her, and likewise all the seven died childless. Finally the woman also died. Now at the resurrection whose wife will that woman be? For all seven had been married to her. Jesus said to them, "The children of this age marry and remarry; but those who are deemed worthy to attain to the coming age and to the resurrection of the dead neither marry nor are given in marriage. They can no longer die, for they are like angels; and they are the children of God because they are the ones who rise. . . . Some of the scribes said in reply, "Teacher, you have answered well." And they no longer dared to ask him anything.
>
> Luke 20:28–36;39–40

To read the complete account in Scripture see Luke 20:27–40.

Our Church Teaches

The Book of Exodus describes one of the most important saving acts of God. The Old Testament is filled with signs of God's love and faithfulness. But the New Testament tells of God's greatest act of love: God the Father sending his Son, Jesus, into the world to save all people. Jesus suffered and died for our sins. Jesus gave his own power to forgive sins to the Church, no matter how great the sin. Jesus Christ rose from the dead and ascended into Heaven. With him we can share in the promised land of Heaven. Because of Jesus' Death and Resurrection, people do not have to be afraid of death. If we love God and others as Jesus taught, death leads to everlasting happiness with God.

We Believe

Jesus Christ conquered death for us. At our Baptism he gives new life to our souls. He will also give new life to our bodies in the Kingdom of Heaven.

ACTIVITIES

1. Jesus said that the Lord is not the God of the dead but of the living. To God, all are alive. The Church has a tradition of praying for both the living and the dead. In the space below, name one person, living or dead, for whom you wish to pray, and write a short prayer for that person.

Name: ______________________________

Prayer: ______________________________

____

____

____

____

2. What questions do you have about life after death?

____

____

____

____

What are some ways that God's people express their need to be free?

Respond

Bound by Faith

In the eighteenth and nineteenth centuries, African people were forced to come to America as slaves. African slaves were robbed of their freedom and self-esteem. They suffered in many of the same ways as the Hebrews did in Egypt. To help them survive, African slaves sang songs called spirituals, which expressed their faith in God. The slaves sang about a journey to spiritual as well as physical freedom and asked Jesus to set them free "on the inside." They called on the heroes of the Old Testament as friends who could help them in their struggles. One person began the spiritual by singing about his or her sadness or joy. A group would sing a response. The following spiritual is called "Go Down, Moses."

Go Down, Moses

Solo: When Israel was in Egypt's land
Group: Let my people go!
Solo: Oppressed so hard they could not stand
Group: Let my people go!
All (refrain): **Go down, Moses,**
'way down in Egypt's land.
Tell ol' Pharaoh to
let my people go!
Solo: The Lord told Moses what to do
Group: Let my people go!
Solo: To lead the children of Israel through
Group: Let my people go!
All (refrain)

Solo: As Israel stood by the water side
Group: Let my people go!
Solo: At God's command it did divide
Group: Let my people go!
All (refrain)
Solo: When they had reached the other shore
Group: Let my people go!
Solo: They sang a song of triumph o'er
Group: Let my people go!
All (refrain)
Solo: Oh, let us all from bondage flee
Group: Let my people go!
Solo: And let us all in Christ be free
Group: Let my people go!
All (refrain)

Did You Know . . .

African slaves used their songs as secret codes? The song "Steal Away to Jesus" was used to call secret meetings. Frederick Douglass, a slave liberator, used the line "I am bound for Canaan" to signal that he was going North.

ACTIVITY

The ancient Egyptian alphabet was made of pictures instead of letters. The pictures are called *hieroglyphics*. The key shows hieroglyphics for the letters in our alphabet. Use it to translate the song Miriam sang when the Hebrews crossed the Red Sea.

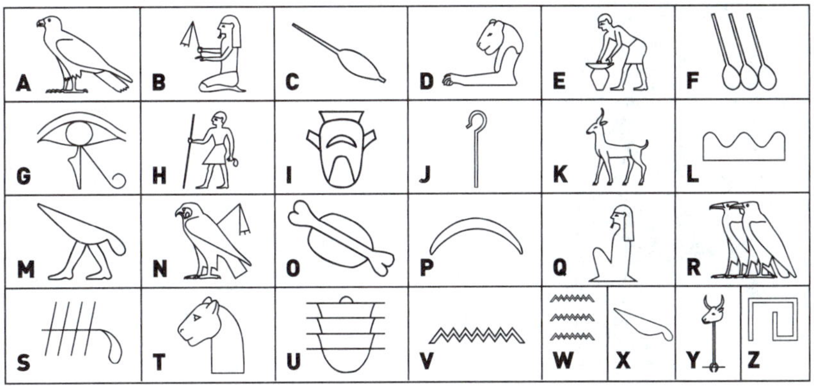

Based on Exodus 15:1

What are some of the ways we can we praise our God, the God of Moses?

A Prayer of Praise

After crossing the Red Sea, the Israelites understood more fully the power of God. Their praises went up to God in a song. God has freed us all from sin and death by his Son, Jesus Christ. Let us stand and praise him, using the words of the Israelites' song.

Leader: Let us sing to the Lord who is covered in wondrous glory.

All: Let us sing to the Lord who is covered in wondrous glory.

Leader: I will sing to the Lord, in glory triumphant;
horse and rider are thrown to the sea.
God of strength, of song, of salvation, God of mine,
hear these praises.

All: Let us sing to the Lord who is covered in wondrous glory.

Leader: My God is a warrior whose name is "The Lord."
Pharaoh's army is thrown to the sea.
Your right hand is magnificent in pow'r,
your right hand has crushed the enemy.

All: Let us sing to the Lord who is covered in wondrous glory.

Leader: In your mercy you led the people you redeemed.
You brought them to your sacred home.
There you will plant them on the mountain that is yours.
The Lord shall reign forever!

All: Let us sing to the Lord who is covered in wondrous glory.

Text: Exodus 15; Naimh O'Kelly-Fischer

Chapter Review 5

A **Identify** who or what is described by each clue, using words from the box.

spiritual
Moses
Exodus
Old Testament
everlasting life
Promised Land
Yahweh
New Testament
Jesus

1. Called Canaan, this is the sacred place God promised to Abraham, Isaac, Jacob, and the Israelites.

   ____

2. The story of how God freed the Hebrews in Egypt; the second book of the Old Testament ______________________

3. He conquered death for us; at Baptism he gives new life to our souls and will give new life to our bodies in the Kingdom of Heaven. ______________________

4. This most sacred name of God, spoken to Moses, means "I am who I am." ______________________

5. This part of the Bible is filled with signs of God's love and faithfulness.

   ____

6. This part of the Bible tells of God's greatest act of love.

   ____

7. Just as God led his people to the Promised Land, he leads us to this.

   ____

8. When he and the Israelites reached the Red Sea, the Lord turned it into dry land. ______________________

B **Explain** the meaning of the statement, "God's love delivers us."

____

____

____

____

5 Chapter Review

C **Complete** the lists below to show ways that people can be enslaved spiritually and materially.

Materially enslaved

1. always asking for things
2. ______________________
3. ______________________
4. ______________________

Spiritually enslaved

1. being jealous of others
2. ______________________
3. ______________________
4. ______________________

D **Describe** the event from Moses' life that Jesus used to teach about everlasting life.

____

____

____

____

E **Respond** to the following.

1. What is God's greatest act of love? ______________________

   ____

2. How did Jesus make it possible for us to share in the promised land of Heaven? ______________________

   ____

   ____

Getting ready for Chapter 6

Take Home

Passover and the Eucharistic Celebration

This chapter recalls the Old Testament story of the Passover, when God delivered his people from the plague of death in Egypt and Pharaoh let the Israelites go. We remember that Jesus' Passover gave us the freedom of salvation. We celebrate this deliverance in the liturgy and on our feast days, especially Easter.

ACTIVITY **Family Identity**

The Israelites were bound together as God's people. To symbolize your family's unity, have everyone dress in the same colors one day this week. Or create a family crest, frame it, and display it in a prominent place in your home.

THROUGH THE WEEK

A Prayer for the Week Dear Lord, you lead us to salvation in the celebration of the Eucharist. By sharing in your Body and Blood, may we one day share in the eternal banquet of the Kingdom of Heaven. Amen.

ON SUNDAY
As you join in the procession to receive the Eucharist at Mass, thank God for his blessings in your life and in the life of your family.

ON THE WEB
BlestAreWe.com
RCLBLectionary.com
SaintsResource.com

Saint Sharbel Makhlouf (1828–1898)

Saint Sharbel was a Maronite Catholic monk in the Monastery of St. Maron in Lebanon. Sharbel lived as a hermit from 1875 until his death. He followed a strict fast and was very devoted to the Blessed Sacrament. His only travel was to nearby villages to administer Holy Communion.

Feast Day: July 24

Take Home

Scripture Background
In the Time of Jesus

THE PASCHAL LAMB During the Exodus, when the plague of death was about to strike Egypt, Moses commanded all Hebrew families to slaughter a lamb and sprinkle its blood on the doorpost of their homes (see Exodus 12:21–22). This slaughtered lamb was called the paschal lamb. Just as on Passover Jews recall the events of their being saved from death and suffering during the Exodus, on Holy Thursday evening we commemorate the Last Supper, when Jesus offered himself as the new Paschal Lamb, saving us from eternal death. Read about the Last Supper in Luke 22:14–20.

Our Catholic Tradition
in Art

THE LAST SUPPER The Last Supper is the subject of one of the world's most famous paintings: Leonardo da Vinci's *The Last Supper*. The masterpiece is a fresco, or wall painting, located in the Church of Santa Maria delle Grazie in Milan, Italy. It miraculously survived bombings in World War II only to be threatened with deterioration from climatic conditions in the church. Fortunately, a vast restoration project completed in 1999 saved da Vinci's painting from destruction.

Passover and the Eucharistic Celebration

Chapter 6

Blessed are you, Lord God of all creation, . . .

The Liturgy of the Eucharist, *Roman Missal*

Share

Many celebrations have unique symbols. The Jewish feast of the Exodus, called Passover, is held around Easter time, and lasts for seven or eight days. On the first night, Jewish families have a meal called the Seder. They share foods eaten by the Hebrews on the night that the plague of death passed over their homes. The Seder foods are symbols. Bitter herbs represent the Hebrews' bitter slavery. Lamb represents the lamb's blood on the Hebrews' doorways. Unleavened bread—bread baked without yeast—represents the hurry to flee Egypt. (There was no time for bread to rise.)

ACTIVITY

Under each symbol write the celebration or holiday it represents.

________________ ________________ ________________ ________________

Choose one of the events above, and name items that are part of your family's celebration of it.

____

____

____

How do Catholics celebrate Jesus' sacrifice?

Hear and Believe **Worship**

Mass of the Lord's Supper

Holy Thursday is a very important day in the Church's calendar of celebrations, known as the **liturgical year**. Holy Thursday honors the night on which Jesus shared the Last Supper with the Twelve Apostles. He washed their feet to teach them about serving others. On that night, the Apostle Judas handed Jesus over to be arrested. Jesus was crucified the next day, Good Friday. The period from Holy Thursday evening until Evening Prayer on Easter Sunday evening is called the *Easter Triduum.*

During the Holy Thursday Evening Mass of the Lord's Supper, we remember the Last Supper and prepare for the remembrance of Jesus' Crucifixion. Priests and parishioners take part in the washing of the feet, symbolic of Jesus' washing the feet of the disciples. The First Reading that evening (Exodus 12:1-8,11-14) tells the story of how the Israelites were passed over when God brought the final plague upon Egypt: death to the firstborns. God told Moses how the Israelites should prepare for, and remember, this event.

A reading from the Book of Exodus.

The LORD said to Moses and Aaron in the land of Egypt: . . . Tell the whole community of Israel: On the tenth of this month every family must procure for itself a lamb, one apiece for each household. . . .You will keep it until the fourteenth day of this month, and then, with the whole community of Israel assembled, it will be slaughtered during the evening twilight. They will take some of its blood and apply it to the two doorposts and the lintel of the houses in which they eat it. They will consume its meat that same night, eating it roasted with unleavened bread and bitter herbs.

This is how you are to eat it: with your loins girt, sandals on your feet and your staff in hand, you will eat it in a hurry. It is the LORD's Passover. For on this same night I will go through Egypt, striking down every firstborn in the land, human being and beast alike, and executing judgment on all the gods of Egypt—I, the LORD! But for you the blood will mark the houses where you are. Seeing the blood, I will pass over you; thereby, when I strike the land of Egypt, no destructive blow will come upon you.

This day will be a day of remembrance for you, which your future generations will celebrate with pilgrimage to the LORD; you will celebrate it as a statute forever. Exodus 12:1,3,6–8,11–14

The Passover of the Lord

Jesus' Death and Resurrection took place during the Jewish feast of **Passover**. The Last Supper was a Passover meal. At the Last Supper, Jesus fulfilled the Jewish Passover. But Jesus gave Passover a whole new meaning. At the Last Supper, Jesus blessed the bread and wine, then distributed them as his Body and Blood. He said, "... [D]o this in memory of me" (Luke 22:19). The Eucharist is a memorial of Jesus' Passover—his work of salvation through his suffering, Death, Resurrection, and Ascension. The Passover of the Lord anticipates the final Passover of the Church when all of his followers find eternal happiness in God's kingdom.

Our liturgies celebrate the great mystery that gave us the chance for happiness in God's kingdom: the Passion (suffering), Death, Resurrection, and Ascension of Jesus. This is the **Paschal Mystery**. We honor it at Mass in Communion, songs, prayers, and readings. The seasons of the liturgical year also celebrate parts of the Paschal Mystery. Easter celebrates Jesus' Resurrection. Lent is a season of sacrifice and preparation for Easter. The Triduum honors the events of Jesus' Death and Resurrection. Jesus' Ascension is celebrated forty days after Easter. Our liturgies also honor people already in Heaven—Mary and the saints.

GO TO page 314 for more information about the liturgical year.

Faith Words

liturgical year
The liturgical year is the Church's yearly calendar of feasts and seasons.

Passover
Passover is the Jewish celebration of the Israelites' Exodus from Egypt.

Paschal Mystery
The Paschal Mystery is Jesus' Passion, Death, Resurrection, and Ascension that saved us from sin and gave us life after death.

ACTIVITY

Explain this statement: "Jesus gave Passover a whole new meaning."

____

____

____

____

____

____

____

What events in the Bible are signs of the Paschal Mystery?

Hear and Believe **Scripture**

The Feeding of the Five Thousand

Jesus, mourning the death of John the Baptist, had wandered off to a deserted place. However, people soon learned where he was headed, and a vast crowd was there to meet him. When Jesus got off the boat and saw the crowd, his heart was moved with pity for them and he cured their sick.

When it was evening, the disciples approached [Jesus] and said, "This is a deserted place and it is already late; dismiss the crowds so that they can go to the villages and buy food for themselves." [Jesus] said to them, "There is no need for them to go away; give them some food yourselves." But they said to him, "Five loaves and two fish are all we have here." Then he said, "Bring them here to me," and he ordered the crowds to sit down on the grass. Taking the five loaves and the two fish, and looking up to heaven, he said the blessing, broke the loaves, and gave them to the disciples, who in turn gave them to the crowds. They all ate and were satisfied, and they picked up the fragments left over—twelve wicker baskets full. Those who ate were about five thousand men, not counting women and children. Matthew 14:15–21

To read the complete account in Scripture see Matthew 14:13–21.

Our Church Teaches

Passover was a sign of the sacrifice of Jesus Christ. Just as a lamb was sacrificed to save the Israelites, Jesus sacrificed his life on the Cross to save all people. The Church also teaches that Jesus' miracle of feeding 5,000 followers with five loaves of bread (see Matthew 14:13– 21) was a sign of the special food he would give the whole world: the Eucharist. We celebrate the Eucharist with confidence that we will one day be able to enjoy the glory of Heaven.

We Believe

The same God who delivered his people from slavery in Egypt delivered us from sin and death through his Son, Jesus Christ.

ACTIVITIES

1. **Reread the Scripture story. Imagine yourself in the story. Using a storybook format, draw the story for a young child.**

2. **Think about the similarities and differences between a Passover feast and a Eucharistic celebration. Then complete the chart below.**

Passover Feast and Eucharistic Celebration	
Similarities	Example: They both celebrate God's love for us.
Differences	

Who teaches us about God's love today?

Respond

The Election of Pope Francis

The election of a new pope is an important event in the life of the Church. All of the cardinals meet in Rome and stay at the Vatican, where the pope lives. They do not read newspapers or watch TV while there. No one tells them how they should vote.

The cardinals pray for the guidance of the Holy Spirit. Catholics from throughout the world gather outside in St. Peter's Square to pray for the cardinals. They join the cardinals in prayer and wait for news regarding the election of the new pope.

The voting process begins when each cardinal writes his vote on a piece of paper. A cardinal then tallies the votes, and if no one has enough votes to be named the new pope, the cardinal burns the papers with chemicals that make black smoke. The black smoke that people see coming from the chimney means that the cardinals have not yet made a decision.

The voting process continues until a cardinal receives enough votes to be named pope. When the cardinals finally elect a new pope, they burn the papers with a different chemical so that people see white smoke coming from the chimney. This signals to all that we have a pope!

In March of 2013, Cardinal Jorge Bergoglio was elected pope. Pope John Paul II named Cardinal Bergoglio, a Jesuit, a cardinal in 2001. He grew up in Argentina, and is the first pope to come from Latin America.

Cardinal Bergoglio chose the name Francis after he was elected pope, in honor of Saint Francis of Assisi. As pope, he is the leader of the Church all over the world. He follows in the footsteps of Saint Peter, who was chosen by Jesus to be the very first leader of the Church on Earth.

Together with the bishops and the College of Cardinals, the pope leads and serves the Church, helping it to grow in holiness and helping us to live as faithful disciples of Jesus.

ACTIVITIES

1. Imagine that you have the opportunity to meet with Pope Francis and interview him. What questions would you ask him? In the space provided, write three questions that you would ask, including one question about his life as a young Catholic.

Soon after he became pope, Pope Francis celebrated the Mass of the Lord's Supper on Holy Thursday, March 28, 2013 at Casa del Marmo, the Prison for Minors in Rome. He washed the feet of twelve inmates. In his homily he challenged the young people to ask themselves this question: "Am I really willing, willing to serve, to help others?"

2. How would you answer Pope Francis' question, "Am I really willing, willing to serve, to help others?" In what ways do you serve and help others?

The Nicene Creed

I believe in one God,
the Father almighty,
maker of heaven and earth,
of all things visible and invisible.

I believe in one Lord Jesus Christ,
the Only Begotten Son of God,
born of the Father before all ages.
God from God, Light from Light,
true God from true God,
begotten, not made, consubstantial with the Father;
through him all things were made.
For us men and for our salvation
he came down from heaven,
and by the Holy Spirit was incarnate of the Virgin Mary,
and became man.

For our sake he was crucified under Pontius Pilate,
he suffered death and was buried,
and rose again on the third day
in accordance with the Scriptures.
He ascended into heaven
and is seated at the right hand of the Father.
He will come again in glory
to judge the living and the dead
and his kingdom will have no end.

I believe in the Holy Spirit, the Lord, the giver of life,
who proceeds from the Father and the Son,
who with the Father and the Son is adored and glorified,
who has spoken through the prophets.

I believe in one, holy, catholic and apostolic Church.
I confess one Baptism for the forgiveness of sins
and I look forward to the resurrection of the dead
and the life of the world to come. Amen.

Roman Missal

Chapter Review 6

A **Complete** the sentences, using words from the box.

liturgical year
Passover
Resurrection
sin
Holy Thursday
Francis
Eucharist
Easter Triduum
Paschal Mystery

1. ______________ is the Jewish celebration of the Israelites' Exodus from Egypt.
2. The Church's yearly calendar of celebrations and seasons is called the ______________.
3. The ______________ is the period from Holy Thursday evening until Evening Prayer on Easter Sunday evening.
4. When Cardinal Jorge Bergoglio became pope, he chose the name ______________.
5. ______________ celebrates the night on which Jesus shared the Last Supper with the Twelve Apostles.
6. The ______________ is a memorial of Jesus' work of salvation through his suffering, Death, ______________, and Ascension.
7. Our liturgies celebrate the ______________, Jesus' Passion, Death, Resurrection, and Ascension that saved us from ______________.

B **Who am I? Write** the name of the person described by each clue.

1. God told me how the Israelites should remember and prepare for the Passover. ______________
2. On Holy Thursday evening, 2013, I washed the feet of twelve inmates. ______________
3. My miracle of feeding 5,000 followers with five loaves of bread was a special sign of the food I would give the whole world: the Eucharist. ______________
4. I grew up in Argentina and became a Jesuit priest. ______________
5. I washed the feet of the Twelve Apostles. ______________

6 Chapter Review

C **Write** what you have learned about the Jewish feast of Passover. Name the foods served at the Seder meal, and tell what each represents.

____

____

____

____

D **Write** a prayer of thanks for the salvation Jesus won for you through the Paschal Mystery.

____

____

____

____

E **Respond** to the following.

1. Tell how Jesus is like the lamb that was sacrificed by the Israelites on Passover.

   ____

   ____

   ____

   ____

2. Give examples of ways you can share in Jesus' mission by making sacrifices for others.

   ____

   ____

   ____

Getting ready for Chapter 7

Take Home

Commandment and Fulfillment

The Israelites traveling in the desert toward what would become their homeland were hungry, thirsty, and angry at Moses. Their complaints were met with miracles from God that filled their physical needs: food falling to the ground each morning and water bursting forth from a rock. God also tended to their spiritual needs by giving them the Ten Commandments. The Commandments helped the Israelites remain in a faithful, rewarding relationship with God.

ACTIVITY **House Rules**

What are your family rules? List them, remembering to include rules that family members follow every day without even thinking about them. Post your family rules. Invite family members to add to the list throughout the coming week.

THROUGH THE WEEK

A Prayer for the Week Lord, through the ages you have sent us holy people to teach us how to live. Open our hearts and minds to their guidance that we may share their joy in eternity with you. Amen.

ON SUNDAY
As the readings are proclaimed at Mass, listen for God's promises and for ways God kept those promises.

ON THE WEB
BlestAreWe.com
RCLBLectionary.com
SaintsResource.com

Saint Teresa of Jesus
(Saint Teresa of Ávila, 1515–1582)

Saint Teresa was born in Spain, the daughter of nobles. Although her father strongly objected, Teresa joined the Carmelite order. Teresa spent much of her life writing about prayer, including how she overcame her difficulties with praying.

Patron Saint of: Spain

Feast Day: October 15

Getting ready for Chapter 7

Take Home

Scripture Background

In the Time of Jesus

TEACHING FROM THE MOUNTAINTOP
On their journey to the Promised Land, God revealed to the Israelites the Ten Commandments, which Moses received on Mount Sinai (see Exodus 19—20). In the New Testament, Jesus delivered the Sermon on the Mount, where he taught his followers the Beatitudes and the Golden Rule from a mountain (see Matthew 5—7). At Mount Sinai, God gave his people laws to guide their relationship with him and with others. In the Sermon on the Mount, Jesus revealed to us the fullness of God's law in the Gospel, the new law of love that finds its home in our hearts and our lives through the power of the Holy Spirit.

Our Catholic Tradition in Sacramentals

ETERNAL LIGHT The Israelites regularly kept oil lamps burning outside the Ark of the Covenant, the sacred box containing the stone tablets of the Ten Commandments. When the Ark was moved to the Temple in Jerusalem, the ritual continued. After their Temple was destroyed, the Israelites began to worship in synagogues, where a continuously burning light called *Ner Tamid* ("eternal light"), representing God's eternal covenant, shines above the Ark, now holding the Torah.

In our churches, at least one oil lamp or candle continually shines near the tabernacle holding the Blessed Sacrament. The light signifies the purity and divinity of Christ, the Light of the World.

Commandment and Fulfillment

Chapter 7

"... I will place my law within them, and write it upon their hearts; ..."
Jeremiah 31:33

Share

You follow rules every day—in school, clubs, sports, and your home. These rules usually keep things running smoothly. Many rules help keep people safe. Try to think of some rules you follow each day that keep people from physical or emotional harm.

ACTIVITY

What do you remember about the rules called the Ten Commandments? In the first column, list everything you already know about the Commandments. In the second column, write a few questions you have about them. Complete the third column when you finish this chapter.

What I Know	What I Want to Know	What I Have Learned

How are the Ten Commandments a covenant?

Hear and Believe **Scripture**

The Covenant at Sinai

After the Israelites left Egypt, God led them through the desert. The journey was rough, and the Israelites grumbled against Moses. But God protected the Israelites and eased their hardships.

The Israelites complained to Moses that they were starving. The next morning, breadlike flakes covered the desert. The Israelites asked, "What is this?" Moses told them, "This is the bread which the Lord has given you to eat." The Israelites called this food *manna*. It was white and tasted like wafers made with honey. The people complained that they were thirsty. At the Lord's command, Moses struck a rock with his staff, and water flowed out for the people to drink.

About three months after they left Egypt, the Israelites came to the desert of Sinai. They camped at the foot of Mount Sinai. Moses went up the mountain to speak to God. The Lord said, "Tell the Israelites: You have seen for yourselves how I brought you here safely to me. Therefore, if you listen to me and keep my covenant, you shall be dearer to me than all other people. You shall be to me a holy nation." Then the Lord told Moses to have the people prepare to meet the Lord in three days.

On the morning of the third day there were peals of thunder and lightning, and a heavy cloud over the mountain, and a very loud blast of the shofar, so that all the people in the camp trembled. But Moses led the people out of the camp to meet God, and they stationed themselves at the foot of the mountain. . . .

Then God spoke all these words:

I am the LORD your God, who brought you out of the land of Egypt, out of the house of slavery. You shall not have other gods beside me.

. . . You shall not invoke the name of the LORD, your God, in vain.

. . . Remember the sabbath day—keep it holy.

Honor your father and your mother, . . .
You shall not kill.
You shall not commit adultery.
You shall not steal.
You shall not bear false witness against your neighbor.
You shall not covet your neighbor's wife . . . or anything that belongs to your neighbor.

Exodus 19:16–17; 20:1,2,7–8,12–17

Moses told the Israelites God's Commandments. They offered sacrifices to the Lord. Then Moses went up the mountain again. When Moses came down the mountain, he was carrying stone tablets upon which God had written the Ten Commandments. But the Israelites were dancing, drinking, and worshiping a golden calf.

Moses angrily threw the tablets and broke them. He went back to the Lord to ask the Lord to forgive the Israelites. The Lord commanded Moses to cut two new stone tablets.

"Here is the covenant I will make," said the Lord. "Before your people's eyes I will work wonders that have never been seen in any nation on Earth. People will see the power of the Lord. But you must keep my Commandments. Write down these words, for with them I have made a covenant with you and Israel."

Faith Words

Ark of the Covenant
The Ark of the Covenant was a special box that held the stone tablets of the Ten Commandments.

manna
Manna is the breadlike food that God gave the Israelites in the desert.

Moses wrote the Commandments on the tablets. Then skillful Israelites created a gold and wood box and a special tent. Moses brought the tablets down the mountain and placed them in the box, called the **Ark of the Covenant**. After that, the Israelites carried the Ark of the Covenant in the tent wherever they traveled.

To read the complete account in Scripture see Exodus 16:13–15,31; 17:5–6;19—20; 32; 34:1–4,10–11,27–29; 35; 40.

God's Love and Laws

The covenant God made with Abraham and his descendants was a two-way relationship. God loved his people, and he would work wonders before their eyes, just as he had done when he fed them **manna**. The people loved God and would keep his Commandments, which he revealed through Moses. The Ten Commandments express the way we all want to live: without offending God or harming other people and ourselves. Because we are created in God's image, we have a natural desire for goodness. We also have a special dignity, as well as rights and duties, such as the right to practice our faith and the duty to love and care for one another.

ACTIVITY

Read the Ten Commandments. Choose two of the Commandments and describe ways you might keep them.

Commandment	Ways to Keep
________________	________________
	________________
________________	________________
	________________

What did Jesus say about the Ten Commandments?

Hear and Believe **Scripture**

Jesus Teaches About the Law

> [The Pharisees] gathered together, and one of them [a scholar of the law] tested [Jesus] by asking, "Teacher, which commandment in the law is the greatest?" [Jesus] said to him, "You shall love the Lord, your God, with all your heart, with all your soul, and with all your mind. This is the greatest and the first commandment. The second is like it: You shall love your neighbor as yourself. The whole law and the prophets depend on these two commandments."
>
> Matthew 22:34–40

Later, Jesus told his disciples, "As for your religious leaders, who have taken the place of Moses as teachers of the law, observe all things they tell you, but do not follow their example. For they preach but they do not practice." Jesus said that such leaders liked to perform their good deeds in public so that everyone could see how great they were.

> [Jesus told his disciples,] "As for you, do not be called 'Rabbi.' You have but one teacher, and you are all brothers. Call no one on earth your father; you have but one Father in heaven."
>
> Matthew 23:8–9

To read the complete account in Scripture see Matthew 22:34–40; 23:1–9.

Our Church Teaches

God is the ultimate authority for our society. God revealed the Ten Commandments. By following them, we show love for God and choose good over evil. God's law from the Old Testament prepares us for the Gospel. Jesus taught us how important it is to keep God's Commandments. He also said, . . . "You shall love the Lord, your God, with all your heart, with all your soul, and with all your mind. This is the greatest and the first commandment. The second is like it: You shall love your neighbor as yourself" (Matthew 22:37–39).

We Believe

Jesus revealed the ultimate meaning of the Ten Commandments and taught us to keep God's laws in the spirit of love.

ACTIVITY

Look at each of the photographs. In the box within each photograph, write the letter of the Commandment that corresponds to it.

a. You shall love the Lord, your God, with all your heart, with all your soul, and with all your mind.

b. Honor your father and your mother.

c. Remember to keep holy the Sabbath day.

How do you show that you love God and others?

Saint Teresa of Jesus (Saint Teresa of Ávila)

As a teenager in Spain in the 1500s, Teresa shared many of the concerns of modern teenagers. She worried about her appearance and what boys thought of her, and she liked to flirt. The last thing on her mind was spending her life in a convent! But Teresa's strict father was worried about his daughter's behavior. When she was sixteen he sent her to a convent.

Teresa soon wanted to spend the rest of her life in service to the Lord. She became a Carmelite nun. Teresa tried to keep Jesus present within her through prayer, which she described as a mental sharing between friends. She believed that prayer should be time spent alone, reflecting only on God. When Teresa prayed, she felt God's presence overwhelm her. People who watched her pray said that her whole body would lift off the ground.

But there was a time in Teresa's life when praying was a struggle. She found it very hard to concentrate. She worked hard to overcome this difficulty. Teresa realized that there were others who also had trouble praying. She wanted to help them experience the beauty of prayer. So she spent much of her life writing and teaching others how to pray.

As an adult, Teresa founded a religious order called the Discalced Carmelites. Members of this order show their love for God by living a simple life of poverty, devoted to prayer. Teresa helped others discover that one finds inner peace through prayer. The Church recognized Teresa for her life of holiness and her contributions to the Church. She was canonized in 1622. In 1970, Saint Teresa of Jesus (Teresa of Ávila) was named a Doctor of the Church. Her feast day is October 15.

ACTIVITY

For each of the Ten Commandments, tell the meaning of the Commandment for today. Four have been done for you.

Bible	Meaning for Today
I, the LORD, am your God. You shall not have other gods besides me.	
You shall not take the name of the LORD, your God, in vain.	
Remember to keep holy the sabbath day.	
Honor your father and your mother.	
You shall not kill.	Respect life. Take care of your health. Work to protect unborn children, the sick, and the elderly.
You shall not commit adultery.	Avoid situations that might lead to sexual sins.
You shall not steal.	Keep promises and agreements. Do not purposely keep things that you have borrowed or things that people have lost.
You shall not bear false witness against your neighbor.	
You shall not covet your neighbor's wife.	Keep your heart pure and your thoughts focused on God. Respect people's marriage vows.
You shall not covet anything that belongs to your neighbor.	

Based on Exodus 20:2–17

How can the Scriptures help us pray?

GO TO page 379 for more information about the Ten Commandments.

Praying with Scripture

Saint Teresa of Jesus (Teresa of Ávila) said that she often started praying by reading Scripture and reflecting upon it. Try her method of prayer. Silently read the following Scripture passage. In it, Moses is speaking to the Israelites.

> **"Hear, O Israel! The LORD is our God, the LORD alone! Therefore, you shall love the LORD, your God, with your whole heart, and with your whole being, and with your whole strength. Take to heart these words which I command you today. Keep repeating them to your children. Recite them when you are at home and when you are away, when you lie down and when you get up."**
>
> Deuteronomy 6:4–7

Quietly reflect on what these words mean for you today. Then write a prayer telling God how you will love him "with all your heart, and with your whole being, and with your whole strength."

Chapter Review 7

A **Circle** the letter of the correct answer.

1. _______ revealed the ultimate meaning of the Ten Commandments and taught us to keep God's laws in the spirit of love.

   a. Moses **b.** Abraham

   c. Jesus **d.** Miriam

2. _______ is the ultimate authority in our society.

   a. Moses **b.** God

   c. The President **d.** The Supreme Court

3. The _______ express the way we all want to live: without offending God or hurting others or ourselves.

   a. Ten Commandments **b.** Israelites

   c. Carmelites **d.** First and Third Commandments

4. Saint Teresa of Jesus (Teresa of Ávila) helped others discover that one finds inner peace through _______.

   a. play. **b.** prayer.

   c. cooking. **d.** the words to a hymn.

B **Match** Column A with Column B by writing the correct number in the space provided.

A	B
1. Ark of the Covenant	_____ laws that guide our moral lives
2. Ten Commandments	_____ "You shall love the Lord, your God, with all your heart, with all your soul, and with all your mind."
3. Sinai	_____ the breadlike food that God gave the Israelites
4. manna	_____ the desert through which the Israelites passed on their journey from Egypt
5. the greatest Commandment	_____ the special box that held the stone tablets of the Ten Commandments

7 Chapter Review

C **Explain** one way that Saint Teresa of Jesus (Teresa of Ávila) showed her love for God. Then explain one way you can show your own love for God.

____

____

____

____

D **Write** an action or behavior that you can carry out to follow each Commandment listed. Examples are provided.

1. Honor your father and your mother.
   Example: Help my parents with chores around the house

   ____

   ____

2. You shall not steal.
   Example: Return things I have borrowed

   ____

   ____

E **Write** a brief summary of what you learned in this chapter, using the words in the box.

Israelites	**Ten Commandments**	**Covenant**
Moses	**neighbor**	**Jesus**

____

____

____

____

____

____

Getting ready for Chapter 8

Take Home

Our Journey and God's Presence

We are a pilgrim people with roots in the wanderings of the nomadic Israelites. We seek a promised land just as they did. Their Promised Land was Canaan, which they reached after forty years in the desert, led by God. Our promised land is Heaven, a land of happiness for our souls, reached by being faithful followers of Christ throughout our lives.

ACTIVITY **Signs of God**

Joshua and the Israelites had to pay careful attention to God's directions when storming the Promised Land. Have each family member draw a symbol of something that keeps him or her in touch with God. Swap symbols, and try to experience another person's way of hearing God's voice this week.

THROUGH THE WEEK

A Prayer for the Week Lord, with your help we can achieve great things. Help us to rely on your love and to see your goodness in the world around us. Amen.

ON SUNDAY
Think of your trip to church as a journey. Identify what makes your destination special.

ON THE WEB
BlestAreWe.com
RCLBLectionary.com
SaintsResource.com

Saint Frances Xavier Cabrini (1850–1917)

From her early childhood in Italy, Frances Xavier Cabrini wanted to be a missionary to China. As a Missionary Sister of the Sacred Heart, she traveled to America instead, where she founded sixty-seven institutions dedicated to the care of the poor.

Patron Saint of:
hospitals and orphans

Feast Day: November 13

Take Home

Scripture Background
Before the Time of Jesus

THE RAM'S HORN The ram's horn (*shofar*) is a powerful image throughout Scripture. Joshua and his soldiers were able to topple Jericho's city walls by blowing horns and shouting (see Joshua 6:1–21). Horns were used as a call to battle, to call assemblies, to announce a new year, and to warn of danger. They were also used in anointings, as when Samuel anointed David as king (see 1 Samuel 16:13). Shofars are still used today. A shofar is sounded at the Jewish new year (Rosh Hashanah) and to signal the end of fasting on the Jewish day of atonement (Yom Kippur).

Russian Orthodox Christians celebrating baptism in the Jordan River

Our Catholic Tradition in Sacramentals

THE JORDAN RIVER Joshua crossed the Jordan River, which was also the river where Jesus was baptized. Blessing rivers or fountains is a custom of Eastern countries. In Africa the Nile is blessed on the Solemnity of the Epiphany of the Lord and in commemoration of the Baptism of the Lord. Christians traditionally would dip themselves in the blessed water three times, and even animals would be herded into the water to receive its blessing.

Our Journey and God's Presence

Chapter 8

In the tender compassion of our God,
the dawn will break upon us, to shine
on those who dwell in darkness.

Based on Luke 1:78–79

Share

The natural world is filled with reminders of God's power and goodness, such as a colorful rainbow that follows a storm, a tiny, detailed snowflake, or a perfect-looking rose. What other events in the natural world remind you of God's love for people?

ACTIVITY

Write the names of three natural wonders that remind you of God's power and goodness. Then write adjectives that describe what each wonder tells you about God.

Natural Wonder ____________________

____

____

____

Natural Wonder ____________________

____

____

____

Natural Wonder ____________________

____

____

____

How did God show his goodness when the Israelites reached the Promised Land?

Hear and Believe **Scripture**

Conquest of the Promised Land

The Israelites had wandered in the desert for forty years. After Moses died, the Lord appointed Joshua to lead the Israelites to the Promised Land, Canaan.

> [The LORD said to Joshua]: Moses my servant is dead. So now, you and the whole people with you, prepare to cross the Jordan to the land that I will give the Israelites. . . . As I was with Moses, I will be with you: I will not leave you nor forsake you. Joshua 1:1–2,5

Joshua secretly sent two of his men to spy on the land. The spies took shelter in the city of Jericho, in the house of a woman named Rahab. The king of Jericho heard about the spies and sent Rahab the order, "Put out the visitors who have entered your house, for they have come to spy on my land." Instead, Rahab hid the men. She told the king's messengers, "The men you speak of came to me, but I did not know where they came from. They left at dark, and I do not know where they went."

> Before the spies lay down, Rahab went up to them on the roof and said, "I know that the LORD has given you the land, that a dread of you has come upon us, and that all the inhabitants of the land tremble with fear because of you. For we have heard how the LORD dried up the waters of the Red Sea before you when you came out of Egypt, . . . Now then, swear to me by the LORD that, since I am showing kindness to you, you in turn will show kindness to my family." Joshua 2:8–10,12

She helped the spies down through the window with a rope. "Go up into the hill country," she said, "so that your pursuers may not find you. Hide there for three days. Then you may go on your way."

The men told Rahab, "Hang a red cord from this window. Gather your family. When we return," they promised, "everyone inside this house will be spared."

Early the next day, Joshua led the Israelites to the banks of the river. They camped out for three days. Then Joshua said to the people, "Tomorrow the Lord will perform wonders among you."

The next day, the Lord told Joshua, "Command the priests carrying the Ark of the Covenant to stop in the waters at the edge of the Jordan." When the priests entered the Jordan River, the river stopped flowing. The priests stood there until the Israelites had crossed the Jordan safely. Then they carried the Ark out and the river flowed back.

> And to Joshua the LORD said: . . . Have all the soldiers circle the city, marching once around it. Do this for six days, with seven priests carrying ram's horns ahead of the ark. On the seventh day march around the city seven times, and have the priests blow the horns.
> Joshua 6:2,3–4

The Israelites followed the Lord's directions. As the horns blew on the seventh day, the people raised a tremendous shout. The walls of Jericho collapsed, and the Israelites stormed the city and conquered it. Rahab and her family were spared.

City by city, the Israelites took the land the Lord had promised. Years later, Joshua called the people together. He reminded them of all that the Lord had done for them. "Acknowledge with your whole heart and soul that every one of the promises the Lord has made to you has been fulfilled. Therefore, love the Lord completely and sincerely, and obey his Commandments."

The Israelites agreed to serve the Lord alone.

To read the complete narrative in Scripture see Exodus 16:35; Joshua 1-6; 24

Faith Words

Chosen People
In the Old Testament the chosen people were Abraham and his descendants, whom God had selected to receive his word.

Listening for God's Voice

The Israelites reached the Promised Land, but they could not have succeeded without God's help. Joshua led the Israelites into Canaan by listening to God's instructions. God told Joshua how the Israelites should cross the Jordan, and it worked. God told Joshua how the Israelites should get inside the city, and they did. Because they talked to and listened to God, Joshua and the Israelites successfully conquered and settled in the Promised Land. With Joshua's guidance, the Israelites promised to continue to listen to God. They wanted to continue to be God's **Chosen People**. God had chosen to reveal his love and fidelity to them so many times. God is love and fidelity.

ACTIVITY

1. What happened to the Israelites after Moses died?

____

____

____

2. How did Joshua know the will of the Lord?

____

____

____

How do people receive God's instructions for their lives?

Hear and Believe

A Man of Prayer: Saint Juan Diego

Juan Diego was an Aztec leader in Mexico in the sixteenth century, a time when most people in Mexico worshiped the Aztec gods and goddesses. Juan became a Catholic when he was about fifty years old. As a new Catholic, Juan had to walk fifteen miles into Mexico City to attend Mass. One day, on this journey, his life changed forever.

This photograph shows the image on Juan Diego's cloak, which is kept in the Basilica of our Lady of Guadalupe in Mexico City.

It was the morning of December 9, 1531. Juan Diego was crossing a hill on his way to Mass when he suddenly heard music and saw an unusual cloud. At the top of the hill, he had a vision of Mary, the Mother of Jesus. She was wearing the colors of an Aztec princess. Mary asked Juan to have the bishop build a church at the spot at which she was standing.

Juan Diego visited the bishop, who was not persuaded by Juan's story. The bishop wanted proof. So Juan Diego returned to the hill. He was amazed to find roses blooming in the frozen ground. Tucking them into his cloak, Juan rushed back to the bishop. This time, Juan convinced the bishop. Not only did the bishop see the unusual roses, but when Juan opened his cloak, he saw a miraculous, colorful image of Mary imprinted on the inside. Wonder and awe filled both Juan and the bishop.

Soon after, the bishop had the church Mary requested built and dedicated to Our Lady of Guadalupe. As the Mother of the Americas, she helped millions of people turn to her son. Many Mexicans converted to Christianity because of her.

And what happened to Juan Diego? After he met Mary, he devoted his life to listening to God. This man of prayer is now a saint. His feast day is celebrated on December 9.

Our Church Teaches

Prayer is talking to and listening to God. We can pray in words, thoughts, gestures, or song. Our Church has certain prayers for each day of the week, for the morning, the middle of the day, and the evening. Praying every day can help us become people who pray continually. Praying continually—during every event of our lives—will help us hear God's instructions for our lives and discover his will for us. Praying as much as we can—every day—will make it easier to discover God's will. This discovery process is called **discernment**. Discernment also happens through seeking God's will in the Scriptures and by reflecting on the teachings of the Church.

We Believe

Prayer will help us know God's will for us. Constant prayer is especially important.

Faith Words

discernment

Discernment is discovering, with God's help, God's will for our lives.

ACTIVITIES

1. What do the stories of Joshua and Saint Juan Diego have in common?

___

___

___

___

2. In what ways can Juan Diego be a model for you of trust in God and commitment to your faith?

___

___

___

___

3. Write a short prayer asking God to help you grow in faith.

___

___

___

___

How do you show that you are listening to God?

Respond

Celebrating the Lord's Wonders

The Scripture story of the Israelites' conquest of the Promised Land tells how God fulfilled his promise to the Israelites. The following prayer is called "The Lord's Wonders at the Exodus." Pray it aloud, and think about how God showed his power and goodness to the Israelites.

When Israel came forth from Egypt,
  the house of Jacob from an alien people,
Judah became God's sanctuary,
  Israel, God's domain.
The sea saw and fled;
  the Jordan turned back.
The mountains skipped like rams;
  the hills, like lambs.
Why was it, sea, that you fled?
  Jordan, that you turned back?
Mountains, that you skipped like rams?
  You hills, like lambs?
Tremble, earth, before the Lord,
  before the God of Jacob,
Who turned the rock into pools of water,
  flint into a flowing spring.

Psalm 114

ACTIVITY

What everyday events, such as seeing a full moon, remind you of the power and goodness of the Lord? List or draw two of these events below.

Constant Prayer

Berahot are short blessing prayers that Jewish people may say throughout the day to praise the power and goodness of the Lord. They pray them upon everyday events, such as noticing a blossoming tree. Here are some examples you can pray.

Upon opening the eyes:

Blessed are you, Lord God of all creation, for you open the eyes of the blind.

Upon going to breakfast:

Blessed are you, Lord God of all creation, for you provide for all my needs.

Based on berahot blessings

ACTIVITIES

1. Choose one of your events from the activity on page 126. Write a berahot prayer for this event.

____

____

____

____

2. Create a berahot prayer for an event or activity that is always a part of your religion. You may work with your classmates to create this prayer, then pray it together at opening or closing prayer each day.

Religion Class Berahot

____

____

____

____

____

How can you make daily prayer a part of your life?

The Canticle of Zechariah

Catholics have certain prayers for the morning, evening, and middle of the day which are treasured as sources of constant prayer. The following prayer, the Canticle of Zechariah, is prayed during the morning prayer of the Church. Zechariah was the father of John the Baptist. This was his prayer after his wife, Elizabeth, gave birth to John. Pray it in the morning, and think about how it makes you feel.

**"Blessed be the Lord, the God of Israel,
for he has visited and brought redemption
to his people.
He has raised up a horn for our salvation
within the house of David his servant,
even as he promised through the mouth of
his holy prophets from of old:
salvation from our enemies and from the hand
of all who hate us,
to show mercy to our fathers
and to be mindful of his holy covenant
and of the oath he swore to Abraham our father,
and to grant us that,
rescued from the hand of enemies,
without fear we might worship him
in holiness and righteousness
before him all our days.
And you, child, will be called prophet of the Most High,
for you will go before the Lord to prepare his ways,
to give his people knowledge of salvation
through the forgiveness of their sins,
because of the tender mercy of our God
by which the daybreak from on high will visit us
to shine on those who sit in darkness
and death's shadow,
to guide our feet into the path of peace."**

Luke 1:68–79

Chapter Review 8

A **Match** Column A with Column B by writing the correct number in the space provided.

A	B
1. prayer	_____ short blessing prayers
2. discernment	_____ helps us know God's will
3. Chosen People	_____ discovering God's will for our lives
4. berahot	_____ Abraham and his descendants; all people who choose to follow God's will

B **Number** the following events from the story of Joshua in the order in which they occurred.

_____ When the priest carrying the Ark of the Covenant entered the Jordan River, its waters stopped flowing so the men could cross safely.

_____ City by city the Israelites took the land the Lord had promised.

_____ The Lord appointed Joshua to lead the Israelites to the Promised Land.

_____ As the horns blew, the people raised a tremendous shout and the walls of Jericho collapsed.

_____ Joshua's spies took shelter in the home of a woman named Rahab.

C **List** some examples of God's blessings that can be a source of prayer in each of the following places.

natural world

____

home

____

school

____

8 Chapter Review

D **Circle** the letter of the correct answer.

1. Where did Juan Diego live?

   a. New Mexico **b.** Mexico **c.** Mexico City **d.** Guadalupe

2. Of whom did Juan Diego have a vision?

   a. Mary **b.** Isaac **c.** Jesus **d.** Abraham

3. Where did Juan Diego pray every day?

   a. at his farm **b.** at Mass

   c. at the bishop's residence **d.** near the church

4. What happened to Juan Diego?

   a. He became a bishop. **b.** He was made a saint.

   c. He became a pope. **d.** He became a Christian.

E **Respond** to the following.

1. How and when can Catholics pray?

   ____

   ____

   ____

2. When do you pray most frequently? During what other times or occasions can you also pray?

   ____

   ____

   ____

3. Write a short prayer that you can say before you go to sleep each night.

   ____

   ____

   ____

Faith in Action

ART TEACHER In addition to learning math, religion, science, social studies, and language arts, young people in elementary school must learn to appreciate the beauty of God's creation, the sacredness of life, and the dignity of each person. One way a Catholic school helps them to do so is through the work of the art teacher, who guides students in learning to observe the details in the world around them so that they can depict what they see in a variety of artistic forms. In doing so, art teachers help students live the Catholic Social Teaching of **Life and Dignity of the Human Person**.

In Everyday Life

ACTIVITY In the space below, use art—such as drawing or poetry—to depict something about the sacredness of life and the wonders of the universe.

In Your Parish

ACTIVITY You can share the talents and skills you develop in school to demonstrate and share your appreciation for life as beautiful and holy in God's eyes. Choose one skill you have developed at school, such as an ability to draw or to sing, or your knowledge of math. Tell how you can use it to help your parish remember that each human life is sacred.

Faith in *Action*

EXTRAORDINARY MINISTERS OF HOLY COMMUNION Those who participate in this ministry help distribute Communion at Mass. They also take the Eucharist to people who are sick and homebound. The people they visit are often elderly and lonely. They look forward to seeing these parish ministers who bring them Communion. They know that through Holy Communion, they are being touched by God's love in a very special way. Extraordinary ministers of Holy Communion honor the Catholic Social Teaching of **Call to Family, Community, and Participation**.

In Everyday Life

ACTIVITY In the left-hand column, describe a time when you helped or cared for someone. In the right-hand column, describe something extraordinary you could have done to walk the extra mile for that person.

A time when I helped someone...	Something extraordinary I could have done...
______________________	______________________
______________________	______________________
______________________	______________________
______________________	______________________

In Your Parish

ACTIVITY An extraordinary minister of Holy Communion takes the Eucharist to those who are ill or homebound. In what ways can you help people you encounter know of God's love?

____

____

____

____

Faith in *Action*

COACHES AND ATHLETICS INSTRUCTORS The development of students involves more than instruction in academic subjects. It involves opportunities to develop intellectually, emotionally, spiritually, and physically. A Catholic school's athletics instructor or coach helps students develop a spirit of teamwork, sportsmanship, and a commitment to living a physically healthy lifestyle. In doing so, athletics instructors encourage students to respect the gifts and talents God has given them. Through their efforts, they model what it means to live out the Catholic Social Teaching on **The Dignity of Work and the Rights of Workers**.

In Everyday Life

ACTIVITY Julia wants to try out for her school's softball team. Her older sister Angela is giving her encouraging advice, saying, "Be sure to get plenty of rest the night before tryouts." What other advice might Angela give Julia?

In Your Parish

ACTIVITY In the space provided, write an announcement for your parish bulletin or parish Web site describing your school's athletics program. Be sure to tell members of your parish how the program helps students develop healthy attitudes about physical fitness. Also tell what you like about the program and the instructors.

Faith in Action

RCIA CATECHISTS Adults and older children who want to learn more about the Catholic faith and are interested in joining the Church participate in the Rite of Christian Initiation of Adults (RCIA). RCIA catechists, along with priests and deacons, help catechumens to discern where God is leading them in the RCIA process. As the catechumens study and pray together, they listen for God's voice to guide them to the next step. With each new step, the RCIA catechists guide the catechumens and candidates closer to their full initiation into the Church. Through their commitment and efforts, these catechists demonstrate the Catholic Social Teaching of **The Dignity of Work and the Rights of Workers.**

In Everyday Life

ACTIVITY Adults and children in the RCIA process are preparing to receive the Sacraments of Christian Initiation—Baptism, Confirmation, and Eucharist. Which of these Sacraments have you received? When did you receive them? What other Sacraments have you received?

____

____

____

____

____

____

____

____

____

____

In Your Parish

ACTIVITY Inquirers in the RCIA process get to ask a lot of questions about what it means to be a Catholic. Write three questions you have about the Church, the Bible, or about living as a committed Catholic.

1. ______________________________

____

____

____

2. ______________________________

____

____

____

3. ______________________________

____

____

____

Unit Wrap-up 2

Each chapter in Unit 2 taught a story about the Hebrews' journey of faith. Match each Scripture quote to the story from which it came.

____ **The Exodus**

____ **The Passover**

1. "Prepare to cross the Jordan River here, with all the people, into the land I will give the Israelites. Do not fear. The Lord, your God, is with you wherever you go."
   Based on Joshua 1:9,11

2. God replied to Moses: I am who I am. Then he added: This is what you will tell the Israelites: I AM has sent me to you.
   Exodus 3:14

3. "Write down these words, for with them I have made a covenant with you and Israel."
   Based on Exodus 34:27

4. This day will be a day of remembrance for you, which your future generations will celebrate with pilgrimage to the LORD; you will celebrate it as a statute forever.
   Exodus 12:14

____ **The Covenant at Sinai**

____ **The Conquest of the Promised Land**

2 Unit Review

A Write the name of the person or group described by each clue.

1. God gave me the Ten Commandments to help people live in love and goodness.

   ____

2. I listened and talked to God and successfully led the Israelites to the Promised Land.

   ____

3. I am a saint and a Doctor of the Church who taught people about prayer.

   ____

4. Because of me, the Church can forgive any sin and no person has to fear death.

   ____

B Circle the letter of the best answer.

1. The same God who delivered his people from slavery in Egypt delivered ____.

   a. the Egyptians from death
   b. us from hunger by giving us fish and bread
   c. us from sin and death
   d. us from slavery to material things through Jesus Christ

2. Jesus' miracle of feeding 5,000 followers with five loaves of bread was a special sign of the food he would give the whole world in ____.

   a. the Eucharist
   b. Easter
   c. Passover
   d. the Seder

3. Jesus' Death and Resurrection took place during the Jewish feast of ____.

   a. Pentecost
   b. Tabernacles
   c. Passover
   d. Atonement

4. Our liturgies celebrate ____.

   a. novenas
   b. the Paschal Mystery
   c. the Promised Land
   d. the Book of Exodus

Unit Review 2

C **Match** Column A with Column B by writing the correct number in the space provided.

A	B
1. Ark of the Covenant	____ Abraham and his descendants, selected by God to receive his word
2. Chosen People	____ Canaan, the sacred place God promised to Abraham, Isaac, Jacob, and the Israelites in Egypt
3. discernment	____ the special box that held the stone tablets of the Ten Commandments
4. Exodus	____ discovering, with God's help, God's will for our lives
5. liturgical year	____ the bread-like food that God gave the Israelites in the desert
6. manna	____ the Church's yearly calendar of celebrations and seasons
7. Paschal Mystery	____ the Jewish celebration of the Exodus from Egypt
8. Passover	____ the most sacred name of God, meaning "I am who I am"
9. Promised Land	____ the Old Testament story of how God freed the Hebrews in Egypt
10. Yahweh	____ the way that Jesus' Passion, Death, Resurrection, and Ascension saved us from sin and gave us life after death

D **Write** a prayer asking God to guide you in following his will.

____

____

____

2 Unit Review

E **Match** Column A with Column B by writing the correct number in the space provided.

A	B
1. greatest Commandment	____ what death leads to if we love God and others as Jesus taught
2. everlasting life	____ praying as much as we can will help us discover this
3. Easter Triduum	____ to love God with our heart, soul, and mind
4. God's will	____ a saint who founded a religious order called the Discalced Carmelites
5. Francis	____ a saint to whom Mary appeared and requested that a church be built where she was standing
6. Teresa of Jesus (Teresa of Ávila)	____ born Jorge Mario Bergoglio, he became the pope in March of 2013
7. Juan Diego	____ the period from Holy Thursday evening until Evening Prayer on Easter Sunday evening

F **Respond** to the following.

1. Name the events of the Paschal Mystery that make it possible for us to live in everlasting happiness with God.

____

____

2. Choose one of the events of the Paschal Mystery and tell what it means for you.

____

____

____

Unit 3

God Invites Us into His Kingdom

God called the people of Israel to build up a kingdom that would be a tribute to his love. Jesus taught us about the Kingdom of Heaven, where God's love will be evident in justice and peace.

> He it is who shall build a house for my name, and I will establish his royal throne forever.
>
> 2 Samuel 7:13

The Temple was built on Mount Zion, the place God chose as his dwelling place for his name (see Deuteronomy 2:11).

Unit 3 SONG

Let Us Go Rejoicing

Michael Joncas

REFRAIN

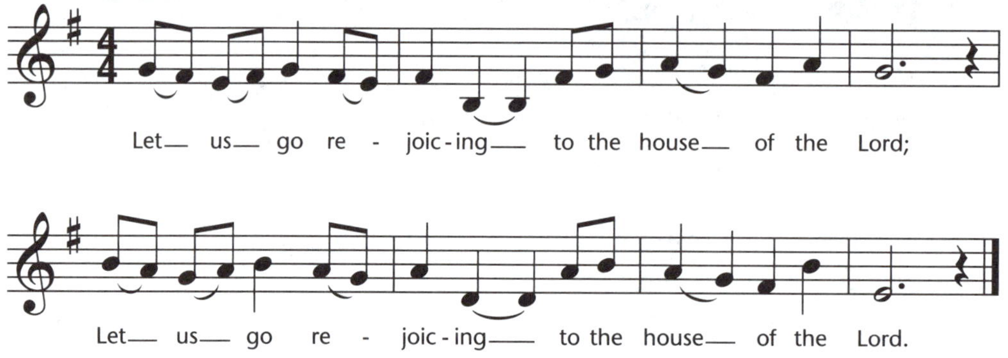

VERSES

1. I rejoiced when I heard them say:
   "Let us go to the house of the Lord,"
   and now our feet are standing
   within your gates, O Jerusalem.
   Refrain

2. Jerusalem is a city built
   with unity and strength.
   It is there, it is there that the tribes go up,
   the tribes of the Lord.
   Refrain

3. For Israel's law is to praise God's name
   and there to give God thanks.
   There are set the judgment thrones
   for all of David's house.
   Refrain

4. Pray for the peace of Jerusalem!
   "May those who love you prosper;
   May peace ever reign within your walls,
   and wealth within your buildings!"
   Refrain

5. For love of my fam'ly and love of my friends,
   I pray that peace be yours.
   For love of the house of the Lord our God
   I pray for your good.
   Refrain

Take Home

Our Land and God's Kingdom

The wisdom of several leaders called *judges* guided the Jewish people in the Promised Land. But some Israelites wanted a king to represent all the tribes of Israel. The judge and prophet Samuel asked God for guidance in choosing a king. God revealed how the people could follow a king and remain loyal to the old Covenant. A family can function well under different styles of leadership, as long as God is behind all its decisions.

ACTIVITY Your Kingdom Is Your Castle

Think of your home as your family's kingdom. Have family members draw, paint, or use a computer to make a sign expressing what this kingdom is all about. The sign may show a popular expression or your last name with symbols of things you value, such as a cross. Hang the sign in a prominent place.

THROUGH THE WEEK

A Prayer for the Week Lord, help us to build your kingdom on Earth as the saints have done, that we may enjoy everlasting happiness with you in Heaven. Amen.

ON SUNDAY
Think of other parishioners as travelers on the journey to God's kingdom. Ask God to bless them.

ON THE WEB
BlestAreWe.com
RCLBLectionary.com
SaintsResource.com

Saint Francis of Assisi (1181–1226)

As a young man Francis enjoyed a rich and easy life. After a conversion experience, he gave up all his wealth to follow Jesus. He began living as a mendicant, begging for his daily needs. He spent his time preaching and caring for the poor and sick. He is the founder of the Franciscan order of religious.

Feast Day: October 4

Take Home

Scripture Background
Before the Time of Jesus

FROM JUDGES TO KINGS During Samuel's rule as a judge, Israel was invaded by its neighbors, the Philistines. Samuel was a man of power and influence, and many looked to him for help in selecting a leader who would protect them. Although Samuel was displeased at their request for a king, he obeyed the Lord's command to listen to them and appoint a king. Read 1 Samuel 8—10 to learn how the monarchy was established in ancient Israel, uniting all Israelites under a single ruler.

Our Catholic Tradition in the Holy Land

ST. CATHERINE'S CHURCH Next door to the Church of the Nativity in Bethlehem is the Roman Catholic Church of St. Catherine. Built by the Franciscans in 1881, the church is situated over a cave where, according to tradition, Saint Jerome lived when he was translating the Scriptures from Greek to the Latin Vulgate in the fourth century. A statue of Saint Jerome stands in the church's courtyard, which was once part of a cloistered convent.

Our Land and God's Kingdom

Chapter 9

Do you not know that your bodies are members of Christ?

1 Corinthians 6:15

Share

God made each of us unique, but we were not meant to live alone. We are part of families, neighborhoods, cities or towns, states, and countries. In many of these communities, people are appointed to lead us.

We are also part of parish communities. What is the name of your parish? Your parish is part of a bigger community, the Catholic Church. Through the leadership of the pope and the bishops of each diocese, the Church guides Catholic parish communities all over the world. We call the Church our mother because she gives birth to the faithful at Baptism and nurtures them in faith. The Church spreads and protects the truth God has revealed. We also call the Church the Bride of Christ because of Christ's sacrifice and love for her.

ACTIVITY

What groups or communities do you belong to? Draw yourself participating in one of these groups or communities.

What are the qualities of a good leader?

Hear and Believe **Scripture**

The First Leaders of Israel

After Joshua died, judges helped the Israelites stay faithful to the old Covenant. Judges were leaders gifted with good judgment. Under their guidance the Israelites enjoyed peace for forty years.

The Israelites had an especially wise judge named Samuel. Samuel was the son of Hannah, a faithful Israelite woman. She could not have children at first. One day she prayed hard for a son. "Lord," she promised, "if you give me a son, I will give him to you as a servant for as long as he lives." God heard Hannah's prayer, and Samuel was born. Hannah brought Samuel to the Temple to live with the priest, Eli. "This child shall be dedicated to the Lord as long as he lives," she told Eli.

Eli taught the boy about serving God. One day, something remarkable happened.

> . . . Samuel was sleeping in the temple of the LORD where the ark of God was. The LORD called to Samuel, who answered, "Here I am." He ran to Eli and said, "Here I am. You called me." "I did not call you," Eli answered. "Go back to sleep." So [Samuel] went back to sleep. Again the LORD called Samuel, who rose and went to Eli. "Here I am," he said. "You called me." But [Eli] answered, "I did not call you, my son. Go back to sleep."
>
> . . . The LORD called Samuel again, for the third time. Getting up and going to Eli, he said, "Here I am. You called me." Then Eli understood that the LORD was calling the youth. So he said to Samuel, "Go to sleep, and if you are called, reply, 'Speak, LORD for your servant is listening.'" When Samuel when to sleep in his place, the LORD came and stood there, calling out as before: Samuel, Samuel! Samuel answered, "Speak, for your servant is listening."
>
> 1 Samuel 3:3–6, 8–10

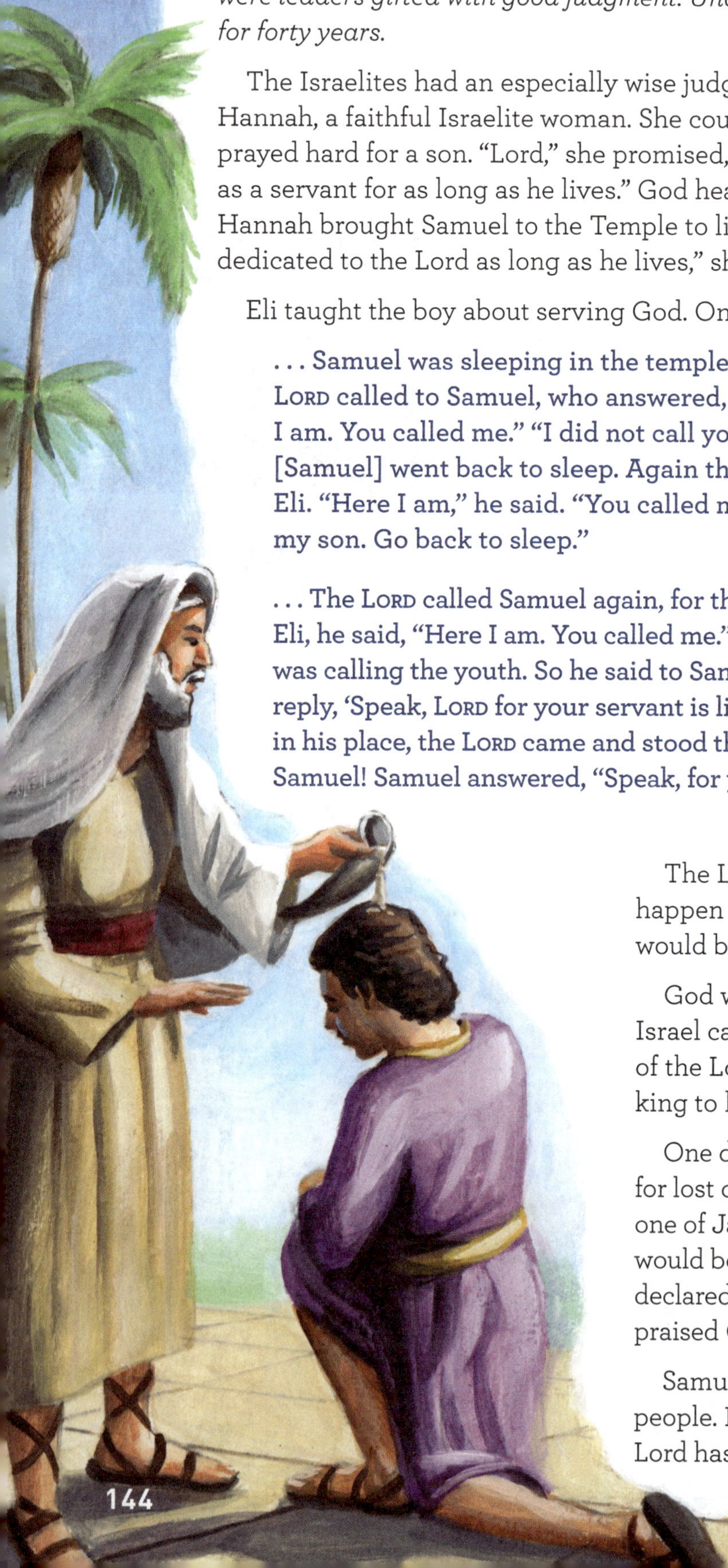

The Lord told Samuel about events that would happen later. Samuel told Eli, and Eli knew Samuel would be a great prophet.

God watched over Samuel as he grew up. All of Israel came to know Samuel as a leader and a prophet of the Lord. When the people wanted him to choose a king to lead them, Samuel asked God for help.

One day, a man named Saul came to the city looking for lost donkeys. Saul was a descendant of Benjamin, one of Jacob's sons. The Lord told Samuel that Saul would be king. Samuel anointed Saul with oil and declared him king in the name of God. The Israelites praised God and said, "Long live the king!"

Samuel reminded them, "The Lord made you his people. Now you have the king you want, a king the Lord has given you. But you must obey the Lord."

As king of Israel, Saul bravely fought Israel's enemies and delivered Israel from its invaders. But then he disobeyed the Lord. Samuel told Saul, "Because you have rejected the Lord's command, the Lord has rejected you as king."

To read the complete narrative in Scripture see Judges 2:16, 18; 5:31; 1 Samuel 1—15.

Kingdoms on the Earth

The Israelites in the Promised Land sometimes failed to keep their part of the old Covenant. Samuel and the Judges helped keep them on the right path. When the Israelites decided they wanted a king, Samuel knew that the king had to be someone who made decisions based on what God wanted. Samuel asked for God's help. God chose Saul to be king. But when Saul failed to obey the Lord, he could no longer lead the people.

God gave the Israelites the Promised Land, and leaders who would help them remain faithful to him. In the same way, God promises us that we will share in his heavenly kingdom and gives us the Church to guide us. Like the Israelites in Canaan, we experience sin and suffering in our world. The Church helps keep us on the path of Jesus. The Church also spreads the saving message of Jesus throughout the world.

Like Samuel, God calls us to carry out the Church's mission and give witness to the kingdom through a **ministry,** or way of serving. We may care for the poor or sick, teach about Christ, help with the liturgy, pray for others, or work for the parish office. All members of the Church, clergy, religious brothers and sisters, and **laity**, can serve the mission of the Church.

Faith Words

ministry
A ministry is a way of serving and caring for others in Christ's name.

laity
The laity are people who are part of the Church and are not clergy or religious brothers or sisters.

ACTIVITY

God calls you to participate in the Church by using your gifts and talents to serve others. In the first column, list gifts and talents that you have. These might be things that you do well, or enjoy doing. In the second column, list ways that you can use the gifts and talents to serve others.

______________	______________________________
______________	______________________________
______________	______________________________
______________	______________________________
______________	______________________________

What ministry did Jesus give to the Apostle Peter?

Hear and Believe **Scripture**

The Keys to the Kingdom

Jesus established the Church to help the Kingdom of God grow on Earth. In the early Church the Apostle Peter took on the role of leader. The Church believes that Jesus himself assigned Peter, whose name means "rock," to this role of leadership. The following passage illustrates this belief.

> When Jesus went into the region of Caesarea Philippi he asked his disciples, "Who do people say that the Son of Man is?" They replied, "Some say John the Baptist, others Elijah, still others Jeremiah or one of the prophets." He said to them, "But who do you say that I am?" Simon Peter said in reply, "You are the Messiah, the Son of the living God." Jesus said to him in reply, "Blessed are you, Simon son of Jonah. For flesh and blood has not revealed this to you, but my heavenly Father. And so I say to you, you are Peter, and upon this rock I will build my church, and the gates of the netherworld shall not prevail against it. I will give you the keys to the kingdom of heaven. Whatever you bind on earth shall be bound in heaven; and whatever you loose on earth shall be loosed in heaven." Matthew 16:13–19

Our Church Teaches

The Church is the beginning of God's kingdom on Earth. The kingdom will reach fulfillment at the end of time when Christ comes again. The Catholic Church welcomes and brings together people of all lands, languages, backgrounds, and races. She is a symbol of the unity of the whole human race. That is why we say the Church is **catholic**, or universal. We also believe that the Church is one (united in faith, worship, and authority), holy (in communion with God), and apostolic (following the tradition and teachings of the Apostles). Jesus gave the Apostle Peter a special authority over the Church that continues with the pope today.

GO TO page 369 to learn more about the Catholic Church.

We Believe

Our mission as Catholics is to prepare the world for the coming of God's heavenly kingdom. We do this by serving others and teaching the saving message of Christ.

Faith Words

catholic
The word *catholic* means "universal." With a capital C, it describes the Church founded by Christ on the Apostles.

ACTIVITIES

1. Reread the Scripture passage on page 146. Put Jesus' statement in your own words.

____
____
____
____
____
____

2. Imagine Jesus is standing in front of you as he was with Peter. What mission do you think Jesus would give to you?

____
____
____
____
____
____

What are some ways we can serve others as Christ did?

Respond

The Franciscans in the Holy Land

In the spirit of Saint Francis, members of the Franciscan order minister to those in need in all parts of the world. In the Holy Land—the place where Jesus lived—Franciscans minister to the needs of Palestinian Christians.

Because of the religious and political disputes between Israelis and Muslim Arabs, Palestinian Christians living in the Holy Land often find themselves caught up in a conflict that forces them to live in war zone conditions. They are deprived of many basic needs, such as jobs and schooling, and even suffer the confiscation of their homes and land. Because of this, many Christians have immigrated to other countries in search of a better life.

The Franciscans, through such organizations as the Franciscan Foundation for the Holy Land, work to ease some of the suffering of Palestinian Catholics and other Christians, as well as non-Christians in the region. They assist families in finding and paying for housing that is safe and livable in cities such as Bethlehem, Jericho, and Nazareth. The Franciscans also help families overcome financial hardship by offering unemployed adults job training, and by hiring them to work in their schools, parish centers, and medical facilities. They also run boys' and girls' schools, and offer university scholarships to Christian Palestinian students in need so they can complete their schooling.

In addition to their humanitarian work in the region, the Franciscans care for and maintain many of the holy sites and shrines, including the Holy Sepulchre and the Church of the Nativity. They also serve pilgrims who visit the Holy Land, providing housing and other services.

The Franciscans have worked in the Holy Land for 800 years, since Saint Francis founded the Order of Friars Minor. Through their work, Christians can continue to live in the land sacred to all Christians, and the holy sites that are so important to our faith will continue to be cared for and available to all Christian pilgrims.

To learn more about the work of the Franciscan Foundation for the Holy Land, visit their Web site at ffhl.org.

ACTIVITIES

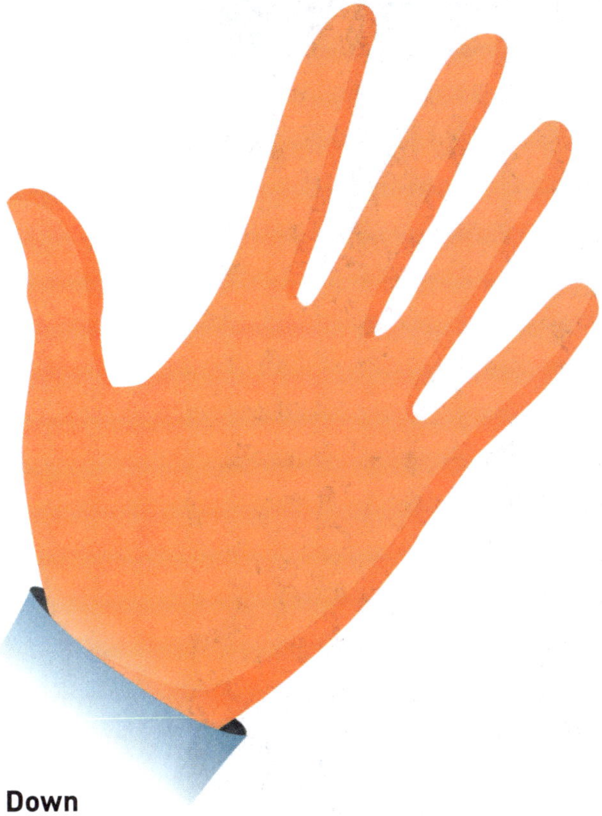

1. Like Samuel in the Old Testament, we may have trouble telling when God is calling us. But as God's children, we all have a mission. The Franciscans in the Holy Land carry out their mission by helping Christians and others in their community, by caring for holy sites and shrines, and by their prayers. How can you work for God's kingdom? On each finger of the hand, write one thing you might do to carry out your mission as a member of the Church.

2. Complete the crossword puzzle with words you learned in this chapter.

Across

1. universal

6. _____ of God, or Heaven

7. following the traditions and teachings of the Apostles

8. united in faith, worship, and authority

9. in communion with God

Down

1. a group of people united in some way

2. a leader with good judgment

3. to put oil on a person who has been chosen

4. a way of serving

5. people who serve in the Church

How can we celebrate our unity as God's children?

A Prayer of Praise

Stand in a circle.

Leader: Grant us, Lord our God,
that we may honor you with all our mind,
and love everyone in truth of heart.
Through our Lord Jesus Christ, your Son,
who lives and reigns with you
in the unity of the Holy Spirit,
one God, for ever and ever. Amen.

Collect for the Fourth Sunday in Ordinary Time, *Roman Missal*

All: **How good and how pleasant it is,**
when brothers and sisters dwell
together as one!

Based on Psalm 133:1

Reader A: All your works give you thanks, LORD
and your faithful bless you.
They speak of the glory of your reign
and tell of your mighty works, . . .

Psalm 145:10–11

Reader B: Your reign is a reign for all ages,
your dominion for all generations.
The LORD is trustworthy in all his words,
and loving in all his works.

Psalm 145:13

All: **Save us, LORD, our God;**
gather us from among the nations
That we may give thanks to your holy name
and glory in praising you.

Psalm 106:47

Chapter Review 9

A **Match** Column A with Column B by writing the correct number in the space provided.

A	B
1. ministry	____ people who are part of the Church but are not clergy or religious brothers or sisters
2. catholic	____ in communion with God
3. holy	____ a way of serving others in Christ's name
4. apostolic	____ united in faith, worship, and authority
5. laity	____ the Church founded by Christ
6. Catholic	____ following the teachings of the Apostles
7. one	____ universal

B **Complete** the paragraph, using words from the box.

covenant	judges	God
Promised Land	heavenly kingdom	

Many of the first leaders of the Israelites were called ____________________.
They helped the Hebrew people remain faithful to the ____________________ they made with God. Samuel was an especially wise judge. He knew that a leader had to make decisions based on what ____________________ wanted.
Just as God gave the Israelites the ____________________, he promises us that we will share in his ____________________.

C **Describe** some ways in which members of the Church contribute to her mission.

____

____

____

9 Chapter Review

D **Complete** the graph, using words from the box.

Church leader: ______	→	diocesan leader: ______	→	______ leader: ______

parish
bishop
pastor
pope

E **Write** a prayer of praise to God for the gift of his kingdom on Earth, the Church. Include examples of how the Church is one, holy, catholic, and apostolic.

____

____

____

____

____

F **Respond** to the following.

1. When will the true Kingdom of God come?

____

____

2. What special mission was given to the Church and to Peter as the head of the Church?

____

____

____

____

____

Getting ready for Chapter 10

Take Home

The Ark and the Temple

To the Israelites, worship before the Ark of the Covenant in the tent was a treasured way to present oneself before God. Washing one's hands and feet before entering, and continually burning lamps outside were rituals that showed respect for God's holy presence. Many of the Israelites' rituals found new meaning in Christ and became the basis for Catholic ways of coming to the Holy Spirit through Jesus. Baptism is one example of this.

ACTIVITY Baptism Anniversaries

Mark the dates of your Baptisms on a household calendar. Celebrate your Baptism anniversaries by reflecting on your mission in spreading God's love. Also have a small celebration on each person's special day, perhaps lighting that person's baptismal candle at mealtime.

THROUGH THE WEEK

A Prayer for the Week Lord, through the intercession of Saint John Vianney, strengthen our faith and enrich your Church through those you have called to the priesthood. Amen.

ON SUNDAY

Meditate before the tabernacle, in which the Blessed Sacrament is kept. Thank God for Christ's presence among us in the priest, in the assembly, in the Word proclaimed, and most especially in the Eucharist.

ON THE WEB

BlestAreWe.com
RCLBLectionary.com
SaintsResource.com

Saint John Vianney (1786–1859)

John Vianney was the parish priest at Ars, a remote French hamlet. His life was one of extreme simplicity and self-deprivation. He was loved by everyone who knew him. He heard confessions for sixteen hours each day, and dedicated his life to bringing people to God.

Patron Saint of: priests

Feast Day: August 4

Take Home

Scripture Background
In the Early Church

BAPTISM AMONG THE EARLY CHRISTIANS

In the Easter Vigil Gospel reading we hear Jesus instruct his disciples, "Go, therefore, and make disciples of all nations, baptizing them in the name of the Father, and of the Son, and of the holy Spirit" (Matthew 28:19). Jesus' followers accepted this call. The Acts of the Apostles contains numerous accounts of baptisms carried out by the Apostles, often of large crowds of people. Peter baptized a crowd of 3,000 (see Acts 2:38–41). Paul preached in Corinth and led many to believe in Jesus and be baptized (see Acts 18:1–8). Philip preached the Good News, and many came to him to be baptized (see Acts 8:12–16).

4th century baptismal font Petra, Jordan

Our Catholic Tradition
in Sacraments

THE BAPTISMAL FONT

In November of 2000, the United States Conference of Catholic Bishops (USCCB) published *Built of Living Stones: Art, Architecture, and Worship*. This set of guidelines emphasizes the importance of giving careful consideration to both the design and the location of the font. Because its waters are a constant reminder to the faithful of their Baptism and of their baptismal promises, the font should be placed where it is visible to all and accessible to all. The shape of the font should also express what we believe about Baptism. Traditional shapes have included cruciform, womb, tomb, step-down, octagonal, and hexagonal.

The Ark and the Temple

Chapter 10

**Springs of water, bless the Lord;
praise and exalt him above all for ever.**

Acclamation, Blessing of Baptismal Water
The Easter Vigil, *Roman Missal*

Share

Your school day may begin with the Pledge of Allegiance. You stand, face the flag, and place your hand over your heart. Sports events usually begin with the singing of our national anthem. These are rituals that remind us of our unity and freedom as Americans.

In the Church, rituals help us honor and prepare for God's presence. Special actions and objects remind us of Jesus Christ and prepare us for God's life in us.

ACTIVITY

The words below relate to rituals of the Church. Find the words in the flame and circle them. You may find them across, up, down, diagonally, or backwards.

anoint	**Sign of the Cross**
bless	**Stations of the Cross**
candle	**crucifix**
oil	**genuflect**
palms	**holy water**
rosary	

S
S
O G
X R S E
I O C S J N
F L R E O I K U
I F A P H R I M U F
C R O S T T C I L Z L L L
U O T R A B F E A U V W E E
R E T A W Y L O H N N G J F C C
I C Y U P U B E E S T I H D D E S S T
A R Y X P L E S S N F O R G L A N O
R S R P A L M S O O T L O X E
B I A Z A N O I N T O L I
A S X P A T G L Y C
Q O E C A I O U
X R B T S R
U V S C

Why is water a special symbol for God's people?

Hear and Believe **Worship**

The Blessing of Water

In the Old Testament, water is a sign of God's power. The first creation story from Genesis says God's Spirit moved over the oceans. Genesis also describes the great flood, sent to destroy evil on Earth. In the Exodus, God parted the Red Sea to help the Israelites escape Egypt, and he gave them water in the desert. God also calmed the Jordan River so the Israelites could cross over to the Promised Land.

In the Sacrament of Baptism, through water blessed with the Holy Spirit, we are cleansed of Original Sin and given new life in Christ. During the Easter Vigil, a priest blesses water that is to be used to baptize people who have been preparing to become Catholics. In the blessing, the priest celebrates Old Testament events as signs of the saving power of the water of Baptism. He sings,

"Father, you give us grace through sacramental signs, which tell us of the wonders of your unseen power.

"In baptism we use your gift of water, which you have made a rich symbol of the grace you give us in this sacrament.

"At the very dawn of creation your Spirit breathed on the waters, making them the wellspring of all holiness.

"The waters of the great flood you made a sign of the waters of baptism that make an end of sin and a new beginning of goodness.

"Through the waters of the Red Sea you led Israel out of slavery, to be an image of God's holy people, set free from sin by baptism.

"In the waters of the Jordan your Son was baptized by John and anointed with the Spirit.

"Your Son willed that water and blood should flow from his side as he hung upon the cross.

"After his Resurrection he told his disciples: 'Go out and teach all nations, baptizing them in the name of the Father, and of the Son, and of the Holy Spirit.'

"Father, look now with love upon your Church, and unseal for it the fountain of baptism.

"By the power of the Holy Spirit give to this water the grace of your Son, so that in the sacrament of baptism all those whom you have created in your likeness may be cleansed from sin and rise to a new birth of innocence through water and the Holy Spirit."

The priest then dips the blessed Easter candle into the water once or three times as he says,

"We ask you, Father, with your Son, to send the Holy Spirit upon the waters of this font. May all who are buried with Christ in the death of this baptism rise also with him through newness of life."

Based on the Blessing of the Water, *Rite of Christian Initiation of Adults* (RCIA) 222A

Signs of God

The Israelites in the Old Testament saw God work wonders through water. They saw water's power to bring purity and goodness. In order to be pure in God's presence, they washed their hands and feet before worshiping God in the tent that held the Ark of the Covenant. Many Jewish people still practice ritual washings for special occasions. Through such rituals, the Israelites and their modern descendants have celebrated God's goodness throughout their history.

The Israelites felt God's presence when they were near the Ark of the Covenant. To honor God, they continually burned oil lamps outside it. When the Israelites settled in Canaan, they needed a permanent holy place to keep the Ark and worship God together. Israel's first two kings, Saul and David, wanted to build a magnificent place to gather for worship. King Solomon, the son of David, finally built the **Temple** on Mount Zion, a hill in Jerusalem during his rule. Israel kept the Ark in the Temple in a sacred space called the Holy of Holies. A continual light shone there, to remind worshipers of the eternal covenant with God.

Faith Words

Temple
The Temple was the Jewish place of worship in Jerusalem that contained the Ark of the Covenant.

ACTIVITY

Look at the diagrams. How are the Temple and a Catholic church alike? How are Catholic and Hebrew, or Jewish, ways of worshiping God similar?

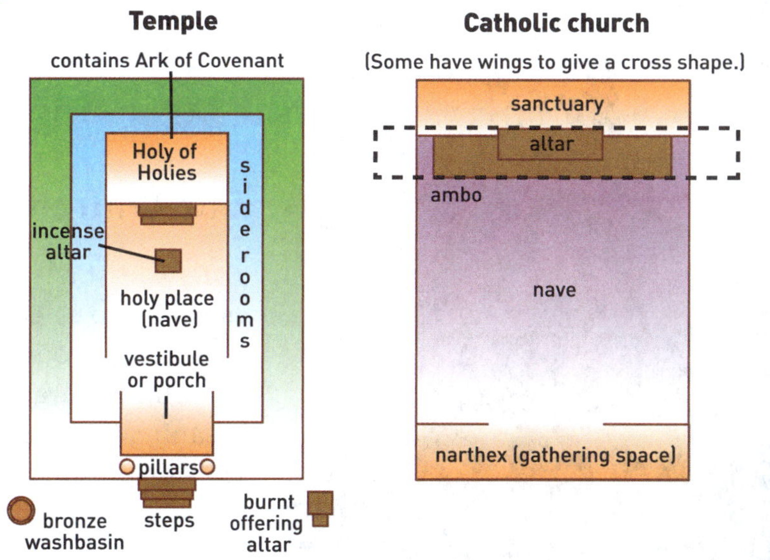

What are some of the ways we can prepare for the kingdom?

Hear and Believe **Scripture**

A Place of God's Presence

Solomon was the Israelite king who built the first Temple. He brought in workers from all over Israel and imported cedar wood from Lebanon. He hired architects and artists from other countries and had much of the Temple covered with gold.

When the beautiful Temple was completed, Solomon ordered the priests to bring the Ark of the Covenant into it. The king and the people offered sacrifices at the Temple.

Solomon stood before the Temple and all of Israel. He prayed, "Can it be that God dwells with people on Earth? If the heavens cannot hold back God's presence, how much less this Temple that I built!"

> [Solomon] stood and blessed the whole assembly of Israel, saying in a loud voice: "Blessed be the LORD who has given rest to his people Israel, . . . May the LORD, our God, be with us as he was with our ancestors . . ."
>
> The LORD said to [Solomon]: I have heard the prayer of petition which you offered in my presence. I have consecrated this house which you have built and I set my name there forever; my eyes and my heart shall be there always. 1 Kings 8:55–57; 9:3

To read the complete account in Scripture see 1 Kings 5—9.

Our Church Teaches

Early Christians adapted some of the rituals used by the Israelites to celebrate the presence of God. For example, Baptism and blessing ourselves with holy water may have grown out of Jewish ritual washings. However, Jewish rituals received new meaning from Jesus Christ. Through Jesus Christ, God could truly be present within us. Baptism and the other **Sacraments** fill us with God's very life and presence, or grace. They are more than symbolic. They help us participate in God's kingdom on Earth as well as prepare us for everlasting life with God. The sprinkling of holy water, as done during a liturgy, is an example of a **sacramental,** a sacred sign that prepares us to receive and live by God's grace. The sacramentals of the Church change us spiritually, but they do not give grace the way the Sacraments do.

In the same way the Israelites went to the Temple to worship and be close to God, Catholics go to church and attend Mass. But we also attend Mass to be filled with Christ. Our churches use blessed candles (which are also sacramentals) and place them by or on the altar. At least one lamp continually shines near the tabernacle holding the Blessed Sacrament, Christ's Body. The light reminds us that Christ is there and that he is the eternal Light of the World.

ACTIVITY

Imagine that objects could speak in much the same way they do in cartoons. What would the following objects tell you about themselves?

a Catholic church

____

____

holy water

____

____

a tabernacle lamp

____

____

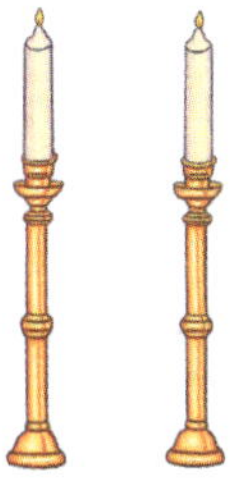

blessed candles

____

____

the Ark of the Covenant

____

____

We Believe

Through the Sacraments, which were instituted by Christ and entrusted to the Church, God's grace is given to us.

Faith Words

Sacrament

A Sacrament is a sacred sign and cause of grace instituted by Christ in the Church to continue his saving action through the Holy Spirit.

sacramental

A sacramental is a symbolic prayer, blessing, object, or action instituted by the Church that can lead us to a fuller participation in the grace of the Sacraments.

What sacramentals are used in the Sacrament of Holy Orders?

Respond The Rite of Ordination

Hector, James, and Nick are in the cafeteria, discussing the weekend.

Hector: My uncle Rodrigo was ordained a priest on Saturday.

Nick: What was that like?

Hector: First, the bishop asked my uncle and the other men if they truly wanted to be priests. They said, "I do." They promised to follow the bishop's guidance.

James: Did your uncle and the others just stand there?

Hector: Well, when they were blessed the first time, they were kneeling. Then they lay on the floor while everyone sang the Litany of the Saints, asking the saints to pray for the new priests.

Nick: Why were they on the floor?

Hector: My uncle says it shows their surrender to God. My uncle and the others became priests when the bishop laid his hands on their heads and prayed over them. Then they received the vestments they'll wear for Mass. Their hands were also anointed with consecrated oil called Sacred Chrism. Once they became priests, they all joined in the celebration of the Mass.

Sacraments at the Service of Communion

Holy Orders and Matrimony are Sacraments at the Service of Communion. Those who receive these Sacraments have a special mission to serve the Church and to work for the salvation of others. In the Sacrament of Holy Orders, baptized men are ordained as bishops, priests, or deacons to serve the Church in the name and Person of Christ. A bishop receives the fullness of the Sacrament of Holy Orders. Under the authority of the pope, he is in charge of a group of church communities. Bishops succeed the Apostles. Priests are coworkers with their bishop in ministering to the community by presiding at Eucharistic celebrations and administering the other Sacraments. They also proclaim God's Word and lead the parish community. Deacons are helpers of bishops and priests and assist with the work of the parish. They can preside at the celebrations of the Sacraments of Baptism and Matrimony. They can also read the Gospel and give the homily at Sunday Mass.

GO TO page 373 to learn more about the Sacraments at the Service of Communion and page 382 to learn more about priests.

ACTIVITIES

1. Using the clues, unscramble the words.

CDRASE MHICRS ______________________________

Clue: oil used to anoint

TRENCSAAMLA ______________________________

Clue: a sacred sign that prepares us to receive and live by God's grace

EEMTLP ______________________________

Clue: the Israelites' center of worship

MASTCRANE ______________________________

Clue: a sacred sign and cause of grace

OHYL DRORSE ______________________________

Clue: the Sacrament by which priests are ordained

2. In Old Testament times, people filled clay jars with water for their ritual washings. In each jar below, write something for which you are sorry—words, actions, choices, or behaviors you would like to wash away.

How do sacramentals bring us closer to Jesus?

A Prayer for Guidance

Some of the sacramentals used by Catholics include holy water and candles. Candles are often used in the liturgy as a reminder that Jesus is the Light of the World. He leads all people out of the darkness of sin and onto the path of salvation. In the space below, write a prayer asking Jesus to be your light and to guide you. Be specific in the ways in which you need Jesus' guidance.

The Sign of the Cross is the sacramental that Catholics use to begin their prayers. Beginning with the Sign of the Cross, quietly and reflectively say your prayer to Jesus.

Pray the Sign of the Cross again.

Chapter Review 10

A **Complete** the sentences, using words from the box.

Matrimony
Baptism
Church
Bishops
Holy Orders
Easter Vigil
Sacraments

1. Through the ______________________, which were instituted by Christ and entrusted to the ______________________, God's grace is given to us.
2. In the Sacrament of ______________________, we are cleansed of Original Sin and given new life in Christ.
3. The Sacraments at the Service of Communion are ______________________ and ______________________.
4. ______________________ are the successors of the Apostles.
5. At the ______________________, a priest blesses water that is to be used to baptize people who are going to become Catholic.

B **Match** Column A with Column B by writing the correct number in the space provided.

A	B
1. sacramental	_____ a baptized man is ordained by a bishop to serve the Church as a deacon, priest, or bishop
2. Holy Orders	_____ the Jewish place of worship in Jerusalem
3. Sacrament	_____ a sacred sign and cause of grace instituted by Christ to continue his saving action
4. Temple	_____ a sacred space that contained the Ark of the Covenant
5. Holy of Holies	_____ a symbolic prayer, blessing, object, or action instituted by the Church

C **Circle** the rituals that the early Christians adapted from the Israelites to celebrate the presence of God.

blessing the water

continually burning a lamp

going to a holy place to worship

exchanging the Sign of Peace

10 Chapter Review

D **Number** the events from the Rite of Ordination for a deacon, priest, or bishop. The first answer is provided.

_____ The men lie on the floor during the Litany of the Saints.

_____ The men promise to follow the bishop's guidance.

__1__ The bishop asks if the men truly want to be ordained.

_____ The men celebrate Mass.

_____ The men receive liturgical vestments.

_____ The men kneel down to be blessed.

_____ The bishop lays his hands on the men and prays over them.

_____ The men are anointed with oil.

E **Circle** the items or actions that are sacramentals.

rosary	genuflect	palms
catholic	Sign of the Cross	holy water
anoint	candle	crucifix
pew	oil	Stations of the Cross

F **Respond** to the following.

1. Describe how someone you know who has received one of the Sacraments at the Service of Communion works for the salvation of others.

____

____

____

2. What can you do to work for the salvation of others?

____

____

____

Take Home

David's Sin and the Story of the Fall

The happiness of many people can be lost by just one person's choosing personal satisfaction over virtue. The biblical account of David and what he did to marry Bathsheba is a prime example. David could not undo the consequences of his actions even though God forgave him. The story of the Fall of Man in Genesis also explains the disobedience of humans and its consequences. But Jesus Christ brought salvation from sin, and God is always there to help us resist temptation.

ACTIVITY Valuable Tears

A tradition holds that Jewish women's tears were collected in jars and later used for special rituals. Have each family member write a one-line prayer for forgiveness on a teardrop-shaped piece of paper, fold it, and drop it into a glass jar. Imagine these prayers are tears poured out to Jesus.

THROUGH THE WEEK

A Prayer for the Week Merciful Father, help us recognize all our sins and failings, lead us to your mercy, and guide us to your eternal kingdom. Amen.

ON SUNDAY
During Mass, pay attention to readings and homilies that focus on forgiveness and mercy.

ON THE WEB
BlestAreWe.com
RCLBLectionary.com
SaintsResource.com

Blessed Laura Vicuña (1891–1904)

From a young age, Laura Vicuña was troubled by the life her mother led. She continually prayed for her mother. When Laura was twelve years old, she was ill and dying. She comforted her mother, saying she was happy to give up her life for her mother's salvation. Upon Laura's death, her mother repented and returned to the Church.

Feast Day: January 22

Take Home

Scripture Background
Before the Time of Jesus

KING DAVID The Bible contains more stories about David than about any other person apart from Jesus. David is honored in Scripture for his accomplishments. As a warrior, David defeated Goliath. After Saul's death, David was crowned king of the tribe of Judah. Seven years later, he became leader of the unified tribes and established Jerusalem as his capital. But David's human weaknesses are also presented in Scripture. A chief example is his adultery with Bathsheba. Read about David's sin in 2 Samuel 11, and about his repentance in 2 Samuel 12.

Our Catholic Tradition in Legend

KING ARTHUR AND KING DAVID The flaw in Camelot in the story of King Arthur was the same as the flaw that brought down David's kingship. The musical *Camelot* tells this story in great detail. Arthur's father had Lady Igraine's husband killed in battle so he could marry the widow. Then Lancelot and Guinevere betrayed Arthur and destroyed the virtue of Camelot. Similarly, David's pursuit of another man's wife damaged his capacity for leading Israel.

David's Sin and the Story of the Fall

Chapter 11

All the paths of the LORD are mercy and truth
toward those who honor his covenant and decrees. Psalm 25:10

Share

Making decisions is not always easy. God gave us free will—the freedom to decide how we are going to act. Think of a time when you had to choose what you knew was right over something that seemed easier to do. Since the beginning of time, people have had to make such choices. Sometimes our choices lead to uncomfortable consequences for us or for others. Sometimes it is hard to admit we have made a mistake.

ACTIVITY

Have you ever been in a situation when you knew the right choice was going to be difficult? What choice did you make? Draw yourself doing what you decided, then answer the questions.

How did the situation influence your choice?

____

____

Did you make the right choice? Why or why not?

____

____

What happens when people do not choose goodness?

Hear and Believe **Scripture**

King David and the Sin of Humanity

God was unhappy with Saul's leadership. God told Samuel to anoint a shepherd boy named David to be the new king of the Israelites. David was the youngest son of Jesse, a man from Bethlehem.

> The spirit of the LORD had departed from Saul, . . . [He] told his servants, "Find me a good harpist, and bring him to me." One of the servants spoke up: "I have observed that a son of Jesse of Bethlehem is a skillful harpist. He is also a brave warrior, an able speaker, and a handsome young man. The LORD is certainly with him."
>
> . . . Thus David came to Saul and entered his service. Saul became very fond of him and made him his armor-bearer.
>
> 1 Samuel 16:14,17–18,21

Saul soon realized that God had chosen David to be the next king of Israel. When David became king, he was a powerful leader. The Lord was with him, and he ruled honorably and fairly for many years. He made Jerusalem the capital of Israel.

But there was a beautiful married woman, Bathsheba, whom David coveted. David sent her husband, Uriah, into battle, and Uriah was killed. David and Bathsheba married and had a son. The baby died soon after it was born. God was not pleased with David's actions. David asked for forgiveness. "I have sinned against the Lord," he said. The Lord forgave David. A new baby, called Solomon, was born.

David's sin might remind us of the story of Adam and Eve. It explains the human weakness for disobeying God.

Out of the soil, God created the first humans, Adam and Eve, to enjoy the beauty of the earth. God gave them a peaceful garden so that they could experience God's love every day. God also made them partners in charge of caring for the other things he had created. In return, God told Adam and Eve to not eat fruit from a certain tree in the garden, the tree of knowledge of good and evil, or they would die.

One day, a serpent tempted Eve to eat the fruit of the tree. Adam and Eve knew God forbade it, but they disobeyed God and ate of the fruit anyway. They knew their choice was wrong. So when God asked what they had done, they were ashamed.

God said, "The humans have become like us, knowing what is good and bad!" God said to Adam:

> By the sweat of your brow
> you shall eat bread,
> Until you return to the ground,
> from which you were taken;
> For you are dust,
> and to dust you shall return.
>
> Genesis 3:19

God banished Adam and Eve from the happiness of the garden. Their sin, which is called Original Sin, has wounded all humans, weakening us in our ability to resist sin and do good.

To read the complete account in Scripture see 1 Samuel 16:14–23; 2 Samuel 1—12; Genesis 2:4—3:23.

True Freedom

The story about Adam and Eve is sometimes called "the fall of humans," or "the Fall." It helps explain the origins and effects of sin. The author tried to help people understand how sin affects everyone and why humans struggle. Because of their human weakness, the Israelites had trouble obeying God's laws and finding true happiness. Even God's anointed, Saul and David, were not free from temptation and its consequences. David gave in to his envy of another man. As we see from his story, envy is a serious sin that can lead to many other sins. David's envy resulted in Uriah's death and damaged David's relationship with God and the kingdom. Like Adam, Eve, and David, people sometimes use their free will to make choices that separate them from God. But David's story shows God's great ability to forgive.

ACTIVITY

From the Bible, we learn about the mystery of evil and God's power to overcome it. The story about Adam and Eve teaches us that evil came into the world because the first humans used their free will to make a sinful choice. The story about David also teaches us that sinful choices have bad consequences, but it shows that God is always ready to forgive us. In the space below, illustrate a story about a person who made a sinful choice but was able to find forgiveness.

How do we decide what is right?

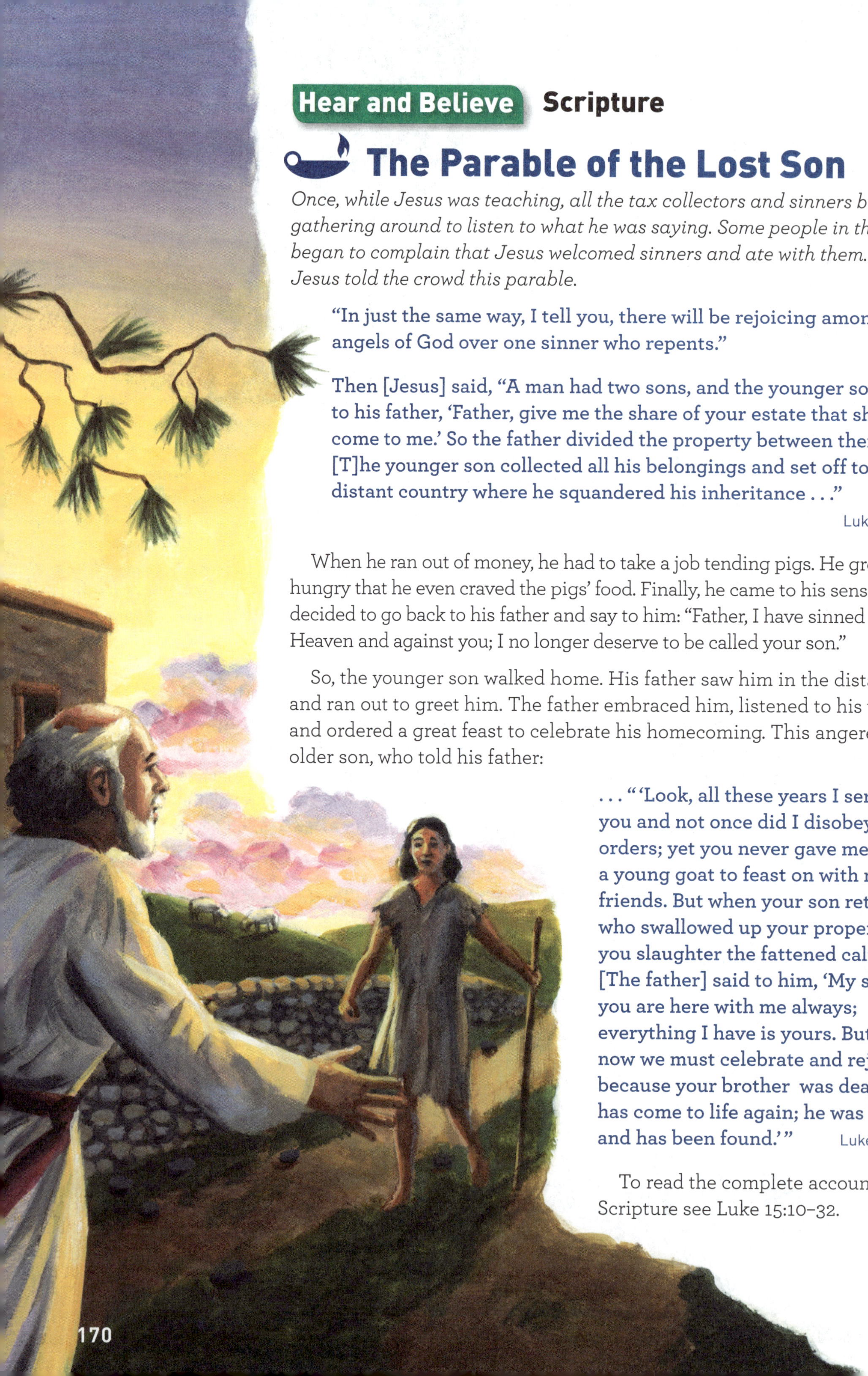

Hear and Believe **Scripture**

The Parable of the Lost Son

Once, while Jesus was teaching, all the tax collectors and sinners began gathering around to listen to what he was saying. Some people in the crowd began to complain that Jesus welcomed sinners and ate with them. So Jesus told the crowd this parable.

> "In just the same way, I tell you, there will be rejoicing among the angels of God over one sinner who repents."
>
> Then [Jesus] said, "A man had two sons, and the younger son said to his father, 'Father, give me the share of your estate that should come to me.' So the father divided the property between them. . . . [T]he younger son collected all his belongings and set off to a distant country where he squandered his inheritance . . ."
>
> Luke 15:10–13

When he ran out of money, he had to take a job tending pigs. He grew so hungry that he even craved the pigs' food. Finally, he came to his senses. He decided to go back to his father and say to him: "Father, I have sinned against Heaven and against you; I no longer deserve to be called your son."

So, the younger son walked home. His father saw him in the distance and ran out to greet him. The father embraced him, listened to his words, and ordered a great feast to celebrate his homecoming. This angered the older son, who told his father:

> . . . "'Look, all these years I served you and not once did I disobey your orders; yet you never gave me even a young goat to feast on with my friends. But when your son returns who swallowed up your property . . . you slaughter the fattened calf.' [The father] said to him, 'My son, you are here with me always; everything I have is yours. But now we must celebrate and rejoice, because your brother was dead and has come to life again; he was lost and has been found.'" Luke 15:29–32

To read the complete account in Scripture see Luke 15:10–32.

Our Church Teaches

Along with free will, each of us has a **conscience**, an ability to know what is right and what is wrong. We must form our conscience properly according to God's law. This means thinking about our choices, whether they reflect God's love, and what their results might be. A good, moral act is more than something that turns out all right in the end. It is something that we start, continue, and finish with good intentions toward ourselves, others, and God. If our conscience tells us that something is wrong, we must not do it, even if it will bring about something good. If we are sure something is right and good, we should choose it. If we do not properly form our conscience, we risk following our conscience when it is not correct. We might be at fault when this happens. To help us develop our conscience, God gives us **guidance**. We are obligated to listen to the guidance of the Church, the Scriptures, and parents or other adults, and to be open to the guidance of the Holy Spirit.

Through the Sacraments God gives us grace, which also helps us make good decisions. **Sacramental grace** is the unique gift of God's love that we receive in each Sacrament. Grace strengthens us to be more holy and to avoid sin. But God's love is always with us, even when we sin. We accept that love in the Sacrament of Penance and Reconciliation. In the Sacrament, and through a bishop or priest, Christ forgives us, frees us from our sins, and gives us the gift of his grace.

ACTIVITY

Below, draw a symbol for sin and a symbol for God's forgiveness.

We Believe

We must form our conscience by following the Word of God, the Church's teaching, and the guidance of the Holy Spirit.

Faith Words

conscience
Our conscience is our ability to judge what is right and what is wrong.

guidance
Guidance is help in making the right choices. God gives us guidance to help us develop our conscience.

sacramental grace
Sacramental grace is the unique gift of God's love that we receive in each Sacrament.

What are some ways we can show our devotion to God?

Respond

Saint Helena

The mother of Emperor Constantine, Saint Helena, did not become a Christian until she was in her sixties. However, she made up for lost time by dedicating her life to her newfound Christian faith.

Helena was born to poor parents in 250 AD. She married Constantius and had one son, Constantine. Constantius divorced Helena to further his political career, but Constantine remained devoted to his mother. When Constantius died and Constantine became emperor, he brought his mother to court, giving her full honors. Under her son's influence, she became a Christian. Although she lived at the royal court, Helena dressed simply and remained humble. She followed Christ's teaching faithfully by helping not only poor people, but also entire communities. She was known for her kindness to soldiers and prisoners.

When she was eighty, Helena went on a pilgrimage to the Holy Land. She carefully explored the sites where it was thought Jesus carried out his ministry. She promised to show her devotion to God by building churches and beautifying existing churches. Legend says that she found the cross on which Jesus had been crucified and had a chapel built to house it. Helena teaches us to trust in God and remain faithful to our calling. Helena died in 330 AD. The Church celebrates her feast day on August 18.

ACTIVITIES

1. In what way did Helena stand firm in her Christian faith?

____

____

____

____

____

____

Saint Helena
Cima da Conegliano Philippe Sauvan-Magnet, 1495

2. Saint Helena showed her devotion to God in a grand way, by building churches and beautifying existing ones. Each of us can help build up and beautify the Church in the simple ways we show our devotion to God. In the spaces below, describe three ways in which you can show your love for God. One can be an everyday way, another can be an extra effort, and the last can be something exceptional you can do.

An everyday way	An extra effort	An exceptional action

3. Saint Helena is believed to have found the true Cross. Reflect on what the cross means to you, and write a prayer to Jesus based on your reflections.

How do we ask God for forgiveness during Mass?

The Confiteor

During the Mass, Catholics celebrate the Penitential Act. The priest invites us to call to mind our sins. Then we pray the Confiteor, a prayer of sorrow for ourselves and for our community. A Catholic tradition is to strike our chest lightly as a sign of regret while praying this prayer.

As you pray the Confiteor, think about your actions during the past week. Did you purposely do or say something that hurt someone else? Did you neglect an opportunity to show kindness to someone who needed it? If you had the chance, would you act differently?

The Confiteor

All: I confess to almighty God
and to you, my brothers and sisters,
that I have greatly sinned,
in my thoughts and in my words,
in what I have done and in what I have failed to do,

(Lightly strike your chest as you pray the following two lines.)

through my fault, through my fault,
through my most grievous fault;
therefore I ask blessed Mary ever-Virgin,
all the Angels and Saints,
and you, my brothers and sisters,
to pray for me to the Lord our God.

Penitential Act, *Roman Missal*

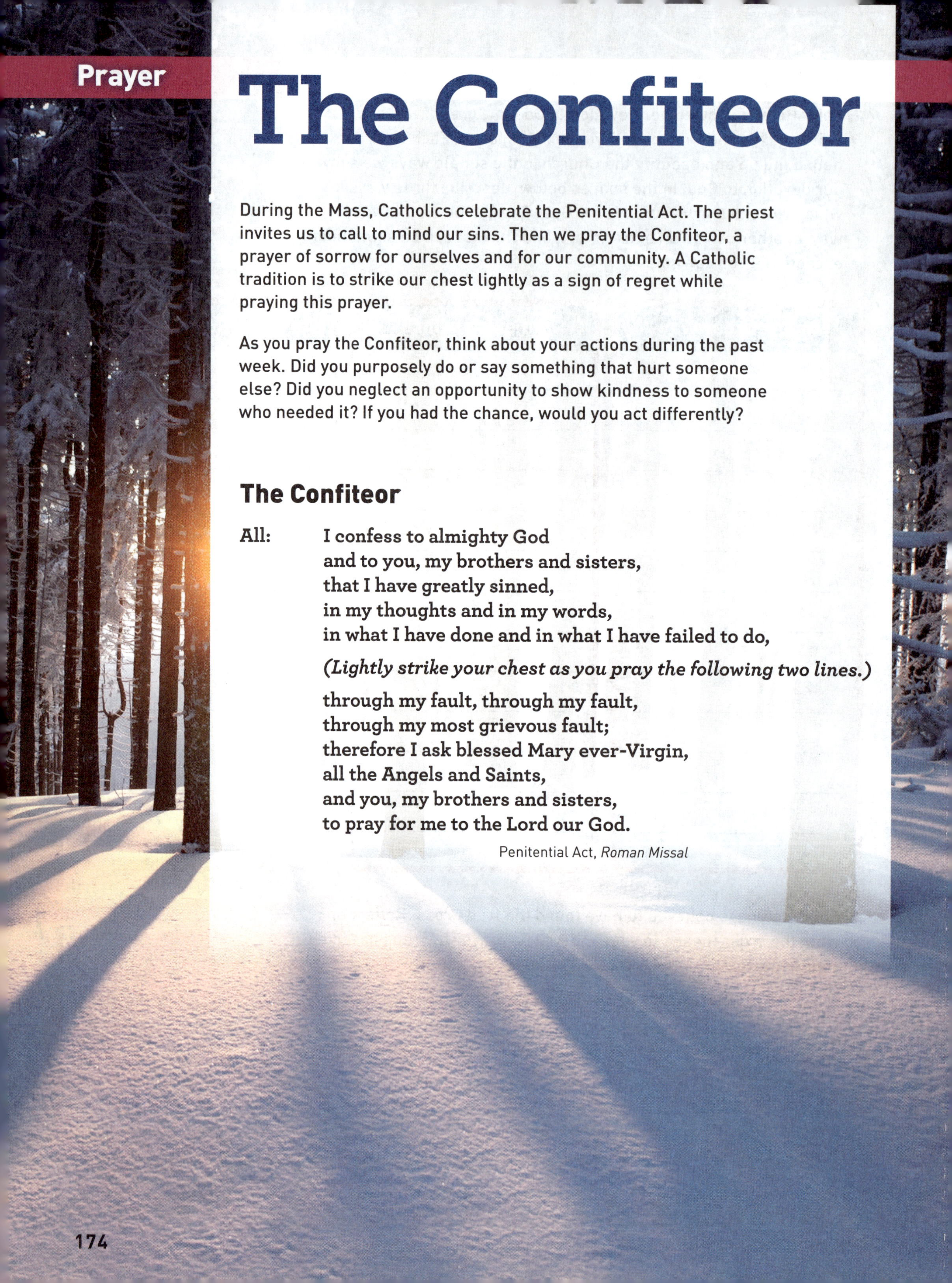

Chapter Review 11

A **Circle** the letter of the correct answer.

1. _____ is the unique gift of God's love that we receive in the Sacraments.

   a. Conscience **b.** Knowledge **c.** Sacramental grace **d.** Guidance

2. The Church, the Scriptures, our parents and other adults, and the Holy Spirit can give us _____ to help us make good decisions.

   a. guidance **b.** free will **c.** permission **d.** happiness

3. Our _____ is our ability to know what is right and what is wrong.

   a. free will **b.** conscience **c.** strength **d.** consequence

4. The story of Adam and Eve helps explain _____.

   a. envy as a sin **b.** the origin and effects of sin

   c. the importance of prayer **d.** the bounty of nature

5. During Mass we pray the _____, a prayer of sorrow for our sins.

   a. Confiteor **b.** Nicene Creed **c.** Hail Mary **d.** Act of Contrition

B **Match** Column A with Column B by writing the correct number in the space provided.

A	B
1. Saint Helena	_____ told parables to teach about God.
2. The lost son	_____ showed his resentment by saying, "You never gave me even a young goat to feast on with my friends."
3. The older son	_____ welcomed the lost son home.
4. Jesus	_____ showed his repentance by saying, "Father, I have sinned. I no longer deserve to be called your son."
5. The forgiving father	_____ converted to Christianity in old age and showed her devotion to God by having churches built.

11 Chapter Review

C **Identify** the person who is speaking in each sentence.

1. God chose me to be king after Saul. I disobeyed God by coveting the wife of another man. ______________________
2. The king sent my husband, Uriah, into battle. When he was killed, the king married me. __________________
3. I was born after my father, King David, asked God's forgiveness. __________________
4. God said to me, "By the sweat of your brow you shall eat bread, until you return to the ground, from which you were taken." __________________
5. A serpent tempted me to eat the fruit of the tree of knowledge. __________________

D **Respond** to the following.

1. Describe ways in which the Church's teaching and the Scriptures guide you in living a moral life.

 ____

 ____

 ____

2. Describe a situation that may lead you to sin. Then tell how conscience can affect the choices you make.

 ____

 ____

 ____

Getting ready for Chapter 12

Take Home

Psalms of Praise and Works of Wonder

Music gives us a different way to experience prayer. The tone of the music can bring joy, consolation, or hope to prayer. Poetry, too, conveys messages of faith in more emotional ways than normal speech. Psalms are prayers, poems, and songs all wrapped up into one. They are a powerful part of the Church's prayer life, with a rich Old Testament history.

ACTIVITY **Prayer Gear**

To show that prayer time is special and sacred, choose a holy item—the Bible, a crucifix, a rosary—that people in your family can keep close by during prayer time.

THROUGH THE WEEK

A Prayer for the Week We praise you, Lord, for your wonderful ways. You have given us many gifts. We especially thank you for the gifts of music and poetry. Amen.

ON SUNDAY
While singing the Responsorial Psalm, try to experience the calm that Saul felt when David sang and played the harp.

ON THE WEB
BlestAreWe.com
RCLBLectionary.com
SaintsResource.com

Pope Saint Gregory the Great (540–604)

Pope Saint Gregory the Great worked to reform the Church by removing unfit clergy and abolishing unjust fees for burial and ordinations. He was responsible for bringing Christianity to England and is credited with initiating Gregorian chant, which is still heard today in the singing of the Responsorial Psalms, Mass acclamations, and many hymns.

Feast Day: September 3

Take Home

Scripture Background
Before the Time of Jesus

THE PSALMS The Book of Psalms contains hymns and laments of ancient Israel—150 altogether. Many psalms are attributed to David. The psalms date from the tenth century BC through the third century BC. Because they were written over such a long period of time, the psalms present varying ways of addressing God. Some speak of the God of a single people and place, while others speak of a God of all people. The psalms describe virtually every aspect of everyday life. The Book of Psalms is truly the common book of prayer of Christians and Jews. Choose a favorite psalm to read.

Our Catholic Tradition in Poetry

GERARD MANLEY HOPKINS
Gerard Manley Hopkins was a Jesuit priest who lived in the nineteenth century. He was the brilliant son of a wealthy English couple, whom he shocked by becoming Catholic and then a priest. He had a unique way of expressing his thoughts and a deep appreciation for God in nature. He ended the poem "Pied Beauty" by reminding the reader to praise God. Hopkins lived only forty-five years and was not published until thirty years after his death.

Psalms of Praise and Works of Wonder

Chapter 12

You are God: we praise you;
You are God: we acclaim you;
You are the eternal Father:
All creation worships you.

Te Deum

Share

How do you feel when someone compliments you? We all feel special when we are noticed for something good. We like it when people see what we have done and say, "Wow!"

What makes you say "Wow!" about God? A sunrise or sunset? A forest? The mountains? Another person? Everything around you shows that God is great and loves you. The world is full of things that remind us of God and make us say, "Wow!"

ACTIVITY

Fill in the following song of praise to God, using the clues for parts of speech to help you.

Every day I will ______________ (verb) you;

I will praise your ______________ (noun) forever and ever.

[I will] ______________ (verb) your abounding goodness and

______________ adverb sing of your ______________ (noun).

The LORD is gracious and ______________ (adjective),

slow to anger and abounding in ______________ (noun).

My ______________ (noun) will speak the praises of the LORD,

all flesh will bless his ______________ (adjective) name

forever and ______________ (noun).

Based on Psalm 145:2,7–8,21

When do we sing songs of praise to God?

Hear and Believe **Scripture**

David's Songs

King David had great faith in the Lord. David used his musical talent to praise God and thank him for coming to his aid in battle.

David had to defend Israel in battle many times. After one victory, he sang the following song to thank God for his protection, power, and faithfulness.

> **O LORD, my rock, my fortress, my deliverer,**
> **my God, my rock of refuge! . . .**
> **Praised be the LORD, I exclaim!**
> **I have been delivered from my enemies.**
>
> **In my distress I called out: LORD!**
> **I cried out to my God;**
> **From his temple he heard my voice,**
> **my cry reached his ears. . . .**
> **The LORD thundered from heaven;**
> **the Most High made his voice resound.**
> **He let fly arrows and scattered them;**
> **lightning, and dispersed them. . . .**
> **He rescued me from my mighty enemy,**
> **from foes too powerful for me.**
>
> 2 Samuel 22:2–3,4,7,14–15,18

Later, when David was too old to rule over Israel, God chose Solomon, the son of David and Bathsheba, to be the next king. David knew Solomon would fulfill his dream of building a magnificent temple in Jerusalem.

"Bless the Lord your God!" David told the people when God had chosen Solomon. David reminded Solomon to honor the Lord's covenant and to be faithful always. David said:

> **LORD, God of our ancestors Abraham, Isaac, and Israel, keep such thoughts in the hearts and minds of your people forever, and direct their hearts toward you. Give to my son Solomon a wholehearted desire to keep your commandments, precepts, and statutes, . . .**
>
> 1 Chronicles 29:18–19

Solomon was anointed king. David soon ended his forty-year rule over Israel. He died a faithful follower of the Lord.

To read the complete account in Scripture see 2 Samuel 22:1–18; 1 Kings 1–2; 1 Chronicles 28:1–21, 29:18–28.

Singing Praise

The Book of Psalms is a collection of 150 religious songs and prayers called **psalms** that are from the Old Testament. The song of David you just read is found in the book. It is believed that David wrote 73 of the 150 psalms in the Book of Psalms. It is also believed that the other psalms are from individual collections and were combined with David's writings to form the one Book of Psalms.

The word *psalm* comes from the Greek word *psalterion*, which was a stringed musical instrument. Often, a psalm's purpose was to express praise, thanksgiving, or sorrow. Stringed or wind instruments often accompanied the singing.

The psalms tell of God's great actions and of people's response to God. The words and themes of the psalms are still fitting today. We can pray them alone or with an assembly.

Faith Words

psalms
The psalms are religious songs and prayers from the Old Testament. Psalms often express praise, thanksgiving, or sorrow.

ACTIVITY

David sang a song to thank God for a victory. Recall a happy time or a special blessing in your life. Write a poem or song lyrics celebrating how God helped you.

____

What do the psalms mean to us today?

Psalm 23: The Lord, Shepherd and Host

For centuries, Psalm 23 from the Book of Psalms has comforted people. This psalm offers simple words of trust in God to carry us through difficult times. Tradition holds that David, the shepherd who became king, wrote Psalm 23. Since it was written, millions of people have memorized it. We believe that even Jesus himself knew it well.

Since its earliest days, the Church has prayed this psalm during liturgies, especially at funerals. Musicians both ancient and modern have composed melodies for the inspirational words of Psalm 23. Read the words of Psalm 23 below.

Psalm 23

The LORD is my shepherd;
  there is nothing I lack.
In green pastures he makes me lie down;
  to still waters he leads me;
  he restores my soul.
He guides me along right paths
  for the sake of his name.
Even though I walk through the valley
    of the shadow of death,
  I will fear no evil, for you are with me;
  your rod and your staff comfort me.
Indeed, goodness and mercy will
    pursue me
  all the days of my life;
I will dwell in the house of the LORD
  for endless days.

Psalm 23:1–4,6

Our Church Teaches

Many of the psalms begin and end with the exclamation *"Hallelujah!"* This word—which means "Praise the Lord!"—is a combination of a Hebrew word for praise, *hallelu*, and the beginning of the word "Yahweh." Today, we say "Alleluia!" when we want to express our joy and praise for God. Another important part of our prayers is the word **amen**, also from the Hebrew tradition of prayer. *Amen* means "I believe" or "So it is."

The Catholic Church has adapted many of the psalms for our liturgical celebrations. In the Liturgy of the Word, we pray the Responsorial Psalm. A leader sings or reads verses from a psalm, and the assembly sings or reads a response after each verse. During the Mass, we may also sing several songs that are based on the psalms. Psalms are simple and loving ways for us to express our **reverence** for God.

We Believe

Through songs and prayers of praise, such as the psalms, we express our adoration for God our Creator.

Faith Words

amen

Amen is a word we usually say at the end of our prayers. It means "I believe" or "So it is."

reverence

Reverence is honor and respect. We can show reverence for God by praying the psalms.

ACTIVITY

As you have learned, many psalms contain certain expressions, such as "Hallelujah!" and "Amen." Expressions often found in psalms are listed in the box. Write a prayer that uses at least five of the expressions.

Amen
Answer me, O Lord
Have mercy on me
O Lord, my king
Hear me, O God
The goodness of the Lord
Give thanks to the Lord
Great is the Lord
The Lord is just
Hallelujah!
Praise the Lord
Sing to the Lord

____

____

____

____

____

____

____

____

____

____

What are some things for which we praise God?

Respond Psalm 8

Read the verses from Psalm 8 below. What does the psalmist say about people's place in the universe? How do humans measure up to the rest of creation?

O LORD, our Lord,
how awesome is your name through all the earth!

When I see your heavens, the work of your fingers,
the moon and stars that you set in place—
What is man that you are mindful of him,
and a son of man that you care for him?
Yet you have made him little less than a god,
crowned him with glory and honor.
You have given him rule over the works of your hands,
put all things at his feet:
All sheep and oxen,
even the beasts of the field,
The birds of the air, the fish of the sea,
and whatever swims the paths of the seas.

Psalm 8:2,4–9

ACTIVITIES

1. Write your own psalm, using Psalm 8 as a model. Address God with reverence, and identify the blessings God has given you.

2. You have been asked to film some of the events that are described in the psalm verses below. The film is called *You Are at My Side*. In the frames, draw scenes to show how God loves his people.

Psalm 27: Trust in God

The LORD is my light and my salvation;
  whom should I fear? . . .
When evildoers come at me
  to devour my flesh,
These my enemies and foes
  themselves stumble and fall.
Though an army encamp against me,
  my heart does not fear;
Though war be waged against me,
  even then do I trust.

One thing I ask of the LORD;
  this I seek:
To dwell in the LORD's house
  all the days of my life,
To gaze on the LORD's beauty,
  to visit his temple.
For God will hide me in his shelter
  in time of trouble,
He will conceal me in the cover of his tent;
  and set me high upon a rock.

Psalm 27:1–5

What are some ways we rejoice over examples of God's goodness?

A Psalm Prayer

This is a song that we might sing at Mass. It is based on Psalm 122. The actual music and lyrics are on page 140.

Group 1: I rejoiced when I heard them say:
"Let us go to the house of the Lord,"

Group 2: And now our feet are standing
within your gates, O Jerusalem.

All: **Let us go rejoicing to the house of the Lord.**

Group 1: Jerusalem is a city built with unity and strength,

Group 2: It is there, it is there that the tribes go up,
the tribes of the Lord.

All: **Let us go rejoicing to the house of the Lord.**

Group 1: For Israel's law is to praise God's name
and there to give God thanks.

Group 2: There are set the judgment thrones
for all of David's house.

All: **Let us go rejoicing to the house of the Lord.**

Group 1: Pray for the peace of Jerusalem!
"May those who love you prosper;

Group 2: May peace ever reign within your walls,
and wealth within your buildings!"

All: **Let us go rejoicing to the house of the Lord.**

Chapter Review 12

A **Complete** the following sentences.

1. When David was too old to rule, God chose ________________ to rule Israel.
2. In our prayers, we say "________________" to express our praise to God.
3. The ____________________________ is a collection of 150 religious songs and prayers.
4. ________________ often express praise, thanksgiving, or sorrow.

B **Circle** the letter of the correct answer.

1. Through songs and prayers of praise, we express our ____ for God our Creator.

   a. adoration **b.** humility **c.** talent **d.** sincerity

2. Amen means "____."

   a. Praise God **b.** I believe **c.** Alleluia **d.** Peace be with you

3. The Catholic Church has adopted many of the psalms for her ____ celebrations.

   a. Old Testament **b.** Christmas **c.** Lenten **d.** liturgical

4. Psalms are simple and loving ways for us to express our ____, or respect, for God.

   a. reverence **b.** humility **c.** enthusiasm **d.** unity

C **Complete** the following prayer to praise God for something he has done for you.

Praised be the Lord, for he has ____

____

____

____

____

____

____

12 Chapter Review

D **Write** a brief summary of what you learned about the Book of Psalms in this chapter.

____

____

____

____

E **Respond** to the following.

1. Read the verses of Psalm 146 that appear in blue in your book on page 68. What do the verses say about God that remind us of his goodness? Rewrite two or three of the verses in blue in your own words.

____

____

____

2. If you could illustrate the verses, what would you draw? Draw two illustrations that go with the verses.

Faith in Action

SOCIAL SERVICE MINISTRIES Catholic social service ministries serve neighbors in need both near and far. They offer relief and hope wherever people need food, clothing, housing, medical care, and the kindness of caring people. Social service ministries change the lives of people every day. Through the volunteering and fundraising efforts of students and teachers, Catholic schools also help people in need near and far. They live the Catholic Social Teaching of **Solidarity**.

In Everyday Life

ACTIVITY Describe two actions that might go along with the statement below, one that will show the statement is true (Action A) and one that might make others doubt its truth (Action B).

I care about people who are suffering in any way, such as from poverty or loneliness.

Action A ______________________________

Action B ______________________________

In Your Parish

ACTIVITY Choose a parish ministry that you are interested in, such as a parish food pantry or outreach to new immigrants, and tell how you can be helpful as a member of the group.

Faith in Action

RELIGION TEACHERS To help young people grow in their faith and become fully participating members of the Catholic Church, religion teachers instruct their students according to the teachings of the Catholic Church. Religions teachers play a special role in helping to prepare students to receive the Sacraments, especially First Penance and Reconciliation, First Holy Communion, and Confirmation. They encourage students to live their Catholic faith. They treat each student with love and respect. They are examples of what it means to live the Catholic Social Teaching of **Life and Dignity of the Human Person.**

In Everyday Life

ACTIVITY List three ways your religion teachers have taught you about the sacredness and dignity of each human life.

1. ______________________________

2. ______________________________

3. ______________________________

In Your Parish

ACTIVITY Describe some ways members of a parish minister to one another. Here are some ideas to get you started.

- Celebrating Catholic beliefs together
- Proclaiming God's Word as lectors
- ______________________________
- ______________________________
- ______________________________
- ______________________________
- ______________________________

Faith in Action

PARISH PASTORAL COUNCIL Like the Church of the first century, Catholics today need help in living out the message of Jesus. Members of your parish pastoral council meet regularly to talk about ways parish leaders can provide this help through ministries of worship, education, service, and stewardship. Through its leadership and guidance, the Pastoral Council helps the parish community live out the Catholic Social Teaching of **Option for the Poor and Vulnerable**. Its most important job is to help us all become more like Jesus in the ways we live, learn, celebrate, and serve together.

In Everyday Life

ACTIVITY Choose two of the qualities below that you think are most important in a good leader. Then explain your choices.

has good ideas	**is generous**
communicates openly	**is respectful**
is a hard worker	**prays regularly**
is a good listener	**is caring**

____

____

____

____

____

____

____

____

____

In Your Parish

ACTIVITY Describe one event or issue you would like to see your parish involved in.

____

____

Do you think Jesus would support this? Why or why not?

____

____

____

____

____

____

____

____

____

Faith in Action

SCHOOL CHOIR It may seem that participating in the school choir is all fun. But don't be fooled! Choir leaders and choir members work hard. The music you hear at Mass and at school events and performances is the result of lots of practicing and a great deal of planning. In liturgy, each song needs to be appropriate for its place in the liturgy and for the season of the liturgical year. At other school events, the music and songs must reflect the spirit of the occasion. And all songs must be directed and sung skillfully and beautifully. When choir directors and choir members share their gifts and talents, they live the Catholic Social Teaching of **Call to Family, Community, and Participation.**

In Everyday Life

ACTIVITY Write the title of one of your favorite liturgical songs. Describe the feelings it evokes or the memory it helps you recall.

Title:

____

____

Feelings/memory:

____

____

____

____

____

____

____

In Your Parish

ACTIVITY Choose a special season of the liturgical year and describe a Church tradition for the season. Then describe some of the musical and liturgical traditions that happen at your parish during these times.

Season:

____

Church tradition:

____

Parish traditions:

____

____

____

____

____

____

Unit Wrap-up 3

The church banners below show the titles of the chapters in Unit 3. Write the main topic of each chapter on the lines below.

9

10

11

12

3 Unit Review

A **Complete** the sentences with words from the box. One word is used twice.

pope
bishops
psalms
Temple
grace
free will
Baptism
forgive
power
kingdom
sins
Book of Psalms

1. The ________________ leads the whole Church. The Church is made up of parish communities that are part of dioceses, which are led by ________________.
2. According to tradition, many of the songs and prayers from the ______________________________ were written by David, the shepherd who became king and the father of Solomon.
3. Just as God gave the Israelites the Promised Land, he promises us a share in his ________________.
4. In the stories of creation, the great flood, and the Exodus, water is a sign of God's ________________.
5. The Sacrament of ________________ may have grown out of Jewish ritual washings.
6. When we repent, God forgives our ________________.
7. The Church has adapted many of the ________________ for its liturgical celebrations.
8. The story of King David shows that God is always ready to ________________ us.
9. King Solomon built the ________________.
10. God gave us ________________ for choosing between right and wrong.
11. The ________________ we receive in the Sacraments strengthens us to avoid sin.
12. Jesus gave Saint Peter a special authority over the Church that continues with the ________________ today.

Unit Review 3

B **Match** Column A with Column B by writing the correct number in the space provided.

A	B
1. amen	____ a sacred sign and cause of grace instituted by Christ
2. catholic	____ a symbolic prayer, blessing, object, or action instituted by the Church
3. conscience	____ a way of serving and caring for others in Christ's name
4. guidance	____ a word meaning "universal" and describing the Church founded by Christ on the Apostles
5. laity	____ our ability to judge what is right and what is wrong
6. ministry	____ help in making the right choices
7. psalms	____ honor and respect
8. reverence	____ people who serve the Church and are not clergy or religious brothers or sisters
9. Sacrament	____ religious songs and prayers from the Old Testament
10. sacramental	____ the Jewish place of worship in Jerusalem that contained the Ark of the Covenant
11. sacramental grace	____ the unique gift of God's love that we receive in each Sacrament
12. Temple	____ a word meaning "I believe" or "So it is"

3 Unit Review

C **Circle** the letter of the best answer.

1. The Church is called _____ because she teaches us about faith and protects the truths God has revealed.

   a. Father **b.** Mother **c.** holy **d.** Catholic

2. Another name for the Church is the "_____ of Christ" because of Christ's love for the Church.

   a. Devotion **b.** Family **c.** Gift **d.** Bride

3. The _____ is the beginning of God's kingdom on Earth.

   a. Old Testament **b.** New Testament **c.** Church **d.** Eucharist

4. Men who receive _____ lead and minister to Jesus' followers in the Church as bishops, priests, and deacons.

   a. the Sacrament of Holy Orders **b.** sacramental grace
   c. Gifts of the Holy Spirit **d.** Christ's Body

5. We develop our _____ by listening to the guidance of the Church, the Scriptures, parents or other adults, and the Holy Spirit.

   a. dignity **b.** conscience **c.** holiness **d.** grace

D **Respond** to the following.

1. Describe what it means when we say that the Catholic Church is one, holy, catholic, and apostolic.

   ____

   ____

   ____

2. Describe two ways in which you can live as a faithful member of the Church.

   ____

   ____

   ____

God Reminds Us to Do His Will

Unit 4

The faith of the Israelites was tested through exile and persecution. We are called to live our faith, even in a world that challenges our Christian values.

For the LORD of hosts will have his day
  against all that is proud and arrogant,
  against all that is high, and it will be brought low; . . .

Isaiah 2:12

Forced into exile, the Israelites carried their possessions on their backs as they traveled to Assyria and Babylon. The map shows their journeys.

We Are Climbing Jacob's Ladder

African-American spiritual

Getting ready for Chapter 13

Take Home

Disobedience and Guidance

This chapter explores what happens when people feel that they no longer need God, concentrating on the period of King Solomon's rule of Israel. Israel enjoyed a time of renown and riches when Solomon ruled. Good fortune began to cloud the people's ability to focus on God. Prophets stepped in and tried to remind the Israelites of the covenant made with God. Who plays the role of prophet in your family's life of faith?

ACTIVITY **There's an Old Saying . . .**

Solomon gained fame for his wise sayings, or proverbs. Work together on a list of the wise sayings, or proverbs, that are popular in your family. Contact grandparents or great-grandparents for their input.

THROUGH THE WEEK

A Prayer for the Week Lord, give us the wisdom and courage to follow your will for our lives and to lead others to you. Amen.

ON SUNDAY
At the Sunday liturgy, listen for wise sayings in the readings that can provide guidance for your family and for particular areas of your life. Be sure to share what you hear with your family.

ON THE WEB
BlestAreWe.com
RCLBLectionary.com
SaintsResource.com

Saint Francis Xavier (1506–1552)

Saint Francis Xavier is known as the "Apostle of the Indies and Japan" because of his missionary work in each of those countries.

As a young man studying at the University of Paris around 1530, Francis met Ignatius of Loyola and became one of the first seven Jesuits.

Patron Saint of:
Catholic missionaries

Feast Day: December 3

Take Home

Scripture Background
Before the Time of Jesus

KING SOLOMON'S WISDOM Solomon was the son of King David and Bathsheba. After David's death, Solomon inherited the throne. Early in his reign, God asked Solomon in a dream to name a gift he wanted. Solomon asked for wisdom (see 1 Kings 3:5–15). Solomon built the first Temple and played an important part in Israel's development, but his reputation as a man of wisdom surpassed all his other accomplishments. Read about Solomon's wise judgment in 1 Kings 3:16–28.

The filbert nut is named after Saint Philibert because it is ripe by his feast day.

Our Catholic Tradition in Language

THE ORIGIN OF EVERYDAY WORDS
Many everyday sayings come from the Bible or from Catholic tradition. Have you ever said that someone "got off Scot free"? This used to refer to being exempt from a tax to support the clergy, paid with a coin called a *sceat*. Do you call important days "red letter days?" This referred to saints' feast days and holidays, traditionally printed in red on calendars. The word *tawdry* is a corruption of the name of Saint Audrey, at whose annual festivals showy, low-quality jewelry once could be seen. When you say, "Leopards never change their spots," you echo the feelings of Jeremiah about the sinfulness of Jerusalem (see Jeremiah 13:23).

Disobedience and Guidance

Chapter 13

When you look for me, you will find me. Yes, when you seek me with all your heart, . . . Jeremiah 29:13

Share

Sometimes when things are going well for us, we forget to thank God. We might even forget about God altogether. We can be so caught up in the good things that are happening and the fun we are having that we forget to take time out for God. It sometimes takes another person to remind us to pray, to worship, and to do good things for other people.

ACTIVITY

Place a check mark next to each person who reminds you to stay faithful to God.

- ☐ parent
- ☐ grandparent
- ☐ coach
- ☐ friend
- ☐ brother or sister
- ☐ priest
- ☐ religious sister
- ☐ teacher
- ☐ neighbor
- ☐ mentor
- ☐ other ____________________
- ☐ other ____________________

How did God remind his people to be faithful?

Hear and Believe **Scripture**

The Rule of King Solomon

When Solomon became king of Israel, he thanked God for allowing him to become king. He asked God for wisdom to lead his people. God told Solomon:

> . . . Because . . . you did not ask for riches, treasures, and glory, . . . but you have asked for wisdom and knowledge in order to rule my people over whom I have made you king—wisdom and knowledge are given you. I will also give you riches, treasures, and glory, such as kings before you never had, nor will those who come after you.
>
> 2 Chronicles 1:11–12

Other kings came to hear the wisdom God had put in Solomon's heart. Solomon had many wise sayings, called *proverbs*. People brought treasures to him, and his nation soon had thousands of horses, chariots, gold and silver items, and garments. Israel became a rich and powerful nation. Solomon decided to build a great temple in Jerusalem to honor the Lord. When it was finished, priests carried the Ark of the Covenant into the Temple. The community of Israel gathered in the Temple. They sang and offered sacrifices to the Lord.

Solomon ruled Israel for forty years. When he died, his son Rehoboam became king. Rehoboam ignored advice from elders who had helped Solomon rule. Seeing that the king would not listen to them, some Israelites revolted. The kingdom divided into Judah in the south and Israel in the north. Many of the people, spoiled by their riches, began to forget their covenant with the Lord. They did not keep God's laws. They worshiped false gods. Rich people mistreated the poor.

The Lord was displeased. He sent people to remind the Jews of Israel and Judah of their covenant with him. One prophet, Elijah, called the people together and said, "The God who answers with fire is God" (1 Kings 18:24). The people prepared a sacrifice. Then Elijah asked the Lord to bring his people back to their senses. Suddenly, the Lord's fire came and consumed the sacrifice. The people fell to the ground and said, . . . "The LORD is God! The LORD is God!" (1 Kings 18:39) But they did not change.

The Lord sent the prophet Hosea, who told the people that their behavior was similar to that of an unfaithful wife. He said that even though they had broken their covenant with the Lord, the Lord still loved them and waited for their return as a loving husband would.

The prophet Micah urged the people:

> You have been told, O mortal, what is good,
> and what the LORD requires of you;
> Only to do justice and to love goodness,
> and to walk humbly with your God.
>
> Micah 6:8

Finally, the prophet Isaiah warned:

Get behind the rocks,
    hide in the dust,
From the terror of the LORD
    and the splendor of his majesty!
. . . For the LORD of hosts will have his day
    against all that is proud and arrogant,
    against all that is high, and it will be brought low; . . .

Isaiah 2:10,12

To read the complete account in Scripture see 1 Chronicles 29:25; 2 Chronicles 1:8–15; 5; 9:23–31; 10:1–19; 36:14–16; Hosea 3—4; 1 Kings 15:22–24; 18:21–39; Micah 2—6; Isaiah 2:6–19.

Guidance from the Lord

When the Israelites were suffering, it was easy for them to remain faithful to God. They needed God's help, so they prayed and worshiped him. After they settled into the kingdom of Israel, they enjoyed great wealth under Solomon's rule. Many of the Israelites stopped praying and worshiping the Lord. Because of this, they were open to distractions that turned them away from God. They eventually began to worship false gods.

God was not about to let his people abandon him. He intended to save them from their sinful ways. The Old Testament **prophets,** such as Elijah, Hosea, Micah, and Isaiah, served God's plan by preaching to the people that God would forgive them, free them from sin, and welcome them back into their covenant with him. Through the prophets, God helped the people begin to hope for **salvation.**

Faith Words

prophet
A prophet is a person sent by God to speak out against behavior that does not follow God's will.

salvation
Salvation is forgiveness of sins and restoration of friendship with God which can be done by God alone.

ACTIVITY

Imagine that the prophets Elijah, Hosea, Micah, and Isaiah were alive today. What sinful ways in our world would these prophets speak out against? Write three tweets that describe one of the prophets speaking about such issues.

What are some of the ways we can be guided back to God today?

Hear and Believe **Scripture**

A Special Gift

When he was still a great king, and long before he began to worship false gods, Solomon enjoyed many gifts from God. God's greatest gift to Solomon was wisdom. The following story illustrates Solomon's special gift of wisdom.

Two women who lived in the same house each gave birth to a son around the same time. But when one woman's baby died, she stole the other woman's baby and put her dead son in his place. Both mothers claimed that the living infant was their own.

To resolve the matter, the women argued their cases before King Solomon. Solomon listened to them, then said to his attendant:

> . . . "Get me a sword." . . . "Cut the living child in two, and give half to one woman and half to the other." The woman whose son was alive, because she was stirred with compassion for her son, said to the king, "Please, my lord, give her the living baby—do not kill it!" But the other said, "It shall be neither mine nor yours. Cut it in two!" The king then answered, "Give her the living baby! Do not kill it! She is the mother." When all Israel heard the judgment the king had given, they were in awe of him, because they saw that the king had in him the wisdom of God for giving right judgment.
>
> 1 Kings 3:24–28

Unfortunately, King Solomon lost his gift of wisdom when he became obsessed with his own power and wealth and chose to stop being faithful to God. This led to the downfall of Solomon's kingdom.

To read the complete account in Scripture see 1 Kings 3:16–28.

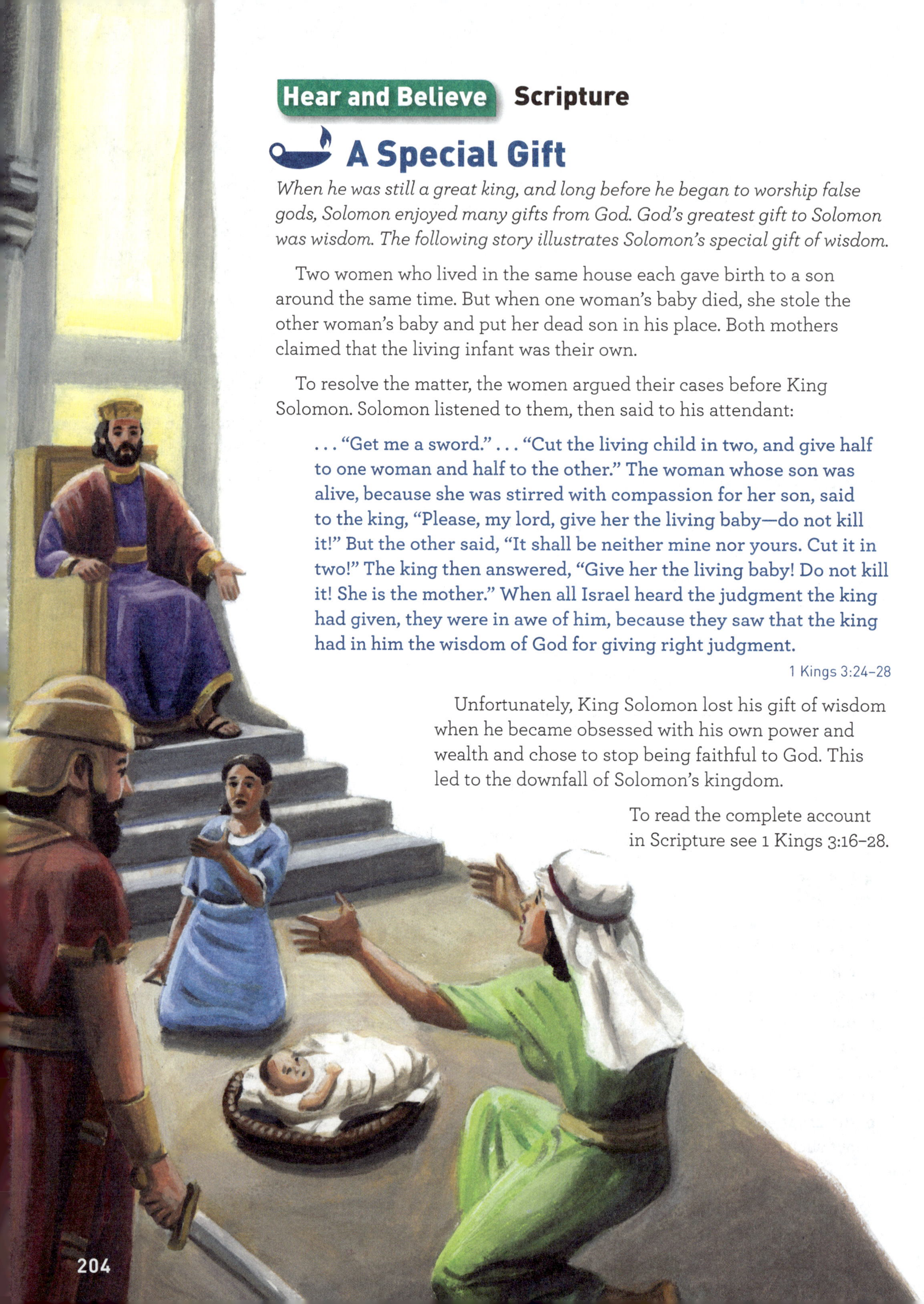

Our Church Teaches

God made the world good and created people to be faithful to him. But as the Bible tells us, the sin of the first humans, Adam and Eve, brought disobedience of God into the world. Sin and death resulted for everyone, and all humans now disobey God's law at times. But Jesus Christ came to save us. He gave us the gift of Baptism, which washes away personal sins and **Original Sin**, the sin of Adam and Eve that was passed on to all human beings.

Jesus' obedience to the will of God the Father brought new life to the world. Jesus is the New Adam and the son of Mary, the New Eve. *Christ* means "anointed one." God anointed his Son, Jesus, with the Holy Spirit. We look to Christ as our Priest, our King, and the Prophet who always guides us back to God the Father. We can find his guidance in the Scriptures, in the Sacraments, in forgiveness, in faithful Christians, and in prayer.

We Believe

Jesus Christ is our Priest, Prophet, and King.

Faith Words

Original Sin
Original Sin is the sin of Adam and Eve, passed on to all human beings. Because of it, we are weakened in our ability to resist sin and do good.

ACTIVITY

The people of Israel sometimes turned their backs on God, and disaster followed. The prophets called them to turn back. Then God sent Jesus Christ, who guides all people back to God.

Below, write ways that people your age might turn their backs on God. Then write a proverb, or wise saying, that could turn them back to God. An example has been done for you.

Backs Turned	Turned Back
Not praying	Seven days without prayer makes one weak.

What can we do to call others back to God?

Respond

Saint Francis Xavier

Francis Xavier was born in his family's castle in Spain in 1506. He studied philosophy at the University of Paris. Francis was a bright student who enjoyed discussing the great thinkers of his time. When Francis graduated, he was hired to teach as a university professor in Paris.

At the university, Francis met Ignatius Loyola, a man who would change Francis' life forever. Ignatius saw in Francis an ability to spread the Gospel to those who had never heard of Jesus. It took Ignatius a while to convince Francis that this was what God wanted him to do, but eventually Francis agreed. Together with a few other interested men, Francis Xavier and Ignatius Loyola began the Society of Jesus, also known as the Jesuits.

In Venice, Italy, in 1537, Francis and Ignatius were ordained to the priesthood. They went to Rome and worked at building up their new order of priests. In 1540, the king of Portugal invited Francis to join his delegation on a sailing trip to Goa, on the west coast of India. This trip became Francis Xavier's first journey as a missionary.

Father Francis traveled farther into India, and then on to Japan and other lands in the Far East. Throughout his missionary travels, Francis introduced thousands of people to Jesus. It is said that he baptized so many people in one day that he could no longer hold up his arms!

Francis would stop at nothing to help people live better lives. He washed the wounds of people with skin diseases and taught religion classes to children. He endured extreme heat and cold in order to work with the poor he met on his travels. Francis even fought off invaders with only his prayers and his crucifix.

Francis' dream was to preach the Gospel to the people of China. At that time, however, China did not allow foreigners. Finally, with the help of the Portuguese government, Francis was given permission to enter China. But he never made it. At the age of forty-six, Francis died of a severe fever on a small island off the coast of China.

Francis Xavier was made a saint in 1602. We celebrate his feast day on December 3. He is the patron saint of sailors and missioners.

Send Me, Lord!

Throughout history, God has sent special messengers to lead people to him. In Old Testament times, when the Israelites turned away from God, God sent prophets such as Hosea to lead them back to him. Throughout the history of the Church, many holy people have worked to lead others to God and to salvation. One of these people was Saint Francis Xavier, who traveled to many parts of the world to bring people the Good News of salvation.

ACTIVITIES

1. **Who do you know who has done extraordinary work in bringing other people closer to God? Tell what this person has done, and which of his or her qualities you would like to develop.**

____

____

2. **It's often difficult to tell other people that we don't approve of their moral choices. What do you do when you see a friend doing something sinful, such as cheating or mistreating someone? Do you speak out, or do you pretend it doesn't matter? Write a diary entry about a time when you observed a friend doing something sinful, and what you did (or should have done) in response.**

What kinds of prayer can keep us focused on God?

A Litany

A litany is a prayer in which we call upon God, Mary, other saints, or holy people, and repeat a response. The repetition gives the prayer rhythm and helps us concentrate on the prayer. Praying litanies helps us focus on God. Litanies are popular in several religions. At a Jewish Day of Atonement service, worshipers may pray this litany.

Leader: Our Father, our King, we have sinned before you. **Response:** **Our Father, our King.**

Our Father, our King, grant us a year of happiness. **Response:** **Our Father, our King.**

Our Father, our King, pardon all our sins. **Response:** **Our Father, our King.**

Based on the Jewish "Our Father, Our King" litany

Our Church has many litanies. The Litany of the Most Holy Name of Jesus is one example. As the leader prays each line about Jesus, pray the response with your eyes closed. Focus on the idea that Jesus is in the center of your being. Whenever you are distracted, return to Jesus by focusing on the repetition.

Leader:	Jesus, Son of the living God:	**All:**	**Have mercy on us.**
	Jesus, our God:		**Have mercy on us.**
	Jesus, king of glory:		**Have mercy on us.**
	Jesus, father of the poor:		**Have mercy on us.**
	Jesus, our way and our life:		**Have mercy on us.**
	Jesus, most powerful:		**Have mercy on us.**
	Jesus, king of patriarchs:		**Have mercy on us.**
	Jesus, God of peace:		**Have mercy on us.**

Based on the Litany of the Most Holy Name of Jesus

Think about the presence of Jesus around and within you.
Slowly and quietly pray the Lord's Prayer.

Chapter Review 13

A **Complete** the sentences, using words from the box.

King
proverbs
Sacraments
prophet
disobedience
covenant
Original Sin
obedience
Scriptures
litany
priest
Salvation

1. A ________________ is a person sent by God to speak out against behavior that does not follow God's will.
2. A ________________ is a prayer in which we call upon God, Mary, other saints, or holy people and repeat a response.
3. Because of Adam and Eve's ________________ sin and death came into the world.
4. ________________ is the forgiveness of sins and the restoration of friendship with God.
5. Jesus' ________________ to the will of God the Father brought new life into the world.
6. Jesus Christ is our ________________, Prophet, and ________________.
7. Solomon had many wise sayings called ________________.
8. Hosea told the Israelites that even though they had broken their ________________ with God, God still loved them.
9. Because of ________________ we are weakened in our ability to resist sin and do good.
10. We find Jesus Christ's guidance in the ________________, in the ________________, in prayer, and in forgiveness.

B **Create** a litany that will help you focus on God. Later, pray your litany at home. A first line is provided below.

A line about God	**The response to repeat**
O Lord, God of Peace	________________
________________	________________
________________	________________

13 Chapter Review

C **Who am I?** Match the description in Column A with the prophet in Column B by writing the correct number in the space provided.

A	B
1. I told the Israelites that their behavior was similar to that of an unfaithful wife.	____ Micah
2. I advised them that "the God who answers with fire is God."	____ Isaiah
3. I urged them to act justly and to love others.	____ Hosea
4. I warned them that "all that is high will be brought low."	____ Elijah

D **Name** a person who acts as a role model for you and his or her words or actions that help you remember to pray, to worship, and to do God's will.

Name: ______________________________

Words or actions: ______________________________

____

E **Respond** to the following.

1. What was the Israelites' relationship with God when they were suffering? How did it change when they prospered?

____

____

____

2. What should your own relationship with God be like, regardless of what is happening in your life?

____

____

____

Take Home

Exile and Remembrance

As time went by, the Chosen People lost sight of the old Covenant and turned away from God. When they were forced into exile, they thought that God had abandoned them. But God was still there for them. God sent the prophets to guide the Israelites back to him. God is always there for us, even though we sometimes turn away from him.

ACTIVITY Exile

Your family or ancestors may have left their homeland to come to America. With your family, explore the feelings of sadness, loss, and hope that such a change brought to your family members, or would bring to anyone making such a life change.

THROUGH THE WEEK

A Prayer for the Week Lord, whatever difficulties our lives bring, help us always stay near to you, trust in you, and follow where you lead us. Amen.

ON SUNDAY
At the Sign of Peace, make an effort to grasp people's hands warmly, look them in the eyes, and smile.

ON THE WEB
BlestAreWe.com
RCLBLectionary.com
SaintsResource.com

Saint Maximilian Kolbe (1894–1941)

Father Maximilian Kolbe was arrested and sent to Auschwitz when Poland was taken over by the Nazis. When ten prisoners at the camp were to be executed, Father Maximilian offered his life in exchange for that of a man in the group who had a family. The man whose life was spared lived to tell the story.

Feast Day: August 14

Take Home

Scripture Background
In the Early Church

THE CALL TO REPENTANCE When the Pharisees complained that Jesus sat with sinners, he said, . . . "Those who are healthy do not need a physician, but the sick do" (Luke 5:31). Jesus is the physician who cures souls and who has come to call sinners to repentance. In the early Church, the Sacrament of Penance and Reconciliation was viewed as a "second baptism." In his first letter to the early Christians, John tells them that if they acknowledge their sins to God, he will forgive them and cleanse them of every wrongdoing. Read all of John's message about confession in 1 John 1:5—2:2.

Our Catholic Tradition in Liturgy

THE LANGUAGE OF PRAYER Synagogues are Jewish places of worship. Synagogue prayer and study may have begun while the Israelites were in exile in Babylon. Prayers and traditions in the synagogue and the home came to replace rituals and sacrifices that had been held in the Temple.

Many elements of Christian prayer and worship have their origins in Judaism. Although Latin was the primary language of the Roman Catholic liturgy for much of the Church's history, a few Hebrew words are part of the Christian liturgy (for example, *amen*, *hosanna*, and *alleluia*). Christian and Jewish worship also share many of the same prayers and acclamations. An example would be the acclamation, "Holy, holy, holy Lord."

Exile and Remembrance

Chapter 14

Lord, your Son laid down his life to gather your scattered children into one family.

Based on the Prayer Over the Gifts, Mass for Refugees and Exiles, *Roman Missal*

Share

Can you remember a time when you were lost? How did being lost make you feel? Who helped you find your way again? We can be lost for many reasons, but God is always there to lead us back to the right path.

ACTIVITY

The people shown in the photographs are all lost in some way. On the lines next to each photograph, explain what the person in the picture might be looking for and what might have caused the person to become lost.

____

____

____

____

____

____

What are some of the ways that God helps those who are lost?

Celebration of the Lord's Passion

The Chosen People had forgotten the covenant with God. When the Lord sent the prophets to remind them to keep the Commandments, they rejected the prophets. In 722 BC, Assyria invaded Israel. The Assyrians captured some Israelites and took them to Assyria. Forced into **exile**, the Israelites felt lost. But God sent more prophets to guide them. One of these prophets was Second Isaiah, a disciple of Isaiah the prophet.

On Good Friday, we gather to remember the Lord's Passion, or suffering, and recall his Death on the Cross. We also adore, or honor, the cross, often by bowing, kissing it, or genuflecting. The First Reading on Good Friday is from Isaiah 53, a prophecy from Second Isaiah. Second Isaiah, chapters 40-55 of the Book of Isaiah, is thought to have been written by a poet who prophesied toward the end of the Babylonian exile. In this passage from Isaiah 53, Second Isaiah explains that the suffering and death of a **messiah** will save the Israelites from their sins. His prophecy gave the Israelites hope and was fulfilled by Jesus Christ.

We had all gone astray like sheep,
all following our own way;
But the LORD laid upon him
the guilt of us all.

Though harshly treated, he submitted
and did not open his mouth;
Like a lamb led to slaughter
or a sheep before shearers,
he did not open his mouth.
Seized and condemned, he was taken away.
Who would have thought any more of his destiny?

. . . He was given a grave among the wicked,
a burial place with evildoers,
Though he had done no wrong,
nor was deceit found in his mouth. . . .

By making his life as a reparation offering,
he shall see his offspring, shall lengthen his days,
and the LORD's will shall be accomplished through him.
Because of his anguish he shall see the light;
because of his knowledge he shall be content;
My servant, the just one, shall justify the many,
their iniquity he shall bear.

Isaiah 53:6–11

Saving Grace

When the Israelites were in exile they could not rise above their failures on their own. They needed the Lord's help. The prophets had told the people that their loving God would send a messiah who would save them from their sins.

Micah, who prophesied around the time of Isaiah, told God's people, "From you [Bethlehem-Ephrathah] shall come forth for me/one who is to be ruler in Israel;/. . . He shall take his place as shepherd/by the strength of the LORD,/. . . he shall be peace" (Micah 5:1,3,4). Jeremiah and Ezekiel prophesied after the time of Isaiah. Jeremiah told God's people, "See, days are coming . . . /when I will raise up a righteous branch for David;/As king he shall reign and govern wisely,/he shall do what is just and right in the land" (Jeremiah 23:5–6). Ezekiel told the people that God would look after them as a shepherd looks after his sheep. The Lord had told him, "I will appoint one shepherd over them to pasture them, . . . " (Ezekiel 34:23).

Faith Words

exile
Exile is the forced removal of people from their homeland to another land. The Israelites captured by the Assyrians were living in exile.

messiah
A messiah is a person chosen to save people from a particular fate. The word means "savior." Jesus Christ is the Messiah, chosen by God to free us from sin and death.

ACTIVITY

The Old Testament prophets described the messiah by likening him to figures from their everyday lives, such as a shepherd or a king. Pretend that you have a prophecy to share about the Messiah. Write your prophecy on the scroll, describing Jesus Christ and what he will do for his people, using figures from everyday life.

How did Jesus describe himself?

Hear and Believe **Scripture**

The Good Shepherd

Like the prophets, Jesus used figures from everyday life to describe who he was. Once, while Jesus was in Jerusalem talking to some people who doubted he was the Son of God, he said:

"I am the good shepherd. A good shepherd lays down his life for the sheep. A hired man, who is not a shepherd and whose sheep are not his own, sees a wolf coming and leaves the sheep and runs away, and the wolf catches and scatters them. This is because he works for pay and has no concern for the sheep. I am the good shepherd, and I know mine and mine know me, just as the Father knows me and I know the Father; and I will lay down my life for the sheep. I have other sheep that do not belong to this fold. These also I must lead, and they will hear my voice, and there will be one flock, one shepherd. This is why the Father loves me, because I lay down my life in order to take it up again." . . .

Again there was a division among the Jews because of these words. . . .

So the Jews gathered around him and said to him, "How long are you going to keep us in suspense? If you are the Messiah, tell us plainly." Jesus answered them, "I told you and you do not believe. The works I do in my Father's name testify to me. But you do not believe, because you are not among my sheep. My sheep hear my voice; I know them, and they follow me. I give them eternal life, and they shall never perish. No one can take them out of my hand."

John 10:11–17,19,24–28

Our Church Teaches

Jesus Christ is the Messiah described by the prophets. He was the shepherd God sent to gather the lost sheep of Israel and of all nations. Christ is always there to bring us back from our own exile—our separation from God because of sin. During our life on Earth we are in exile from Heaven. In the Sacraments, especially the celebration of the Eucharist, we meet Christ and receive grace to continue our journey to our heavenly home. All the members of the Church—those here on Earth and those already in Heaven—form one Body of Christ. The example of those in Heaven encourages us. We celebrate their memory throughout the liturgical year. We join them in praise and thanksgiving for God's goodness.

We Believe

God's love for his people is everlasting. Even in our sufferings God is with us, loving us.

ACTIVITY

Reread Jesus' teaching about the Good Shepherd. Try to figure out what the everyday figures that Jesus uses, such as the wolf, might symbolize. Then complete the following chart. One answer has been provided.

Figure	What It Symbolizes
good shepherd 	____________
sheep 	____________
hired man who is not a shepherd 	____________
wolf 	____________
fold belonging to the good shepherd 	Jesus' followers
sheep that do not belong 	____________
one flock 	____________

Who can teach us to make sacrifices for others?

Respond

Saint Maximilian Kolbe

Raymond Kolbe was born in Poland in 1894. He came from a devout Catholic family. When he was twelve, Mary appeared to him in a dream. She held out two crowns: one white, the other red. The white crown meant that he should keep himself pure, the red one meant that he would be a martyr. In the dream, Raymond accepted both crowns.

Raymond entered a Franciscan seminary at age thirteen. In 1918, he was ordained a priest and took the name Maximilian Mary.

Soon after his ordination, Father Maximilian discovered he had tuberculosis, a disease of the lungs. In spite of his poor health, Maximilian worked hard to promote devotion to the Blessed Mother. He began to publish *Knight of the Immaculata*, a monthly magazine dedicated to Mary, and started a Franciscan friary dedicated to her.

The Nazi Invasion and Auschwitz

When the Nazis invaded Poland in 1939, they killed many people and drove others out of their homes. The Nazis were taking "undesirables"—Jews, Roma (gypsies), and Catholic priests and nuns, among others—to concentration camps. Maximilian's community became a haven for refugees. As many as 1,500 refugees were housed there at a time, cared for by the Franciscan friars. Father Maximilian wondered how long it would be before the Nazis came for him and his brothers.

In May 1941, Father Maximilian and four other priests at the friary were sent to Auschwitz. At Auschwitz, Maximilian secretly heard confessions and offered Holy Communion from his daily ration of bread. Later in 1941, some prisoners tried to escape from Auschwitz. In order to discourage others from doing the same thing, the guards decided to kill ten men. One of the ten men cried in despair. He would never see his family again. Father Maximilian stepped forward and said, "I am a Catholic priest from Poland. I would like to take his place because he has a wife and children."

Witnesses say Father Maximilian prayed, sang hymns, and recited the Rosary while waiting to die by starvation. After two weeks, when the guards saw that he was still alive and encouraging others, they killed him by lethal injection.

We celebrate the Feast of Saint Maximilian Kolbe on August 14, the date of his martyrdom.

ACTIVITIES

1. While waiting to die by starvation, Maximilian Kolbe said prayers, sang hymns, and recited the Rosary. How might his actions have provided encouragement to the other prisoners?

2. Saint Maximilian Kolbe gave up his own life to save another person from death. Describe at least three everyday sacrifices you can make for others.

3. His faith in Mary was a source of inspiration and strength for Maximilian. In the space provided, write a short prayer to the Blessed Mother, asking her to help you grow spiritually.

How can our prayers express our trust in God?

Praying in Jesus' Words

According to the Scriptures, as Jesus died, he called out to God saying, "My God, my God, why have you abandoned me?" (Psalm 22:2). We hear these words during the reading of the Passion in the Good Friday liturgy.

Leader: Now let us pray Psalm 22.

Reader 1: My God, my God, why have you abandoned me?
Why so far from my call for help,
from my cries of anguish?
My God, I call by day, but you do not answer;
by night, but I have no relief.
Yet you are enthroned as the Holy One;
you are the glory of Israel.

Reader 2: In you our fathers trusted;
they trusted and you rescued them.
To you they cried out and they escaped;
in you they trusted and were not
disappointed. . . .

All the ends of the earth
will remember and turn to the LORD;
All the families of the nations
will bow low before him.

Reader 3: For kingship belongs to the LORD,
the ruler over the nations.

. . . The generation to come will be told of the Lord,
that they may proclaim to a people yet unborn
the deliverance you have brought.

Psalm 22:2–6,28–29,32

Chapter Review 14

A **Who am I?** Write the name of the person described by each clue.

1. I am the prophet who told the people that God would look after them as a shepherd looks after his sheep. ____________________
2. I am the prophet who told the people that the ruler of Israel would come forth from Bethlehem. ____________________
3. I am the prophet who compared his people to sheep who had gone astray. ____________________
4. I am the prophet who said that the Lord would raise up a descendant of David to reign as king. ____________________
5. I am the Messiah described by the prophets. ____________________

B **Complete** the sentences, using words from the box.

sin
Messiah
Psalm 22
Passion
prophets

1. According to the Scriptures, as Jesus died he called out to God in the words of ______________________.
2. Christ is the ______________________, chosen by God to free us from ______________________.
3. In church on Good Friday, we remember Jesus' ______________________, or suffering, and his Death on the Cross.
4. Many ______________________ foretold of the coming of a messiah.

C **Define** the following.

Exile: ____

____

Messiah: ____

____

14 Chapter Review

D **Complete** the sentences, using words from the box.

covenant	exile	sin	Israelites
Commandments	prophets	Messiah	

1. The ______________________, the Chosen People, had forgotten the ______________________ God made with them.

2. The Lord God sent the ______________________ to remind them to keep the ______________________.

3. Christ is the ______________________ who brings us back from our own ______________________, our separation from God because of ______________________.

E **Reread** the prayer at the top of page 211 in your book. Think about its meaning. How does this prayer reflect the main idea of Chapter 14?

____

____

____

F **Respond** to the following.

1. How is Jesus like a Good Shepherd and why are we like his sheep?

____

____

2. Describe a time a young person might especially need to be led by Jesus as a shepherd leads his sheep.

____

____

Take Home

Hope and Faithfulness

When the people of Judah lived in exile, the prophet Ezekiel helped them realize that even though they might temporarily turn away from God, God would always be ready to welcome them back. We have this same relationship with God and are called to share it with others.

ACTIVITY **For the Greater Good**

Look for a parish, school, neighborhood, or community volunteer opportunity in which your family can participate. Check your school newsletter, your parish bulletin or Web site, and your community calendar for possibilities.

THROUGH THE WEEK

A Prayer for the Week Help us appreciate the gift of faith, Lord. Keep us strong in faith, and strong in our hope in you. Amen.

ON SUNDAY
Listen for messages of faith and hope during the readings and the homily. Invite family members to share the messages they hear.

ON THE WEB
BlestAreWe.com
RCLBLectionary.com
SaintsResource.com

Blessed Andrew of Phu Yen (1625–1644)

As a young Catholic Vietnamese, Andrew became a catechist. He was arrested and advised to renounce his faith, but he refused. Even as he was about to be executed, Andrew continued to encourage the Christians present to remain firm in their faith.

Vietnamese Catholics have a special devotion to Blessed Andrew.

Feast Day: July 26

Take Home

Scripture Background
Before the Time of Jesus

EZEKIEL'S TEACHINGS OF SALVATION
The prophet Ezekiel had a strong influence on the exiled community of Jews. Under his guidance, the Jews came to believe that God was with them wherever they were exiled. Ezekiel told the people that they were like a flock of sheep that had gotten lost, and that God was like a shepherd who would lead them back to safety (see Ezekiel 34:11–16). Just as Ezekiel tells the Israelites that God will care for them like a shepherd for his sheep, Jesus reminds us that he is the Good Shepherd who will lay down his life for his sheep (see John 10:11–18).

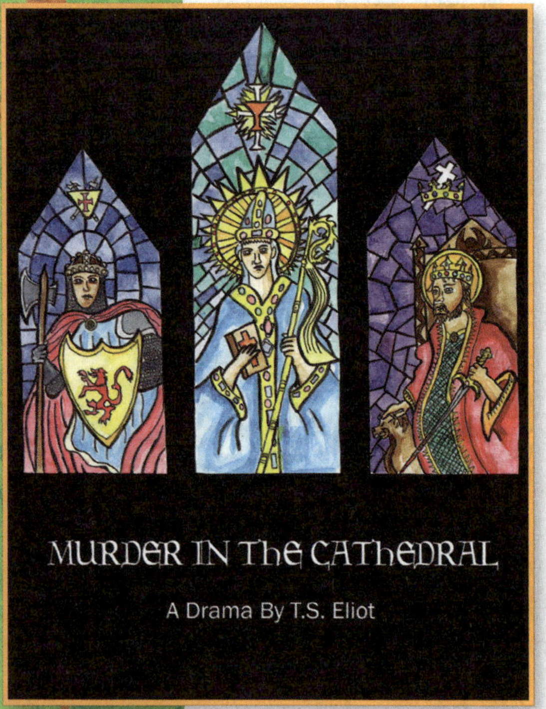

Our Catholic Tradition in Literature

T. S. ELIOT T. S. Eliot, who converted to Anglo-Catholicism in 1927, was one of the most renowned literary figures of the twentieth century. (Anglo-Catholicism is a tradition in the Anglican Church which is close to Catholicism in its doctrine and worship.) Born in the United States in 1888, Eliot gained fame while living in England. He was a prolific writer of poetry, essays, and plays. Eliot's devotion to religion had a profound impact on his work. In his famous poem, "The Waste Land," Eliot used the imagery of the dry bones from Ezekiel 37:1–14, which is discussed in this chapter. His well-known play, *Murder in the Cathedral*, is about the death of Saint Thomas Becket in the twelfth century. Eliot received the Nobel Prize for Literature in 1948. He died in London in 1965.

Hope and Faithfulness

Chapter 15

"Wherever you go I will go,
wherever you lodge I will lodge." Ruth 1:16

Share

Do you have friends, cousins, grandparents, or other relatives who live far away? When you are not able to see them very often, you probably begin to miss them and look forward to a visit with them.

ACTIVITY

Try to remember the last time you saw a friend or a relative whom you missed very much. Then complete the story by writing in the information and circling the bold words that describe that experience.

I remember the last time I saw my **friend** **cousin** **grandmother** **grandfather** **aunt** **uncle** **other**: ______________________,

whose name is______________________.

When we first saw each other, we ______________________.

It was a very happy time. ______________________ is special to me because______________________.

I miss ______________________ because **he** **she** has always shown love for me by ______________________

______________________.

It has been ____________ **months** **years** since the last time I saw

______________________.

I am looking forward to the next visit with lots of hope!

How did God give hope to the Jews in exile?

Hear and Believe **Scripture**

Vision of the Dry Bones

The Babylonians conquered Judah, the southern kingdom, and exiled its citizens around 587 BC. *The Babylonians destroyed the Temple. Without their Temple in Jerusalem, the Jews in exile had to find other ways to feel God's presence. Prophets helped them learn that God did not just exist in Jerusalem and in the Temple. God was with them wherever they went. The prophet Ezekiel taught the exiles how to have faith again by telling them of a vision he had.*

> The hand of the LORD came upon me, and he led me out in the spirit of the LORD and set me in the center of the broad valley. It was filled with bones. . . . Then he said to me: Prophesy over these bones, and say to them: Dry bones, hear the word of the LORD! Thus says the Lord GOD to these bones: Listen! I will make breath enter you so you may come to life. I will put sinews on you, make flesh grow over you, cover you with skin, and put breath into you so you may come to life. Then you shall know that I am the LORD. I prophesied as I had been commanded. A sound started up, . . . rattling like thunder. The bones came together, bone joining to bone. As I watched, sinews appeared on them, flesh grew over them, skin covered them on top, but there was no breath in them.

Ezekiel 37:1,4–8

Then the Lord said to me, "Prophesy to the spirit and say, 'Thus says the Lord God: Come, O spirit, and breathe into these so that they may come to life.'" I prophesied as he told me, and the spirit came into them; they came alive and stood upright, a vast army. Then he said:

> . . . Son of man, these bones are the whole house of Israel! They are saying, "Our bones are dried up, our hope is lost, and we are cut off." Therefore, prophesy and say to them: Thus says the Lord GOD: Look! I am going to open your graves; I will make you come up out of your graves, my people, and bring you back to the land of Israel. . . . I have spoken; I will do it—oracle of the LORD.

Ezekiel 37:11–12,14

To read the complete account in Scripture see Ezekiel 37:1–14.

Together Again

Ezekiel's vision of the dry bones gave people hope that God would bring them back to their kingdom. The plain scattered with bones represents the Jews scattered across foreign lands during the Exile. The coming together of the bones represents the coming together of God's people after the Exile. Ezekiel said that God told him to prophesy over the bones so that God's spirit would bring life to them. Then the bones became live people, united as an army. This represents God's bringing the exiles home to Israel. Ezekiel's vision came true.

In 539 BC, Cyrus, leader of the Persians, conquered the Babylonians. He said that the exiles could return home. The Jews who returned had high hopes. They rebuilt the Temple. They also prayed and studied God's Word in synagogues, smaller places of worship. Jerusalem again became the center of worship and government. New prophets led the people in worshiping God. People honored God with feasts and celebrations.

The Sabbath is an important occasion for the Jewish people. For them it is a memorial of Israel's freedom from Egypt. The Sabbath also recalls the seventh day in the Bible account of creation, when God rested. During the Exodus, God commanded the Israelites to always keep holy the Sabbath. For Christians, we recall and celebrate Jesus' Resurrection on Sunday as the Lord's Day. The Lord's Day symbolizes the "eighth day" because Christ's Resurrection brought into the world a new creation.

ACTIVITIES

1. God was faithful to the covenant and did not allow the Israelites to remain in exile for long. Identify and write the ways the Israelites honored God after the Exile.

____

____

____

2. Ezekiel's vision of the Dry Bones captured the exiles' interest and gave them hope that they would return to their kingdom. Reread what Ezekiel said. Draw the part of Ezekiel's vision that is the most interesting to you.

As Christians, what do we hope for?

Hear and Believe

Celebrating the Lord's Day

It was Sunday, and Alicia needed to talk to someone. She had a lot of things on her mind. She was getting bad grades in math. Her teacher had accused her of disturbing the class on Friday. Her best friend, Max, was mad at her about something she had said.

In addition, Alicia's grandmother, who was called Nona, had been taken to the hospital with a heart condition a few days earlier. Not only was Alicia worried about her grandmother, but she was also feeling lonely. Nona had always spent time with Alicia, but now she wasn't around. Alicia's mom had been spending most of her free time at the hospital visiting Nona. Alicia's father also wasn't home as often, now that he was working two jobs to pay college tuition for Alicia's older sister, Olivia. And Olivia always wore earbuds and locked herself in her bedroom.

Whom could Alicia turn to? Normally when her family went to Sunday Mass together, Alicia noticed that Nona spent extra time before and after Mass silently talking to God. When Alicia asked her about this once, Nona had said, "God always makes time for us if we make time for him."

So, this Sunday, before Mass began, Alicia spent extra time praying. She asked God to heal Nona, reflected on how her behavior could have been better that week, and resolved to apologize to Max. At the end of Mass, she asked her sister to wait for her while she knelt before the tabernacle and talked to God about her worries and problems. At the end of her prayers, a sense of hope came over Alicia. She felt that God had really listened to her. Maybe her grandmother was on to something.

Our Church Teaches

We obey God's Commandment to keep holy the Lord's Day by attending Mass each Sunday. We must also attend Mass on holy days of obligation, confess our sins in Penance and Reconciliation at least once a year, receive the Eucharist at least during the Easter season, observe the Church's days of fast and abstinence, and contribute to the Church to provide for its material needs. These are the **precepts of the Church**. They are our obligations as Catholics. Above all, we are required to do good and avoid evil, showing respect for the value of human life.

By living according to the teachings of our Catholic faith, we can hope for everlasting happiness that God promises us. Hope is our trust in God to help us achieve everlasting life. Hope is one of the **Theological Virtues**, three spiritual qualities that come from God and help us become more holy. The other two Theological Virtues are faith and charity. Through faith we believe in God, in everything God has revealed, and in all that the Church teaches us to believe. Faith is necessary for salvation. Charity is the love we show for others and for God. **Moral Virtues** help us avoid sin, which separates us from God. Temperance is a Moral Virtue. It means not doing too much of any one thing, such as eating too much, driving too fast, or abusing alcohol. Temperance helps prevent danger or sin. For example, speeding and drunk driving can kill or hurt people, and endangerment of human life is a serious sin.

GO TO page 376 to learn more about the virtues.

ACTIVITY

Charity is the love we show for God and others. It is made up of many ingredients. Write your own recipe for charity (for example, a cup of courage, a teaspoon of patience, and so on).

CHARITY

We Believe

Sin separates us from God and makes us people in exile. We come closer to God by making good moral decisions and following the teachings of our faith.

Faith Words

precepts of the Church
The precepts of the Church are the Church's teachings about our obligations as Catholics.

Theological Virtues
The Theological Virtues—faith, hope, and charity—come from God and help us become more holy. They connect us with the Holy Trinity.

Moral Virtues
The Moral Virtues—temperance, prudence, justice, and fortitude—are four spiritual qualities that help us avoid sin.

What are some ways that you can be an example of faith, hope, and charity?

Respond

Faith and Charity

The Book of Ruth in the Old Testament tells this special story about faith and charity.

A Jewish woman named Naomi moved from Bethlehem, in Judah, to Moab with her husband and two sons. But soon after leaving Bethlehem, Naomi's husband died. Naomi's sons married Moabite women, Orpah and Ruth.

For ten years the widow and her family lived peacefully. Then suddenly, both of Naomi's sons died. Now she was in a foreign land without her husband or her sons. And her native people, the Jews, were far away. Naomi decided it was time to return to Bethlehem. Both of her daughters-in-law decided to go with her.

On the road to Bethlehem, Naomi said to Orpah and Ruth, "Go back to your mothers' houses! May the Lord grant each of you a husband and a home in which you will find rest."

Orpah kissed her mother-in-law goodbye and returned to her homeland.

> **But Ruth said, "Do not press me to go back and abandon you!**
>
> **Wherever you go I will go,**
> **wherever you lodge I will lodge.**
> **Your people shall be my people**
> **and your God, my God."**
>
> Ruth 1:16

Naomi and Ruth continued their journey and arrived in Bethlehem during the harvest. They were desperately poor and needed food to eat. Ruth went into someone's fields and picked up grain left behind by the harvesters. For many hours she gathered food for Naomi and herself.

Then the owner of the fields, Boaz, approached Ruth. "I have heard what you have done for your mother-in-law," he said. "You have left the land of your birth and have come to a foreign land. May the Lord reward you for what you have done!" Over time, Boaz came to love Ruth. He knew that she was a good woman who lived a life of faith and charity. Boaz and Ruth married. They became the great-grandparents of David, the king.

ACTIVITIES

1. Complete each sentence with a Theological Virtue.

Ruth's decisions to stay with Naomi and to gather food for her are examples of ____________________. When Ruth said, "Your God will be my God," she showed that she had ____________________ in Naomi's beliefs.

2. Ruth put Naomi's needs above her own. Think about ways you can follow Ruth's example of charity. Write your ideas below.

My Needs	Other People's Needs
______________________	______________________
______________________	______________________
______________________	______________________
______________________	______________________

What I Can Do to Meet Others' Needs

____

____

____

____

3. The end of the Exile showed the Jewish people once again that God was faithful and loving. Describe ways in which you experience God's love and kindness in your life.

____

____

____

____

How can you express hopefulness?

An Act of Hope

O my God,
relying on your infinite goodness and promises,
I hope to obtain pardon of my sins,
the help of your grace,
and life everlasting,
through the merits of Jesus Christ,
my Lord and Redeemer.
Amen.

What other hopes do you have for your relationship with God? Silently ask God to help fulfill your hopes.

Chapter Review 15

A **Match** Column A with Column B by writing the correct number in the space provided.

A	B
1. Ruth	____ faith, hope, and charity, which come from God and help us become more holy
2. Book of Ruth	____ helps us believe in God and what he has revealed, and in the Church's teachings
3. faith	____ conquered Judah, sent its citizens into exile, and destroyed the Temple
4. Ezekiel	____ the Church's teachings about our obligations as Catholics
5. precepts of the Church	____ the Persian leader who allowed the exiles to return home
6. Moral Virtues	____ had the vision of the dry bones, which gave the exiles hope that God would bring them together again
7. Theological Virtues	____ remained faithful to her mother-in-law; married Boaz
8. Sabbath	____ tells a special story about faith and charity
9. Babylonians	____ temperance, prudence, justice, and fortitude, which help us avoid sin
10. Cyrus	____ the day that recalls the seventh day in the story of creation, when God rested

B **Write** a brief summary of the Christian hope that is expressed in the Act of Hope found on page 232 in your book.

____

____

____

____

15 Chapter Review

C **Complete** the sentences about the story of Ruth, using words from the box.

family	faith	Naomi	homeland
Ruth	David	charity	Orpah

1. ________________ lived with her two daughters-in-law, ________________ and ________________, in Judah.
2. Ruth chose to leave her ________________ and her ________________ in order to care for Naomi.
3. Ruth's love for God and Naomi is an example of the Theological Virtue of ________________.
4. Ruth's belief in the God of Naomi is an example of the Theological Virtue of ________________.
5. Ruth and Boaz became the great-grandparents of ________________, the king.

D **Respond** to the following.

1. How is being apart from God because of sin like the Israelites' exile from their homeland?

____

____

____

2. Ruth showed charity toward Naomi. In what ways can you show charity for family members?

____

____

____

Take Home

Trust and Prayer

God invites us into a relationship of trust and caring. We sustain that relationship through faith and prayer. The Old Testament story of Esther shows us that we can overcome even extraordinary challenges if we put our faith in God and pray for the strength to carry out his plan for us.

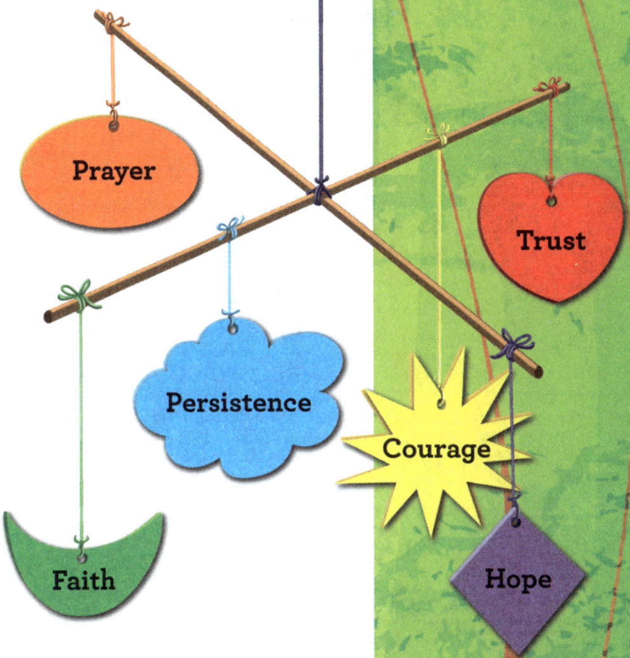

ACTIVITY **What's in a Word?**

Together, make a mobile that displays some words that exemplify the main ideas of this chapter, such as faith, prayer, and trust. Display the mobile in a prominent place in your home.

THROUGH THE WEEK

A Prayer for the Week Even when we grow tired, Lord, give us the faith to trust in your goodness and to pray always. Amen.

ON SUNDAY
As the Universal Prayer (Prayer of the Faithful) is said, pray that you will be a courageous and trustworthy friend.

ON THE WEB
BlestAreWe.com
RCLBLectionary.com
SaintsResource.com

Saint Monica (333–387)

For seventeen years, Saint Monica prayed for her son's conversion to the Christian faith. Her persistence was rewarded. Augustine, later to be known as Saint Augustine, was baptized in 387. Saint Monica died later that same year.

Patron Saint of: wives and mothers

Feast Day: August 27

Take Home

Scripture Background
Before the Time of Jesus

ESTHER AND THE VIRGIN MARY Esther's name comes from the Persian word for "star." Esther was a Jew, but for a time she hid her Jewish identity. When King Xerxes of Persia met Esther, he made her his queen. In this role, Esther was able to intercede with the king to save the Jews from death according to a plot devised by the king's adviser, Haman. For Catholics, Esther is a model of virtue and courage. She is even seen as prefiguring the Virgin Mary in her beauty, chastity, and especially in her ability to intercede for others. Read how Esther saved the Jews in the Book of Esther 2—8.

Our Catholic Tradition
in World History

POPE PIUS XII During World War II, the Nazis, under the leadership of Adolph Hitler, killed more than 12 million people, including 6 million Jews. In Vatican City in Italy, Pope Pius XII worked to save the Jewish people, concealing many Jews in the Vatican and at Castelgondolfo, the papal summer home. He told bishops, priests, and nuns to help the Jewish people whenever they could, and asked that convents and monasteries be opened to Jews. He gave many Jewish people Vatican citizenship and helped them escape Europe.

At Pope Pius XII's death in 1958, Golda Meir, Israel's foreign minister, said, "When fearful martyrdom came to our people in the decade of Nazi terror, the voice of the pope was raised for its victims. . . . We mourn a great servant of peace."

Trust and Prayer

Chapter 16

It is truly right and just . . . to acclaim our God invisible, the almighty Father.

Based on the Easter Proclamation (Exsultet), *Roman Missal*

Share

Think about the people who take care of you, such as your parents or grandparents. Although you may not stop to think about it, every day these people take care of your needs and wants in several ways. What kinds of things do they provide for you daily?

ACTIVITY

Needs are things that you require to live a healthy life. Wants are things that make your life more pleasurable. Complete the chart by writing in the needs and wants that people meet for you during each part of the day.

	Needs	Wants
Morning		
Afternoon		
Night		

How does God take care of us?

Hear and Believe **Scripture**

A Prayer for Her People

Esther was a beautiful young Jewish woman who lived about 500 years before the birth of Christ. She was adopted by a relative, Mordecai, after her parents died. Mordecai, a Jew, lived in exile in Persia (present-day Iran), where he was appointed to the royal court after saving the king's life.

Soon after Esther went to live with Mordecai, the king decreed that all the young women in his empire move to the royal palace. He planned to choose one of them to be the new queen. Esther then moved to the palace. When the king met Esther, he was struck by her kindness and her great beauty. He made her the queen.

At this time, a man named Haman was the highest official in the royal court. Haman was greedy for fame and power. All the king's servants had to bow down in his presence. Mordecai refused. As a Jew, he would not honor a man in the way he would honor the Lord. Haman was angry about this. He vowed to destroy all the Jews in Persia. He wrote a royal order stating, "All Jews, young and old, including women and children, should be killed in one day."

When Mordecai learned of Haman's plan, he requested that Queen Esther ask the king to save the Jews from death. To plead for the lives of her people, Esther would have to tell the king that she was a Jew. Knowing that this could lead to death, Esther prayed to the Lord for guidance and courage.

> **. . . "My Lord, you alone are our King. Help me, who am alone and have no help but you, for I am taking my life in my hand. . . . Put in my mouth persuasive words in the presence of the lion, and turn his heart to hatred for our enemy, . . . Save us by your power, . . ."**
>
> Esther C:14–15, 24–25

Then Queen Esther went to the king and enjoyed a great banquet with him. While dining, Esther told the king that she was a Jew. She told him of Haman's plan. She said, . . .

> **"If I have found favor with you, O king, . . . I ask that my life be spared, and I beg that you spare the lives of my people. For we have been sold, I and my people, to be destroyed, killed, and annihilated."**
>
> Esther 7:3–4

The king was enraged about Haman's plan. He ordered that Haman be punished and appointed Mordecai to fill Haman's position in court.

To read the complete account in Scripture see Esther 2—8.

Faith and Prayer

Esther had great faith in the goodness and power of God. In her time of need, she prayed a prayer of **supplication** to the Lord. She humbly and earnestly asked God for help. She asked God to give her the courage to face the king and the wisdom to convince the king to spare her people. Esther prayed with **persistence**. Her prayer arose from her faith that God could really answer her. She trusted that God would meet the needs of his people. Esther's petition, or solemn prayer of request, was granted.

ACTIVITY

In five words or less, write a prayer of supplication that you can pray at any time, such as "Give me courage, Lord" (Queen Esther's prayer).

____

Faith Words

supplication

Supplication is humbly and earnestly asking for help. Like Esther, we address prayers of supplication to God.

persistence

Persistence is the act of continually pursuing something in spite of obstacles. Prayer often requires persistence.

How should we pray if we are in need?

Hear and Believe **Scripture**

The Trials of Job

In the Old Testament, there is a special narrative that illustrates persistence and complete trust in God. It is found in the Book of Job. Here is a summary of that story.

Job was a holy man who honored God above all else. Job was blessed with good health, good fortune, and a good family. But all of a sudden, everything changed. Job lost his fortune, witnessed the deaths of his children, and suffered from sores all over his body. As each terrible thing happened, Job refused to believe that God had abandoned him.

Soon friends came by to tell Job that God must have been punishing him for past sins. They urged him to repent. Job replied, "Repent for what? I am innocent of any sin."

Finally, Job questioned God. He demanded that God explain the reasons for his tragic situation. He accused God of breaking the covenant with him. To the amazement of Job's friends, God actually answered Job. God spoke in a mighty voice, explaining that he was the almighty Creator and asking for Job's trust.

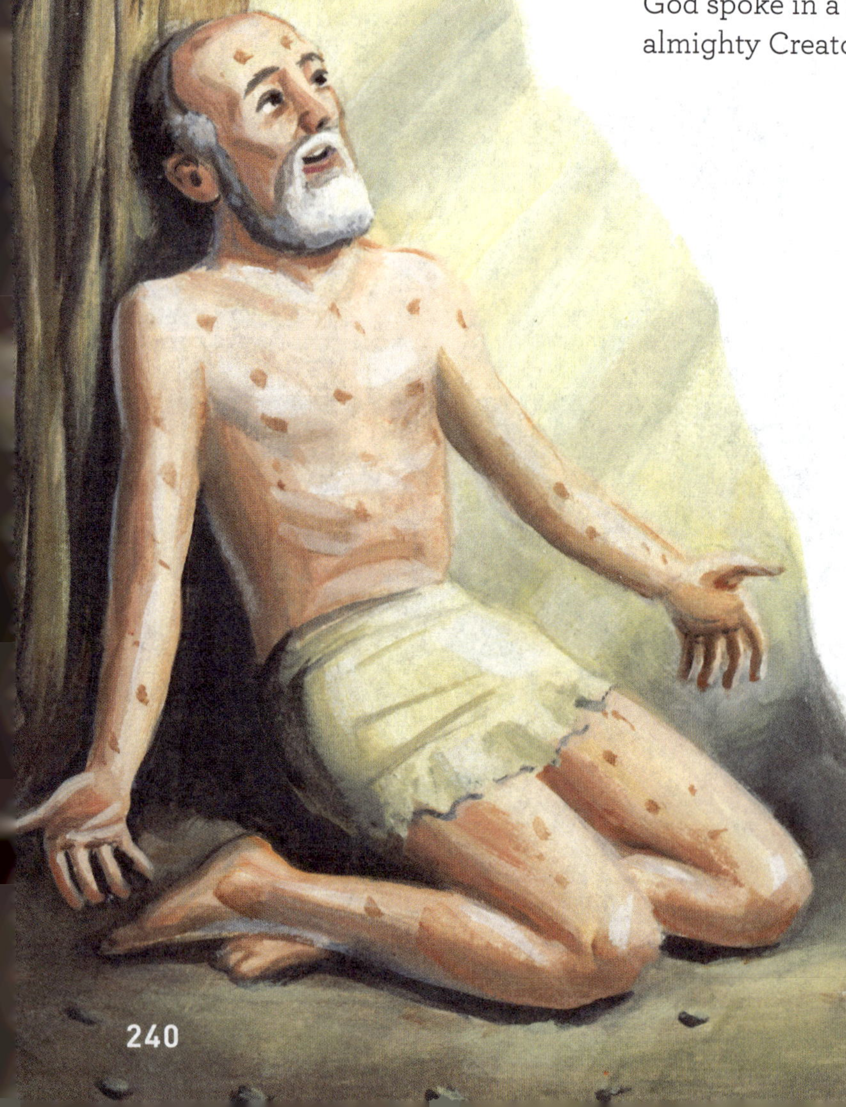

God's words satisfied Job, and the suffering man placed his trust in his Creator. Job praised God, saying, "I was born with nothing, and I shall die with nothing. The Lord gave, and the Lord has taken away; blessed be the name of the Lord!"

Job prayed because he believed firmly in God. He knew that God really heard him.

To read the complete account in Scripture read the Book of Job.

Our Church Teaches

When we pray, we raise our minds and hearts to God and request good things from him. God meets our needs through those who care for us and who take care of our needs every day. Our prayers may require persistence. God answers our prayers if we have faith in his power and goodness.

Prayer arises from faith. We pray because we believe that God really hears us. To grow in our relationship with God, we must pray frequently and with patience.

We Believe

Prayer requires faith and persistence. The sources of prayer are the Word of God, the liturgy, and the Theological Virtues of faith, hope, and charity.

ACTIVITIES

1. Think of someone you know, or someone you have read or heard about, who demonstrates trustful prayer. Give an example from this person's life that illustrates his or her ability to trust God in the face of trial.

____

____

____

____

2. Give an example of trustful prayer from Jesus' life.

____

____

____

3. Now write a prayer of trust that you can say in your own life when you are facing challenges or hardships.

____

____

____

____

____

What did Jesus teach us about prayer?

Respond

The Parable of the Persistent Widow

Jesus taught his disciples about the necessity of praying without becoming weary by telling this parable.

> [Jesus] said, "There was a judge in a certain town who neither feared God nor respected any human being. And a widow in that town used to come to him and say, 'Render a just decision for me against my adversary.' For a long time the judge was unwilling, but eventually he thought, 'While it is true that I neither fear God nor respect any human being, because this widow keeps bothering me I shall deliver a just decision for her, . . .'" The Lord said, "Pay attention to what the dishonest judge says. Will not God then secure the rights of his chosen ones who call out to him day and night? Will he be slow to answer them? I tell you, he will see to it that justice is done for them speedily."
>
> Luke 18:2–8

ACTIVITIES

1. Think about the parable. Imagine you are the widow. Think about how you feel when the judge denies your request. Then think about how you feel when your request is finally granted. Reflect on the message Jesus wants to send you through this story.

What is that message? ____

____

Name needs that you or other people have. ________________________

____

Write a short prayer asking God to fulfill those needs. ______________

____

____

____

Quietly and reflectively address your prayer to God.

"That Would Have Been Enough!"

A Jewish custom is to praise God before asking him for something. The *Dayenu* is a Hebrew song that praises God. *Dayenu* means, "That would have been enough!" The song celebrates how God delivered the Israelites every time they needed help, and then went even further than just meeting each need. It is sung during Passover. Here is a version you can pray.

Leader:	Had he brought us out of Egypt, and not fed us in the desert, brought us out of Egypt we'd be satisfied.
Response:	**That would have been enough!**
Leader:	Had he fed us with manna, and not then ordained the Sabbath, fed us with the manna we'd be satisfied.
Response:	**That would have been enough!**
Leader:	Had he ordained the Sabbath, and not brought us to Mount Sinai, ordained the Sabbath we'd be satisfied.
Response:	**That would have been enough!**
Leader:	Had he brought us to Mount Sinai, and not given us the Torah, brought us to Mount Sinai we'd be satisfied.
Response:	**That would have been enough!**
Leader:	Had he given us the Torah, and not led us into Israel, given us the Torah we'd be satisfied.
Response:	**That would have been enough!**

Based on the Dayenu

2. Think about the ways that God has shown his presence in your class this year. Work with a partner to write some verses for your own class *Dayenu*.

____

____

____

____

____

____

How is Jesus' Resurrection an answer to our prayers?

The Exsultet

The Easter Proclamation, or *Exsultet*, also celebrates God's glorious acts. It is sung during the Easter Vigil. It is filled with praises and rejoicings about the Resurrection of Jesus Christ.

Exult, let them exult, the hosts of heaven,
exult, let Angel ministers of God exult,
let the trumpet of salvation
sound aloud our mighty King's triumph!

Rejoice, let Mother Church also rejoice,
arrayed with the lightning of his glory,
let this holy building shake with joy,
filled with the mighty voices of the peoples.

This is the night,
when once you led our forebears, Israel's children,
from slavery in Egypt
and made them pass dry-shod through the Red Sea.

This is the night
that even now, throughout the world,
sets Christian believers apart from worldly vices
and from the gloom of sin,
leading them to grace
and joining them to his holy ones.

O wonder of your humble care for us!
O love, O charity beyond all telling,
to ransom a slave you gave away your Son!

O happy fault,
that earned so great, so glorious a Redeemer!

Portions of the Exsultet, Easter Vigil, *Roman Missal*

Chapter Review 16

A **Complete** the sentences, using words from the box.

parable	Dayenu	Theological Virtues
supplication	persistence	liturgy
Exsultet	Esther	faith

1. The ____________, or Easter Proclamation, is prayed during the Easter Vigil.
2. ____________ is humbly and earnestly asking God for help.
3. Esther prayed with ____________. Her prayer arose from her ____________ in God.
4. Jesus' story of the persistent widow is called a ____________.
5. ____________ married the king of Persia and convinced him to spare her people.
6. The ____________ is a Hebrew song that praises God and means, "That would have been enough!"
7. The sources of prayer are the Word of God, the ____________, and the ____________ of faith, hope, and charity.

B **Respond** to the following.

1. What did the woman in the parable of the Persistent Widow need the judge to do?

____

____

2. What lesson about prayer and asking God for help did Jesus want to teach us in this parable?

____

____

____

16 Chapter Review

C **Complete** the sentences, using words from the box. Each word will be used more than once.

faith
persistence

1. Esther prayed because she had ________________ that God could really answer her.
2. Despite the bad things that happened to him, Job continued to pray with ________________.
3. Job prayed even during bad times because he had ________________ that God really heard him.
4. Prayer often requires ________________.

D **List** three things for which the Exsultet on page 244 in your book praises God.

____

____

____

E **Respond** to the following.

1. Explain Jesus' message about prayer in the parable of the Persistent Widow.

____

____

____

2. How might you apply this message in your prayers?

____

____

____

Faith in Action

AUXILIARY MISSIONARIES From her beginnings, the Church has cared for the needs of others and has shared individual gifts and possessions with those who are poor or in need. Students in Catholic schools contribute to this important work by volunteering to help the less fortunate in their own communities and by supporting missionaries in faraway places. Groups of students working together to support the Church's mission of serving the poor live out the Catholic Social Teaching of **Option for the Poor and Vulnerable**. They help spread Jesus' message of love and goodness to people in need far and near.

In Everyday Life

ACTIVITY Think about a time when you encountered someone in your family, school, or community who was in need of special care. Describe the need you saw, and how you or others helped meet the needs of that person.

____

____

____

____

____

____

____

____

____

____

____

____

In Your Parish

ACTIVITY Discuss with classmates how you would spend a $100 donation to help a family in need in your own community or a community nearby. Be sure to consider both the needs and the feelings of the people you help. Fill in your budget on the lines provided.

Amount	**Purpose**

Faith in Action

LECTORS A trained lector prayerfully prepares to proclaim God's Word at Mass. The Holy Spirit, who inspired the writing of Scripture, also inspires, or breathes life into, its proclamation. When we prayerfully prepare to hear the Word of God, we open ourselves to the blessing of growing closer to God. Even when we have heard a Scripture story over and over again, hearing someone new read it can be like hearing it for the very first time. Through his Word and through the ministry of lectors, God speaks to us and reveals himself and his love for us. Lectors live the Catholic Social Teaching of **Call to Family, Community, and Participation.**

In Everyday Life

ACTIVITY Put a check mark next to each item that presents a good way for others to know more about you. Then circle the three items that would most accurately reveal your personality to others.

____ my group of friends

____ sports I participate in

____ my musical talents

____ Web sites I visit

____ music I listen to

____ my neighborhood

____ where I like to hang out

____ my favorite movies

____ the books I read

____ the clothes I wear

In Your Parish

ACTIVITY Use your Bible to look up and read the First Reading from last Sunday. Write the reference to the verses in the space provided. Write in your own words what you think God is trying to say to you in that reading.

Reference: ____________________

What God is saying to me: ____________________

____

____

____

____

____

____

____

____

____

Faith in Action

PARENT AND FAMILY VOLUNTEERS It takes the contributions of many people to ensure the success of a school community. In a Catholic school, parent volunteers offer their time and assistance to help create an environment where children can grow in learning and in their faith. Parents share their time and talents in many ways—whether helping with fundraisers, serving in the school cafeteria, working in the school library, or serving as class parents. Parent volunteers live the Catholic Social Teaching of **Call to Family, Community, and Participation.** They make an invaluable contribution to the mission and success of a Catholic school.

In Everyday Life

ACTIVITY Being part of a team or a family means sharing a similar goal and working together to meet that goal. Describe one or two goals of a group that you participate in, who motivates you to stay focused on the goals, and how you and other participants work together to achieve them.

Goal 1: ______________________________

____

Goal 2: ______________________________

____

Motivator: ______________________________

____

How our team or group works together:

____

____

____

In Your Parish

ACTIVITY Describe one of your parish's goals and tell how members of the parish community work together to meet that goal.

Goal: ______________________________

____

How parishioners work together:

____

____

____

____

____

____

____

____

____

____

____

Faith in Action

RESPECT LIFE MINISTRY Helping people to understand and appreciate the Church's teachings about the sanctity, or holiness, of all human life is the most important goal of Respect Life or Pro-Life committees in Catholic parishes. It is one way we live out the Catholic Social Teaching of **Life and Dignity of the Human Person**. Being pro-life means protecting the rights of the unborn, people who are elderly and handicapped, and even people on death row. Through prayer, education, and fundraising, pro-life ministries support activities that demonstrate respect and love for all life as a precious and valuable gift from God.

In Everyday Life

ACTIVITY For each decision, write an **F** to indicate that it is a decision made out of fear or a **C** to indicate that it is a decision made with courage. Then write about the most courageous decision you've ever known somebody to make.

_____ Apologize to someone I know I have hurt

_____ Audition for the school talent show

_____ Visit my grandmother at the hospital

_____ Lie to my parents about a test grade

_____ Refuse to help a friend cheat on a test

A most courageous decision: ____________

In Your Parish

ACTIVITY List two or three concerns that a young unmarried pregnant woman might have about having a baby. Then tell how your parish might help the woman resolve these concerns. Be sure to identify specific help the parish can provide, including spiritual guidance.

Concerns: ____________

How the parish can help: ____________

Unit Wrap-up 4

Using at least five of the key words below and your own words, write a summary of what you have learned in this unit.

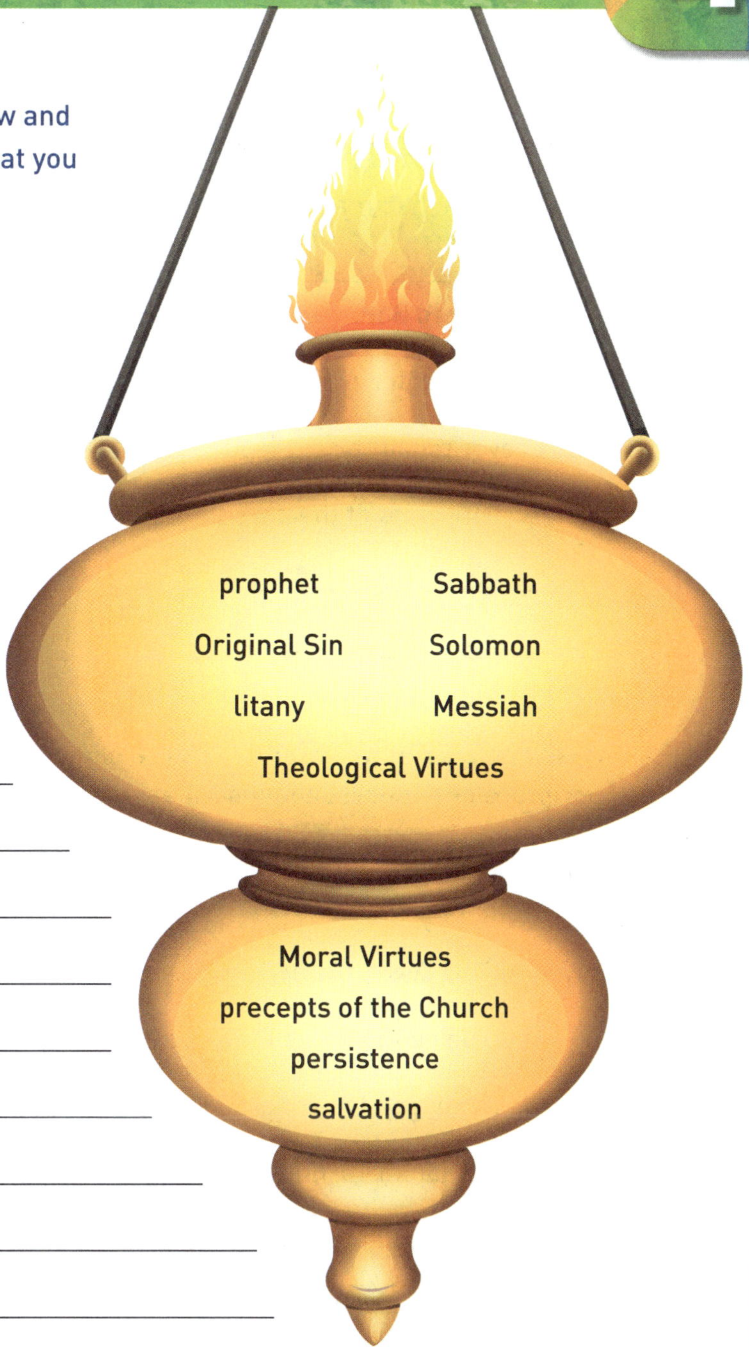

4 Unit Review

A **Complete** each sentence with the correct word or words.

1. Solomon had many wise sayings, called ____________________.

2. ____________________________ is our Priest, our King, and the Prophet who guides us back to God.

3. Even though we ____________________, God's love for us is everlasting.

4. Prayer requires ____________________ and persistence.

5. Two precepts of the ____________________ are that we attend Mass each ____ and that we confess our sins in ____ at least once a year.

B **Read** each Scripture verse. Write the name of the person who spoke the words in Scripture or the person it describes. Use the names in the box to help you.

Micah	Ruth	Jesus	Ezekiel	Job	Solomon

1. ". . . The LORD gave and the LORD has taken away; blessed be the name of the LORD!" (____________________ 1:21).

2. "I am the good shepherd. / A good shepherd lays down his life for his sheep" (John 10:11). ____________________

3. ". . . [B]ut you have asked for wisdom and knowledge in order to rule my people over who I have made you king— . . ." 2 Chronicles 1:11. ____________________

4. "Only to do justice and to love goodness, / and to walk humbly with your God" (____________________ 6:8).

5. ". . . Son of man, these bones are the whole house of Israel!" (____________________ 37:11)

6. "Your people shall be my people / and your God, my God" (____________________ 1:16).

Unit Review 4

C **Match** Column A with Column B by writing the correct number in the space provided.

A	B
1. exile	____ a person chosen to save people from a particular fate
2. messiah	____ a person sent by God to speak out against accepted behavior that does not follow God's will
3. Moral Virtues	____ faith, hope, and charity
4. Original Sin	____ forgiveness of sin and restoration of friendship with God
5. persistence	____ humbly and earnestly asking for help
6. precepts of the Church	____ temperance, prudence, justice, and fortitude
7. prophet	____ the act of continually pursuing something
8. salvation	____ the sin of Adam and Eve that was passed on to all human beings
9. supplication	____ the Church's teachings about our obligations as Catholics
10. Theological Virtues	____ the forced removal of people from their homeland to another land

D **Explain** how Jesus, the New Adam, is different from the first Adam.

___

___

___

4 Unit Review

E **Match** Column A with Column B by writing the correct number in the space provided.

A	B
1. Christ	_____ invaded Israel in 722 BC and forced its people into exile
2. Esther	_____ offered his own life for that of a prisoner condemned to die
3. litany	_____ a prayer in which we call upon God, Mary, the saints, or holy people, and repeat a response
4. charity	_____ washes away Original Sin
5. Assyrians	_____ the love we show for others and for God
6. Ruth	_____ an Easter Vigil song about the Resurrection of Jesus Christ
7. Exsultet	_____ a Jewish woman who saved her people through prayer
8. Sacrament of Baptism	_____ a word that means "anointed one"
9. Maximilian Kolbe	_____ a Moabite woman who showed great charity toward her Hebrew mother-in-law

F **Respond** to the following.

1. What are the sources of guidance for Christians today?

____

____

____

2. How can you be a source of guidance for others through your example?

____

____

Unit 5

God Promises Us Everlasting Life

John called people to a baptism of repentance. He foretold the Baptism we would receive in Christ. Through Christ, our Baptism calls us to turn our attention toward the Kingdom of God and to be its witnesses by the way we live.

> "I am baptizing you with water, for repentance, but the one who is coming after me is mightier than I."
>
> Matthew 3:11

John baptized Jesus in the Jordan River. Early Christians first drew pictures of baptismal scenes in the catacombs of ancient Rome.

Unit 5
SONG

Creator of the Stars of Night

Words: Latin, 9th c.

CONDITOR ALME SIDERUM, Chant Mode IV

Tune: accomp. by Carol E. Browning

Getting ready for Chapter 17

Take Home

A New Life and a Coming Messiah

Some years after their return from exile, the Jewish people were ruled by nations that tried to prevent them from practicing their faith. The Temple was filled with statues of false gods. A group of Jewish warriors led a revolt and reclaimed the Temple. Out of the struggles of God's people grew the hope that God would send a messiah and reward his faithful ones with peace after death.

ACTIVITY **Family Time Capsule**

The Jewish people drew strength from recalling past experiences of God. Collect items that remind your family of happy times. Store the items in a decorated box. Set a date to open the box.

THROUGH THE WEEK

A Prayer for the Week Lord, to believe in you is to believe that even when we walk in darkness a great light awaits us. Help us to remain firm in our faith. Amen.

ON SUNDAY
Light a candle for someone in your family who is struggling, ill, or deceased. Ask God to give that person happiness and peace.

ON THE WEB
BlestAreWe.com
RCLBLectionary.com
SaintsResource.com

Saint Lucy (285–304)

Saint Lucy is honored as a young martyr from the early Church. She was denounced for her faith, and the governor ordered her killed. After torture that included being blinded, she was executed. Legend says her eyesight was restored before her death.

Patron Saint of:
people with eye diseases

Feast Day: December 13

Take Home

Scripture Background

Before the Time of Jesus

RECLAIMING THE TEMPLE When Antiochus became ruler of the Syrian Empire in 175 BC, the empire included Palestine. Antiochus wanted to promote Greek culture and suppress Judaism. In 167 BC, when Antiochus offered a sacrifice to the false god Zeus in the Temple, a priest named Mattathias killed the emperor 's representative. Mattathias and his sons fled to the hills and gathered an army. By 164 BC, the Jews again controlled most of Jerusalem, and they cleansed and restored the Temple. The Jewish feast of Hannukah commemorates this event. Read about the purification of the Temple in 1 Maccabees 4:36–56.

Our Catholic Tradition in Sacramentals

LIGHTING CANDLES Many Catholic churches feature rows of votive candles in front of statues or sacred images of Jesus and the saints. A churchgoer can light a candle and pray for a special intention. The burning candle suggests a continual rising of the intention toward Jesus or the saint who has been asked to intercede. Burning candles have a long history of religious symbolism. Candles or oil lamps burned outside saints' tombs in the third century. In the Middle Ages people sometimes lit candles as tall as themselves before they prayed, to signify their coming into the light of faith. Lighting candles in a menorah is also an important part of the Jewish feast of Hanukkah.

A New Life and a Coming Messiah

Chapter 17

"... [T]he King of the universe will raise us up to live again forever, ..." 2 Maccabees 7:9

Share

Can you recall a time when you were very happy? Why were you happy? Was it the people you were with? A fun activity? A gift you received? If we had to choose between being happy and being sad, we all know what we would choose.

Now imagine what it would be like to enjoy happiness forever. Jesus promised us everlasting happiness and taught us how to achieve it.

ACTIVITY

Circle the things that make you happy, and draw a line through the things that are not important for your happiness.

_____ Winning a game

_____ Giving presents

_____ Having a lot of possessions

_____ Volunteering to help people

_____ Having name-brand clothes

_____ Texting back and forth with your friends

_____ Making fun of people

_____ Being a good friend

_____ Getting away with breaking a rule

_____ Following Jesus

_____ Loving my family

_____ Respecting my parents

_____ Earning good grades in school

_____ People thinking I'm attractive

Now see how close you are to Jesus' idea of happiness. Write the letter J on the line next to the things that seem close to Jesus' way to happiness.

How many of your ideas of happiness seem to be the same as those of Jesus?

What would make the Jews of the Old Testament happy?

Hear and Believe **Scripture**

The Struggles Under Greek Rule

The period before Christ's birth was difficult for the Jewish people. The Persian rule of Israel ended in 332 BC, and the Jews came under the control of other foreign rulers, such as the Greeks. The Greeks did not worship the God of Israel. People who worshiped false gods were called pagans *or* Gentiles.

There sprang from these a sinful offshoot, Antiochus Epiphanes, son of King Antiochus, once a hostage at Rome. He became king in the one hundred and thirty-seventh year of the kingdom of the Greeks.

In those days there appeared in Israel [men who were breakers] of the law who seduced many, saying: "Let us go and make a covenant with the Gentiles all around us; since we separated from them, many evils have come upon us." The proposal was agreeable; some from among the people promptly went to the king, and he authorized them to introduce the ordinances of the Gentiles. Thereupon they built a gymnasium in Jerusalem according to the Gentile custom. They . . . abandoned the holy covenant; they allied themselves with the Gentiles and sold themselves to wrongdoing.

Then the king wrote to his whole kingdom that all should be one people, and abandon their particular customs. All the Gentiles conformed to the command of the king, and many Israelites delighted in his religion; they sacrificed to idols and profaned the sabbath.

. . . [I]n the year one hundred and forty-five, the king erected the desolating abomination upon the altar of burnt offerings, and in the surrounding cities of Judah they built pagan altars. . . Whoever was found with a scroll of the covenant, and whoever observed the law, was condemned to death by royal decree.

1 Maccabees 1:10–15, 41–43, 54, 57

A group of devout Jews known as the Maccabees conquered the armies of the king. They took back the Temple, removed the pagan objects, and built a new altar. The Temple was rededicated, and according to tradition a one-day supply of lamp oil for the Temple lasted eight days. The eight-day Jewish feast of Hanukkah celebrates these events.

Everlasting Joy

The belief in **resurrection** is gradually revealed in the Old Testament. The Maccabees believed that God's faithful people would have a rewarding life after death. The Maccabees prayed for the souls of fellow soldiers who were killed.

Catholics, too, pray for the souls of the deceased. We believe we will be resurrected because of Christ's Resurrection. We believe that people who die in God's grace experience everlasting happiness, or **Heaven**. Those who die in God's friendship but are in need of purification from venial sins and the temporal punishment due to sin experience **Purgatory**, so as to achieve the holiness necessary to enter Heaven. Praying for the souls in Purgatory helps speed their entry into Heaven. People who die in a state of mortal sin risk eternal separation from God, or **hell**. A mortal sin is a serious act against God's law done purposely. It separates us from God's grace and normally requires the Sacrament of Penance and Reconciliation in order to be forgiven.

The community of people in the Church on Earth, in Purgatory, and in Heaven is the Communion of Saints.

Faith Words

resurrection
Resurrection is the new life given to us when our bodies reunite with our souls at the end of time.

Heaven
Heaven is a life of everlasting happiness with God, and with all people who love him.

Purgatory
Purgatory is a final purification from sin after death.

hell
Hell is everlasting suffering and separation from God after death.

ACTIVITY

The Maccabees regained the Temple under the Lord's guidance, and the Jews dedicated the Temple to God again. They burned incense and lighted lamps. They bowed down and begged the Lord to spare them from such misfortune again. They asked God to protect them from sin. Then they celebrated joyfully for eight days, remembering all God had done for them (see 2 Maccabees 10:1–6).

Why should we too ask God to protect us from sin?

____

____

____

What help from God can we too celebrate in our lives?

____

____

What are some of the ways that the Holy Spirit leads us?

Hear and Believe **Scripture**

Praying for the Dead

Once, after a great battle, the Maccabees went off to bury their dead. To their surprise, some of the fallen soldiers were wearing pagan charms. These good soldiers had fought and died bravely for God's cause, but they had worshiped pagan idols. The Maccabees prayed to God that the soldiers' sinful deeds might be erased.

> The noble Judas exhorted the people to keep themselves free from sin, for they had seen with their own eyes what had happened because of the sin of those who had fallen. He then took up a collection among all his soldiers, . . . which he sent to Jerusalem to provide for an expiatory sacrifice. In doing this he acted in a very excellent and noble way, inasmuch as he had the resurrection in mind; . . . Thus he made atonement for the dead that they might be absolved from their sin.
>
> 2 Maccabees 12:42–43, 46

The Maccabees trusted that God would listen to their prayers for the forgiveness of the otherwise good men. In the same way, we trust that God will hear our prayers for all the souls, both living and dead, in the Communion of Saints. We are especially hopeful because we know that God the Father sent his Son, Jesus, to save all people.

To read the complete account in Scripture see 2 Maccabees 12:38–46.

Our Church Teaches

The Jews believed that God would send a messiah to bring peace, justice, mercy, and salvation to all. Jesus Christ is that Messiah. God's promises to people in the Old Testament were completely fulfilled in Jesus Christ. Jesus is both true God and true man, united in One Divine Person.

Believing in Jesus Christ and in God the Father who sent him is necessary for salvation from sin. Jesus said, "No one comes to the Father except through me" (John 14:6). God desires us to come to him through Christ so that we can become more God-like. The Holy Spirit makes this possible. The grace of the Holy Spirit and our desire to be with God cause us to believe in Jesus and say, "You are the Christ, the Son of the living God."

The Holy Spirit inspired the Old Testament writers and is revealed in their writings, including the creation story, the Exile, and stories about the poor. It is also in the Scriptures that God revealed himself as Father, Son, and Holy Spirit, or the Holy Trinity.

GO TO page 368 to learn more about the Holy Trinity.

We Believe

Jesus Christ is the Son of God and the Savior, as foretold in the Old Testament. Jesus makes everlasting happiness in Heaven possible.

ACTIVITIES

1. Why do Catholics pray for the dead?

____

____

2. Explain why Jesus Christ is our Messiah.

____

____

____

____

____

____

From whom can we learn to stand firm in our faith?

Respond Saint Lucy

When we have a problem, it is good to talk to someone who understands how we feel. We may also talk to God in prayer. We can ask saints to pray for our special needs, too.

Because saints overcame certain difficulties, many saints are patrons, or helpers, of people with certain needs or characteristics. One of the saints Catholics honor is Saint Lucy. Lucy is the patron saint of people with eye disease, blindness, or throat ailments. Here is the legend that explains why.

Lucy lived in Sicily—part of what is now Italy—in the third century after Christ's birth. At that time Christianity was against the law and Christians were often persecuted. When Lucy was a teenager, her mother chose a rich young man for Lucy to marry, even though he wasn't a Christian. Lucy didn't want to marry at all. She had made a vow to live for Christ only. She prayed to God to help her mother accept her decision.

Lucy's mother had been ill for some time. Lucy accompanied her on a pilgrimage to the tomb of Saint Agatha to find healing, and she was miraculously healed. In gratitude to God for his goodness, she accepted Lucy's decision to devote her life to Jesus.

The rich young man was unhappy with Lucy's decision. To get revenge, he informed the authorities that she was Christian so she would be persecuted. Soldiers came to arrest Lucy, but she would not leave her house. They tried to pull her out by attaching a herd of oxen to her, but they could not move her. The soldiers decided to torture her. First, they poked out her eyes, then they tried to burn her. But by a miracle she would not burn. Then, one of the soldiers stabbed her in the throat. Before she died, her eyesight was restored. Saint Lucy's feast day is December 13.

St. Lucy Altarpiece by Francesco Figini Pagani

ACTIVITIES

1. On the line, write the name of the patron saint of your parish, the saint you are named after, or your favorite saint. Then draw something you know about the saint.

2. Name a person you know who is a model of Christ. List three qualities this person has that you would like to imitate.

Person: ____________________

Qualities I can learn from:

____

____

____

3. Describe an everyday thing you do or can do to be a model of Christ.

____

____

____

How can the saints help us pray?

A Litany Prayer

Here are two litanies, one that requests help from the saints in Heaven and one for the forgiveness of people who have died. After the leader speaks, pray the response while making the gestures shown.

Leader: Holy Mary

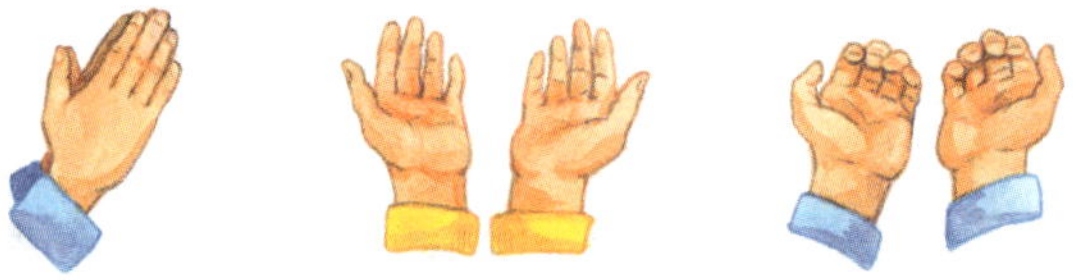

Response: **Pray** **for** **us**

Leader:	Mother of God	**All:**	**(response)**
	Angels of God		**(response)**
	Saint Peter and Saint Paul		**(response)**
	All holy apostles		**(response)**
	All holy martyrs of Christ		**(response)**
	Saint Lucy		**(response)**
	Saint (name a favorite saint)		**(response)**
	All holy men and women		**(response)**

Leader: Now we will pray to God for other people.
Lord, show us your kindness.

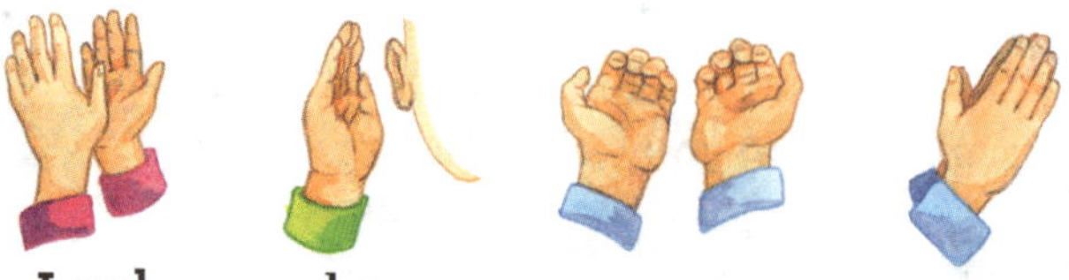

Response: **Lord,** **hear** **our** **prayer.**

Leader:	Save our friends and family.	**All:**	**(response)**
	For (*name people you know*).		**(response)**
	Grant eternal rest to all who have died, especially (*name people who have died*).		**(response)**
	Bring all people together in trust and peace.		**(response)**
	Lord Jesus, hear our prayer.		**(response)**

Chapter Review 17

A **Complete** the sentences, using words from the box.

1. The community of people in the Church on Earth, in Purgatory, and in Heaven is the ______________________________.
2. ______________________ is a final purification from sin after death.
3. The new life given to us when our bodies reunite with our souls at the end of time is called ______________________.
4. ______________________ makes everlasting happiness in Heaven possible.
5. ______________________ is everlasting suffering and separation from God after death.
6. A life of everlasting happiness with God and with all people who love God is called ______________________.
7. God's promises to people in the ______________________________ were completely fulfilled in Jesus.
8. The ______________________ inspired the Old Testament writers and is revealed in their writings.
9. A ______________________ separates us from God's grace and normally requires the Sacrament of Penance and Reconciliation to be forgiven.

Purgatory
mortal sin
Old Testament
hell
Communion of Saints
Heaven
Jesus
Holy Spirit
resurrection

B **Describe** how the example of Saint Lucy might inspire you today.

____

____

____

____

17 Chapter Review

C **Complete** the following sentences, which relate Old Testament beliefs to Catholic beliefs today.

1. Some Jews came to believe in life after death. In a similar way, we believe in ______________________.
2. The Maccabees prayed for their soldiers who had died in battle. In a similar way, we pray for all souls, both living and dead, in the ____.
3. The Old Testament describes the Jews' hope that God would send a messiah. We believe that _______________________________ is the Messiah.
4. The ______________________ inspired the Old Testament authors.
5. God revealed himself as Father, Son, and Holy Spirit in the Scriptures. This is how we know about the ______________________.

D **Respond** to the following.

1. How do saints help us?

____

____

____

2. Recall one saint story you have read either in this book, on SaintsResource.com, or elsewhere. Name the saint and tell how you can learn from him or her how to grow closer to God.

____

____

____

____

Getting ready for Chapter 18

Take Home

Baptism and Repentance

John the Baptist prepared people for the Messiah, Jesus Christ. John preached repentance and the need to wash away one's sins in the waters of Baptism. His story reminds us of the importance of the Sacraments and of our need to prepare spiritually for Christ. What helps your family live as people who are ready for God's kingdom?

ACTIVITY **The Spirit of Advent**

Preparation for Christ is appropriate any time of the year. Research the date for the upcoming First Sunday of Advent and find out more about Advent symbols and rituals. After your research you can make note of how you want to celebrate with your family and begin gathering materials you may need.

THROUGH THE WEEK

A Prayer for the Week God, thank you for the gift of the Sacrament of Baptism and for all the Sacraments. May they bring your life and love into our hearts. Amen.

ON SUNDAY
As you sing the Lamb of God, think of instances in which you need Christ's mercy.

ON THE WEB
BlestAreWe.com
RCLBLectionary.com
SaintsResource.com

Saint Josephine Bakhita (1869–1947)

As a child, Josephine Bakhita was kidnapped from her village in Darfur, Sudan, and sold into slavery. She was rescued about ten years later and taken to Italy. In 1890, Bakhita was baptized—taking the name Josephine—and confirmed, and she received the Eucharist. In 1896, she took religious vows. She went on to live an exemplary life of virtue.

Feast Day: February 8

Patron Saint of: Sudan

Take Home

Scripture Background
In the Time of Jesus

JOHN THE BAPTIST Like the prophets of the Old Testament, John the Baptist warned the Jewish people of their need to repent. Yet John stood apart from the prophets of old in that he proclaimed that God's kingdom was at hand and he announced the coming of the Messiah. Similarly, John's baptisms were based on the Hebrew tradition of ritual washings, but they were performed in expectation of the coming Messiah. When Jesus asked John to baptize him, John was reluctant at first. He knew that Jesus was the Lamb of God, who was without sin and who takes away all sin. Read how John the Baptist prepared people for the coming of Jesus in Matthew 3:1–11.

Subiaco Abbey, a Benedictine monastery in Subiaco, Arkansas

Our Catholic Tradition
in Religious Orders

THE BENEDICTINES John the Baptist was called to proclaim to people the news of the coming Messiah. From the Church's early history, there have been Christians with a special vocation to serve and build up the Church. As the Church grew, communities of people sharing this special calling began to develop. One of the earliest of these is the religious order founded by Saint Benedict. In 529, Benedict founded a monastery at Monte Cassino in southern Italy. In the Middle Ages, hundreds of Benedictine monasteries sprang up throughout Europe and played an important role in passing on the Christian faith. Today, Benedictine monasteries can be found in many parts of the world.

Baptism and Repentance

Chapter 18

I will give you a new heart, and a new spirit I will put within you.

Ezekiel 36:26

Share

Think about your household when a holiday is coming. Your family will make preparations so that everybody enjoys the holiday. Special meals and activities are planned, especially if guests are visiting. Special occasions are even more special when we have time to get ready. God gives us plenty of time to prepare ourselves for his kingdom—a lifetime!

ACTIVITY

This calendar shows events that require preparation. In each box with an event, write something you would do to prepare for it.

Sunday	Monday	Tuesday	Wednesday	Thursday	Friday	Saturday
1 Mass	2	3 science test	4	5 piano lesson	6 sleepover party	7
8 cousin's Baptism	9 Mom's birthday	10	11 gymnastics competition	12	13	14 receive Penance and Reconciliation
15 Mass	16 book report due	17	18	19 doctor's appointment	20	21
22 friend's Confirmation	23	24	25	26 sing in school play	27	28 vacation starts
29 Mass	30					

Who prepared people for Jesus' coming?

Hear and Believe **Scripture**

Advent Gospel Reading

About 2,000 years passed since Abraham first encountered the Lord. The Jews had survived the Exile and foreign rule. They still believed in the God who revealed himself to Abraham and Moses, and in the covenant. In different ways they tried very hard to obey God's law. The **Pharisees** were Jews who were devoted to the Commandments from the Old Testament. They also followed the spoken teachings of religious leaders. The **Sadducees** followed only the written laws from the Old Testament and valued the Temple rituals. The **Essenes** lived simply in the desert. They may have performed special washing rituals. They also believed in life after death. Some scholars think that John the Baptist was one of them.

During Advent, we prepare to celebrate the birth of Jesus. The following Scripture passage is proclaimed on the Second Sunday of Advent, Year A. It tells how John the Baptist prepared people for the coming of Jesus.

> . . . John the Baptist appeared, preaching in the desert of Judea [and] saying, "Repent, for the kingdom of heaven is at hand!" It was of him that the prophet Isaiah had spoken when he said:
>
> "A voice of one crying out in the desert,
> 'Prepare the way of the Lord,
> make straight his paths.' "
>
> John wore clothing made of camel's hair and had a leather belt around his waist. His food was locusts and wild honey. At that time Jerusalem, all Judea, and the whole region around the Jordan were going out to him and were being baptized by him in the Jordan River as they acknowledged their sins.
>
> When he saw many of the Pharisees and Sadducees coming to his baptism, he said to them, "You brood of vipers! Who warned you to flee from the coming wrath? Produce good fruit as evidence of your repentance. And do not presume to say to yourselves, 'We have Abraham as our father.' For I tell you, God can raise up children to Abraham from these stones. Even now the ax lies at the root of the trees. Therefore every tree that does not bear good fruit will be cut down and thrown into the fire. I am baptizing you with water, for repentance, but the one who is coming after me is mightier than I. I am not worthy to carry his sandals. He will baptize you with the holy Spirit and fire."

Matthew 3:1–11

The Kingdom Is Coming

John the Baptist prepared people to receive Jesus as the Messiah by telling them to repent, or be sorry for their sins and change their behavior. Some people believed that the coming of the Messiah was a sign of the final judgment of all humans and the resurrection of the dead.

We recognize Jesus as the Messiah. We are baptized in the Holy Spirit. At our Baptisms, water and the words "I baptize you in the name of the Father, and of the Son, and of the Holy Spirit" give us the seal of eternal life and mark us as belonging to Christ. In Confirmation, Sacred Chrism, the laying on of hands, and the words "Be sealed with the gift of the Holy Spirit" complete the grace of Baptism. Baptism and Confirmation are called Sacraments of Christian Initiation. Both give us a permanent character, or seal, that strengthens us to live as members of the Church and to spread Jesus' message.

ACTIVITY

John the Baptist said, "Repent, for the Kingdom of Heaven is at hand!" He meant that there would be no room for sinful ways in the kingdom. Fill the space below with words describing things that the kingdom will have room for, such as kindness and mercy. Add a design to the space that shows what you imagine the Kingdom of Heaven to be like.

Faith Words

Pharisees
Pharisees were Jewish people who accepted both the written law of the Old Testament and spoken teachings and tradition.

Saddducees
Sadducees were Jewish people who accepted only the written law of the Old Testament and rejected spoken teachings and tradition.

Essenes
Essenes were devout Jewish people who lived simply in the desert.

What happened when John the Baptist met Jesus at the Jordan River?

Hear and Believe **Scripture**

The Baptism of Jesus

John the Baptist's preaching was so powerful that crowds flocked to the Jordan River to listen to him. Many people were in awe of John and thought he was the Messiah. But one day, a day for which John had long hoped, he stood in awe of another Person, Jesus. As John was baptizing people, Jesus had stepped out of the crowd and asked John to baptize him. John did not feel worthy of baptizing him.

> [John said to Jesus], "I need to be baptized by you, and yet you are coming to me?" Jesus said to him in reply, "Allow it now, for thus it is fitting for us to fulfill all righteousness." Then he allowed him. After Jesus was baptized, he came up from the water and behold, the heavens were opened [for him], and he saw the Spirit of God descending like a dove [and] coming upon him. And a voice came from the heavens, saying, "This is my beloved Son, with whom I am well pleased."
>
> Matthew 3:14–17

To read the complete account in Scripture see Matthew 3:5–6, 13–17.

Our Church Teaches

The Sacraments of Baptism and Confirmation affect our souls permanently, so we celebrate them only once. On the other hand, we should celebrate the Sacrament of Penance and Reconciliation frequently—at least once a year. This Sacrament, instituted by Christ, helps us spiritually in many ways. It reconciles us with God if we have committed a mortal sin, giving us God's grace again. It also reconciles us with the Church. It excuses us from eternal punishment for mortal sins and from some of the punishment due for all sin after death. Finally, it brings us peace of mind, comfort, and the strength to avoid temptation. Through this Sacrament, we prepare for the Final Judgment at the Second Coming of Christ.

Before confessing our sins to the priest, we carefully examine our consciences, reflecting upon how we have sinned. The Church teaches that we should confess to the priest all unconfessed grave sins. This is the only ordinary way to be reconciled with God and the Church. The Church does not require that venial, or less serious, faults be confessed. However, it strongly recommends it. After we confess our sins and express our sorrow, the priest will absolve us, saying, “God, the Father of mercies, through the death and resurrection of his Son has reconciled the world to himself and sent the Holy Spirit among us for the forgiveness of sins; through the ministry of the Church may God give you pardon and peace, and I absolve you from your sins in the name of the Father, and of the Son, and of the Holy Spirit” *(Rite of Penance)*.

We Believe

To obtain reconciliation with God and with the Church, we must confess grave sins to a priest.

ACTIVITIES

1. Match the word to the sentence that describes it.

_________ Saddducees _________ Essenes

_________ Pharisees _________ Penance and Reconciliation

a. These Jews accepted both the written law and the spoken teachings and tradition.

b. These devout Jews lived simply in the desert.

c. This Sacrament reconciles us with God.

d. These Jews accepted only the written law of the Old Testament.

2. Under to each event below, write how Christians prepare for it, based on what you have learned in this chapter.

Christmas ____

____

The coming of the Kingdom of Heaven ____

____

The final judgment at the Second Coming of Christ ____

____

The Sacrament of Penance and Reconciliation ____

____

How do the Sacraments lead us to holiness?

Respond

ACTIVITIES

1. Fill in the missing information about the Sacraments.

Type of Sacrament	Sacrament	What is it?	Who may receive it?
Christian Initiation	Baptism		babies, children, or adults who have not been baptized
	Confirmation	seals us with the gift of the Holy Spirit	baptized people who are ready to boldly proclaim the Gospel
	Eucharist		
Healing	Penance and Reconciliation		
	Anointing of the Sick	an anointing of people suffering from serious illness or old age, giving special graces, including forgiveness of sin	people who are sick or dying
At the Service of Communion	Matrimony	a lifelong covenant between a husband and wife to love and serve one another and to raise and love children, teaching them to follow Christ	
	Holy Orders	a commitment to serve the Church as a bishop, priest, or deacon	

GO TO pages 371–373 if you need help with this activity.

2. Fill in the blanks with names of the Sacraments to complete the story of how one young person experienced them.

When Arthur was a baby, he was welcomed into the Catholic Church through the Sacrament of ______________________________. When he was seven, he experienced the Sacrament of ______________________________ for the first time, in which he celebrated God's forgiveness. Soon after, Arthur celebrated the Sacrament of the ______________________________ and received the Body and Blood of Christ. At thirteen, he was sealed with the gift of the Holy Spirit in ______________________________. As an adult, instead of celebrating ______________________________ and having a family, Arthur chose to receive the Sacrament of ______________________________ and become a priest. He was then able to administer the Sacraments, including the ______________________________, in which elderly and ill people receive special grace from God to help them in their suffering.

3. Write a prayer asking God to help you choose the vocation that is right for you when you are older. ______________________________

____

____

What are some of the ways that prayer renews us?

Prayer

A Prayer of Renewal

What images from nature remind you of birth? The prophet Ezekiel told the Jewish people that God would make Israel "born again" after the Exile. At Baptism, the following passage from the thirty-sixth chapter of the Book of Ezekiel may be read. The reading reminds us that Baptism gives us new life.

Close your eyes and quietly listen to the passage. The leader will pause after each sentence and ask you to imagine a beautiful flower or plant growing step by step.

Leader: **Thus says the Lord God:**

I will take you away from among the nations,
gather you from all the foreign lands,
and bring you back to your own land.

Imagine hands planting seeds in soil.

I will sprinkle clean water upon you
to cleanse you from all your impurities,
and from all your idols I will cleanse you.

Imagine a watering can over the soil and water sprinkling out.

I will give you a new heart and place a new spirit within you, taking from your bodies your stony hearts and giving you natural hearts.

Imagine tiny green sprouts shooting up from the soil.

I will put my spirit within you and make you live by my statutes, careful to observe my decrees.

Imagine a green stem beginning to grow, with buds and leaves slowly appearing.

You shall live in the land I gave your fathers;
you shall be my people, and I will be your God.

Imagine the stem growing into a beautiful plant or a flower in full bloom, with sunlight shining on it. Imagine a meadow of flowers around it.

Based on Ezekiel 36:24–28

Leader: Let us pray together.

All: **Thank you, God, for the new life you gave us in Baptism. Help us grow in faith and love. Amen.**

Chapter Review 18

A **Match** Column A with Column B by writing the correct number in the space provided.

A	B
1. The Sacrament of Penance and Reconciliation	_____ Jewish people who accepted only the written law of the Old Testament
2. The Sacrament of Confirmation	_____ consenting to the lifelong covenant between a baptized man and a baptized woman
3. Pharisees	_____ ordained man is enabled to act in the Person of Christ
4. John the Baptist	_____ seals us with the gift of the Holy Spirit
5. The Sacrament of Matrimony	_____ devout Jewish people who lived simply in the desert
6. Sadducees	_____ the Sacrament administered to those who are suffering from serious illness or old age
7. The Sacrament of Holy Orders	_____ told the Jewish people that God would make Israel "born again" after the Exile
8. Essenes	_____ Jewish people who accepted both the written law and tradition
9. Ezekiel	_____ preached in the desert and baptized in the Jordan River
10. The Sacrament of Anointing of the Sick	_____ reconciles us with God if we have committed a mortal sin; should be celebrated at least once a year

B **Explain** how the following Scripture verse relates to Baptism: "I will give you a new heart, and a new spirit I will put within you" (Ezekiel 36:26).

____

____

18 Chapter Review

C **Complete** the sentences, using words from the box.

Kingdom of Heaven	Penance and Reconciliation
Baptism	Confirmation

1. The Sacraments of Baptism, Confirmation, and Penance and Reconciliation prepare us for the ______________________.
2. The Sacrament of ______________________ excuses us from eternal punishment for mortal sin and brings us peace of mind.
3. The Sacraments of Baptism and ______________ affect our souls permanently.
4. Catholics receive ____________ and Confirmation once in a lifetime.

D **Circle** the best answer.

John the Baptist preached in the **(desert, community)** of Judea.

He **(baptized, confirmed)** many people in the **(Tigris, Jordan)** River.

He told people to **(repent, forgive)** and change their **(souls, behavior)**.

E **Respond** to the following.

1. What are some ways in which the Sacrament of Penance and Reconciliation helps us spiritually?

____

____

____

2. In what ways can you benefit by making the celebration of the Sacrament of Penance and Reconciliation a regular part of your spiritual life?

____

____

____

Getting ready for Chapter 19

Take Home

Christians and the Reign of God

The New Testament story about the boy Jesus in wise conversation with Temple priests inspires us to reflect upon the great love of God, who let us share in his own divinity through a seemingly ordinary boy. When we value our dignity as Christians and as God's children, we are able to understand that all people deserve our love and that we can become holy people and saints ourselves.

ACTIVITY **The Star Prayer**

Have each family member draw an outline of a star and write *Holy Spirit* on the left and right of it, *Jesus Christ* in the center, and *God* above its top point. Inside the star, each person should jot down anything for which he or she would like to pray. With the help of the Holy Spirit, the "beams" of your prayers rise up to God through Jesus Christ.

THROUGH THE WEEK

A Prayer for the Week Lord Jesus, you became one of us and taught us how to live. Help us learn from your example and from the example of the holy people who live lives of goodness and virtue. Amen.

ON SUNDAY
Live the message of the Sign of Peace at Mass by continuing to pray for peace in the world, at work, at school, and at home in the coming week.

ON THE WEB
BlestAreWe.com
RCLBLectionary.com
SaintsResource.com

Saint Teresa of Calcutta (1910–1997)

Mother Teresa worked among the "untouchables" of India's society. With the sisters of the religious order she founded, she cared for the most neglected people of Calcutta. She founded orphanages for unwanted children and homes for the sick and dying, and cared for them physically, emotionally, and spiritually. Mother Teresa was named a saint of the Church in 2016.

Take Home

Scripture Background
In the Time of Jesus

JESUS BEFORE HIS MINISTRY Jesus' life is known almost solely from the Gospels, and although the Gospels provide details about Jesus' birth and early infancy, they provide little other information about Jesus before his public ministry. The exception is the story of Jesus in the Temple when he was twelve, where we see him speaking with the teachers. In Luke's story of Jesus in the Temple, we see that even before he began his public ministry, and even as a boy, Jesus was aware of his unique relationship with God. Read about Jesus in the Temple in Luke 2:41–51.

Our Catholic Tradition in Ireland

CELTIC MONKS A well-known path called Saints' Road winds through the Dingle Peninsula in County Kerry, Ireland. Beginning in the sixth century, monks traveled such paths to convert Christians to the monastic life. Christians lived, studied, and worshiped on the Dingle Peninsula between the sixth and tenth centuries. Ruins of early Christian settlements are abundant on the coast, from oratories to holy wells to Celtic crosses to small stone huts once belonging to the monks. Some sites remain remarkably intact from the time they were abandoned in the twelfth century. Saints' Road connects the holy site of Mount Brandon to Gallarus Oratory, a stone church more than 1,100 years old (shown at left).

Christians and the Reign of God

Chapter 19

"Blessed are they who hunger and
thirst for righteousness,
for they will be satisfied."

Matthew 5:6

Share

Have you ever made something out of clay? From a lump of clay you can form something beautiful in any shape you want.

God lovingly shaped us in his own image, giving us his goodness and love within us. God gave each person beautiful gifts and talents. God sees beauty in all of us—inside and out. When we recognize the beauty within ourselves, we are better able to respect the inner beauty of others.

ACTIVITY

This photograph shows a situation in which God's image is not respected. In the space provided draw an opposite situation, in which God's image is honored.

What are ways we can show that we are all created in God's image?

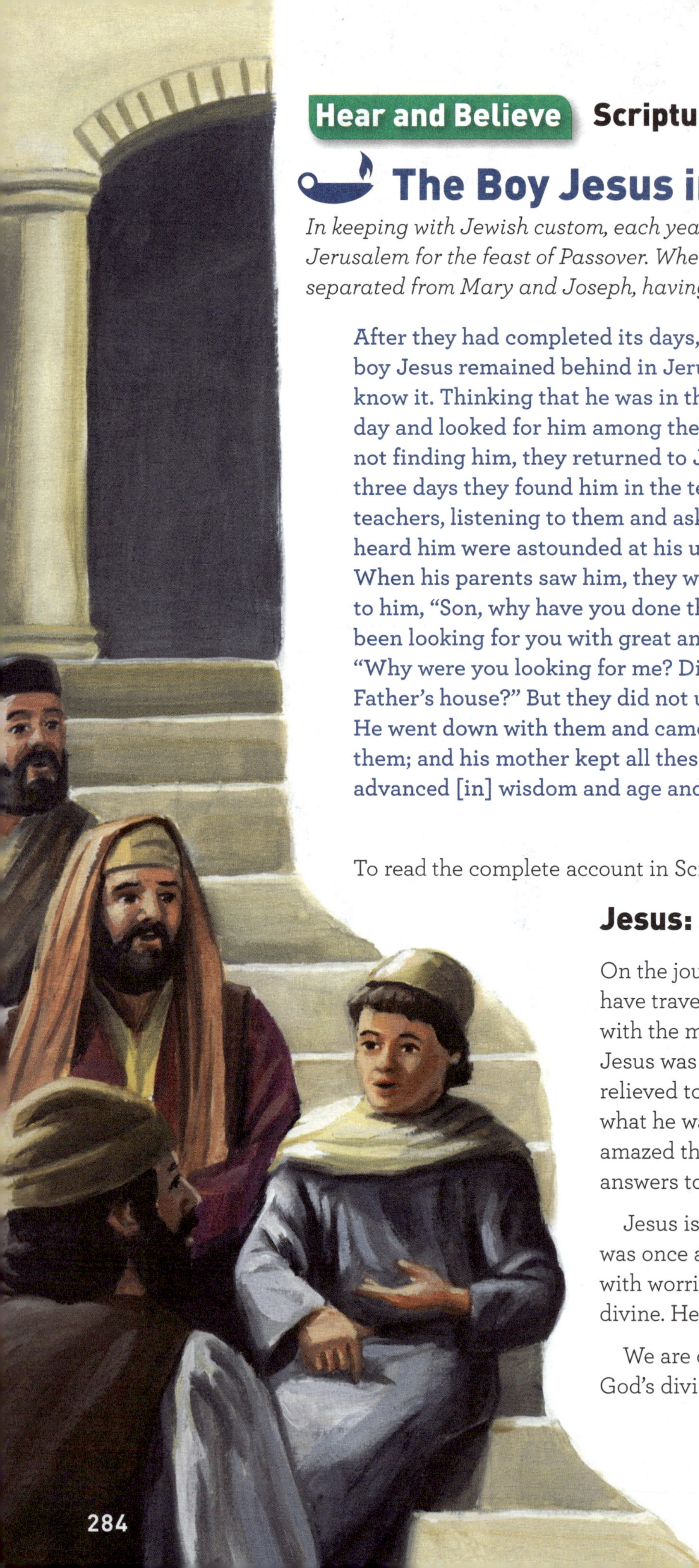

Hear and Believe **Scripture**

The Boy Jesus in the Temple

In keeping with Jewish custom, each year Jesus and his parents went to Jerusalem for the feast of Passover. When Jesus was twelve years old, he was separated from Mary and Joseph, having stayed behind in the Temple.

After they had completed its days, as they were returning, the boy Jesus remained behind in Jerusalem, but his parents did not know it. Thinking that he was in the caravan, they journeyed for a day and looked for him among their relatives and acquaintances, but not finding him, they returned to Jerusalem to look for him. After three days they found him in the temple, sitting in the midst of the teachers, listening to them and asking them questions, and all who heard him were astounded at his understanding and his answers. When his parents saw him, they were astonished, and his mother said to him, "Son, why have you done this to us? Your father and I have been looking for you with great anxiety." And [Jesus] said to them, "Why were you looking for me? Did you not know that I must be in my Father's house?" But they did not understand what he said to them. He went down with them and came to Nazareth, and was obedient to them; and his mother kept all these things in her heart. And Jesus advanced [in] wisdom and age and favor before God and man.

Luke 2:43–52

To read the complete account in Scripture see Luke 2:41-52.

Jesus: Son of God, Son of Man

On the journey back to Nazareth, Mary would have traveled with the women, and Joseph with the men. Each parent probably thought Jesus was with the other one. They were relieved to find Jesus, but did not understand what he was doing in the Temple. Jesus amazed the teachers in the Temple with his answers to their difficult questions.

Jesus is the Son of God, the Messiah. He was once a missing twelve-year-old Jewish boy with worried parents. He is both human and divine. He is true man and true God.

We are created in God's image and share in God's divine nature through Jesus Christ.

All people have dignity as God's children. Human dignity gives people certain rights. People have a right to make moral choices, to have religious freedom, and to express belief in God. People have a right to govern their families, which are formed by married men and women and their children, without interference from other institutions.

ACTIVITY

Listed below are some ways of showing others that we respect the human dignity of others. As a follower of Jesus, how can you do each of the things listed? Give specific examples on the lines.

Helping others do what is right

____

____

Giving advice to those who are doubtful

____

____

Praying for others

____

____

Comforting the suffering

____

____

Forgiving people

____

____

Being patient with others

____

____

Why do we respect others' dignity?

Hear and Believe **Scripture**

Jonah, the Reluctant Prophet

Sometimes, respecting other people's dignity can be a struggle. Our own pride or prejudices can get in the way. In the Old Testament, the Book of Jonah tells the story of someone who struggled with God's call to help others do what was right. The following is a summary of that story.

Jonah was a prophet, but not a willing one. He tried to run away after the Lord told him:

> **Set out for the great city of Nineveh, and preach against it; for their wickedness has come before me.** Jonah 1:2

God wanted Jonah to warn the citizens that if they did not repent, God would destroy them. But Jonah, like other Jewish people, did not like the wicked Assyrians who lived in Nineveh. He hoped that God would punish them. So Jonah refused to undertake his mission. He hopped aboard a ship headed in another direction.

God, however, had other plans. During Jonah's sea voyage, violent winds hurled the ship back and forth, until Jonah's passengers turned to him and said:

> **. . . "Tell us why this evil has come to us! What is your business? Where do you come from? What is your country, and to what people do you belong?"** Jonah 1:8

Jonah said:

> **. . . "Pick me up and hurl me into the sea and then the sea will calm down for you. For I know that this great storm has come upon you because of me."** Jonah 1:12

After Jonah was thrown overboard, the Lord sent a large fish to swallow him. After three days, the fish heaved him upon the shore, and the Lord again told Jonah to go to Nineveh. Reluctantly, Jonah went and preached God's message. To his surprise, his hated enemies paid attention. They changed their wicked ways. Jonah's success really angered him. He asked God, "Why did I have to be the instrument of your mercy?"

The Lord answered:

> **"And should I not be concerned over the great city of Nineveh, in which there are more than a hundred and twenty thousand persons . . . ?"** Jonah 4:11

From Jonah's story, we learn that God sends his mercy to everyone, including those whom we consider our enemies. Just as God is merciful to all people, we too must show mercy to all people.

To read the complete account in Scripture, read the Book of Jonah.

Our Church Teaches

We respect people's dignity by treating them with love and kindness. We can do this by practicing the **Spiritual Works of Mercy** and the **Corporal Works of Mercy**, loving deeds that fulfill the needs of other people. The Spiritual Works of Mercy include helping others do what is right, praying for others, comforting the suffering, forgiving people, and being patient with others. The Corporal Works of Mercy fulfill the physical needs of others. They include feeding the hungry, sheltering the homeless, visiting the sick, and burying the dead.

GO TO page 381 to learn about the Corporal and Spiritual Works of Mercy.

Saint Paul said, "Do you not know that you are the temple of God, and that the Spirit of God dwells in you?" (see 1 Corinthians 3:16). Each Christian is a **temple of the Holy Spirit**. As temples of the Holy Spirit, we are called to respect our bodies. For example, God's gift of sex is noble and honorable, and should be shared only by a husband and wife for the creation of children and as an expression of love and commitment.

As temples of the Holy Spirit, we are also called to be saints, holy people who follow the example of Jesus. Holiness comes from living simply, as the saints did. The saints denied themselves possessions and avoided distractions that prevented them from serving God. Holiness comes from the struggle of overcoming temptation and trying to imitate Christ.

GO TO page 378 to learn about the Beatitudes.

We Believe

We are made in God's image. We must respect our dignity and the dignity of all God's children

Faith Words

Spiritual Works of Mercy
The Spiritual Works of Mercy are loving deeds to meet the spiritual needs of others.

Corporal Works of Mercy
The Corporal Works of Mercy are loving deeds that relieve the physical suffering of others.

temple of the Holy Spirit
Each of us is a temple of the Holy Spirit because the Holy Spirit dwells within us. As temples of the Holy Spirit, we are called to imitate Jesus.

ACTIVITY

Complete the sentences.

1. Jonah refused his mission and was thrown into the ____________.
2. Like other Jewish people, Jonah did not like the ________________.
3. The people of Nineveh ____________ after Jonah preached God's message.
4. We are called to show ________________ to others.

What are some of the ways we can use our gifts to help others?

Respond

Saint Teresa of Calcutta
(Mother Teresa)

Saint Teresa of Calcutta understood that every human being has dignity, and dedicated her life to working with the weakest members of society—the poor, the orphaned, the sick, and the dying.

Mother Teresa was born Agnes Bojaxhiu in Yugoslavia in 1910. When she was fourteen years old, she read about the missionary work of the Loreto sisters working in Calcutta, India. She knew with certainty that this was work she wanted to do. A few years later, she made her final profession as a Loreto sister and took the name Teresa, after Saint Thérèse of the Child Jesus (Thérèse of Lisieux). As a Loreto nun she went to India, where she first worked as a teacher. But as she saw the less fortunate members of the city, Teresa longed to help them.

Teresa heard God's call and left the convent. She traveled to Calcutta to live and work among the poor. Encouraged by the archbishop of Calcutta, Teresa started her own order of sisters, the Missionaries of Charity. Their habit was a white sari trimmed with a blue border. Led by Mother Teresa, they cared for the poorest of the poor in India. They founded homes where they could bring the dying people that lay on the streets of the city, so that they might spend their last hours in the company of people who treated them with love and compassion. The sisters then established a home for children, a place where orphaned and unwanted children could be nurtured and loved.

Mother Teresa and her sisters worked tirelessly among the "untouchables" of India's society. They cared for the poor, the sick, those afflicted with leprosy, AIDS, tuberculosis, or any illness, and the neglected and unloved. Following the example of Jesus, Mother Teresa sought out the lowliest members of society and brought them comfort, love, and the joy of knowing God's infinite love for them.

Mother Teresa died on September 5, 1997. Today the Missionaries of Charity number in the thousands and carry out their ministry in countries around the world. Mother Teresa was declared a saint of the Church on September 4, 2016.

ACTIVITIES

1. Jesus said, "You are the light of the world. . . . Just so, your light must shine before others, that they may see your good deeds and glorify your heavenly Father" (Matthew 5:14,16). Imagine that you are the lighthouse in the picture. Each boat is named with a difficulty it must overcome. On each light beam, write a gift you have that will guide each boat to shore unharmed.

2. Following the example of Saint Teresa of Calcutta (Mother Teresa), name some simple ways you can help someone in need.

____

____

____

____

____

How can we pray for holiness?

A Prayer for Holiness

Group 1: Lord, I pray that you may be a lamp for me in the darkness. Touch my soul and kindle a fire within it, that it may burn brightly and give light to my life.

Group 2: Thus my body may truly become your temple. And may the light within me shine on my friends that it may drive away the darkness of ignorance and sin from them also.

All: **Thus together let us be lights to the world, manifesting the bright beauty of your Gospel to all around us. Amen.**

Based on a prayer by Saint Columbanus, AD 540–615

Chapter Review 19

A Circle the letter of the correct answer.

1. Each year Jesus went to Jerusalem with Mary and Joseph for the feast of ______.

   a. Hanukkah
   b. Purim
   c. Passover
   d. Yom Kippur

2. When Mary and Joseph were looking for Jesus, they found him in the ______ talking to the ______.

   a. market, high priest
   b. Temple, teachers
   c. Temple, Pharisees
   d. caravan, elders

3. Loving deeds that relieve the physical suffering of others are the ______.

   a. Corporal Works of Mercy
   b. Theological Virtues
   c. Moral Virtues
   d. Spiritual Works of Mercy

4. Loving deeds to meet the spiritual needs of others are the ______.

   a. Corporal Works of Mercy
   b. Theological Virtues
   c. Moral Virtues
   d. Spiritual Works of Mercy

B Complete the following sentences.

1. Each of us is a ________________ of the Holy Spirit because the Holy Spirit dwells in us.
2. All people are made in God's ________________.
3. Jesus is both human and ________________.
4. ________________ comes from living simply, as the saints did.
5. Human ________________ gives people certain rights, including the right to make moral choices and to express belief in God.

C Rewrite the prayer of Saint Columbanus from page 290 in your own words. Then silently pray what you have written.

____

____

____

19 Chapter Review

D **Label** each of the following actions with an **S** if it is a Spiritual Work of Mercy and with a **C** if it is a Corporal Work of Mercy.

_____ forgiving someone who hurt us

_____ helping a friend avoid a sin

_____ praying for others

_____ visiting a sick relative

_____ donating food to a soup kitchen

_____ being patient with a younger sibling

_____ consoling someone who is suffering

_____ sharing possessions with the needy

E **Describe** ways in which Saint Teresa of Calcutta's example teaches us that every human person has dignity.

____

____

____

F **Respond** to the following.

1. Explain what it means to say that as a Christian you are a temple of the Holy Spirit.

____

____

____

2. Name two ways that you can live as a temple of the Holy Spirit and grow in holiness.

____

____

____

Getting ready for Chapter 20

Take Home

Hope for the Ages

Jesus, the hope of the ages, not only taught us how to pray in words but through his actions. Jesus ordinarily prayed alone in silence. He depended on prayer to help him through the most difficult moments in his life. Periods of silence and prayer may be rare in our lives, but Jesus' example shows us how to achieve a richer life of prayer.

ACTIVITY **A Family Prayer**

Write each part of the Lord's Prayer (see page 384) on a separate slip of paper. Have each family member read a line out loud, and discuss its meaning together.

THROUGH THE WEEK

A Prayer for the Week Lord, through the intercession of the Blessed Mother, we come to you in prayer for all our needs. Hear and answer us. Amen.

ON SUNDAY
Listen to what the priest says just after the Lord's Prayer. What should you do when you are worried and why?

ON THE WEB
BlestAreWe.com
RCLBLectionary.com
SaintsResource.com

Our Lady of Czestochowa

The image of Our Lady of Czestochowa is sometimes called Our Lady of Jasna Góra, after the monastery in Poland in which it has been kept for six centuries. Many miracles have been attributed to the image, including the halt of an impending Russian invasion of Poland in 1920. Polish Catholics have a special devotion to Our Lady of Czestochowa.

Take Home

Scripture Background

In the Time of Jesus

THE LORD'S PRAYER The prayer that Jesus taught, the Lord's Prayer, was called "the most perfect of prayers" by Saint Thomas Aquinas. He said, "In it we ask not only for the things we can rightly desire, but also in the sequence they should be desired." The prayer is seen as a model prayer that features essential elements of all Christian prayers. In the Lord's Prayer, Jesus taught us to call God "our Father." Read how Jesus taught the Lord's Prayer in Matthew 6:9–13 and Luke 11:2–4.

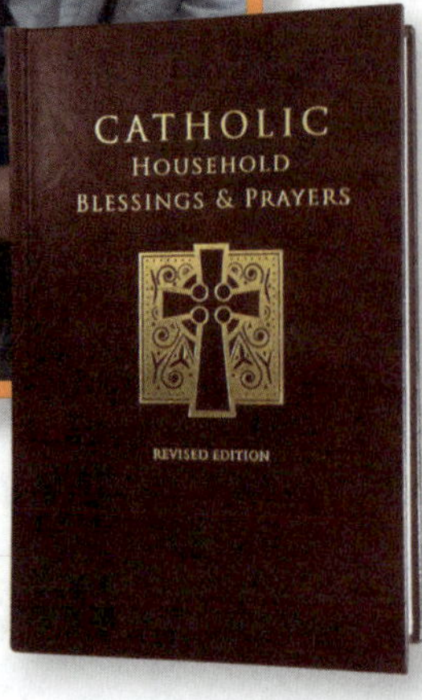

Our Catholic Tradition in Prayer

CATHOLIC HOUSEHOLD BLESSINGS AND PRAYERS The introduction of *Catholic Household Blessings and Prayers* states: "It is in the family that we learn to recognize the love of God and to turn to him in prayer. It is in the family that we first learn the language of prayer and the virtues of Christian living." The United States Conference of Catholic Bishops (USCCB) encourages families to use this book, and to create a space for prayer and a time for prayer in the home, the domestic Church. The book includes traditional and newly-written prayers—blessings, daily prayers, prayers for the liturgical seasons and feast days of the Church year, family prayers, prayers for Catholic living, and prayers for the Church and the world.

Chapter 20

Hope for the Ages

The spirit of the Lord GOD is upon me,
because the LORD has anointed me;
He has sent me to bring good news to the afflicted, . . . Isaiah 61:1

Share

Parents or other adults who care for us love us and want us to be happy. They do much more than meet our material needs. They are also there to guide us when we need help making decisions. Like Jesus, we have earthly caregivers and our heavenly one, God. Mary and Joseph were Jesus' earthly parents, who guided him on Earth. God the Father was Jesus' heavenly Father, who guided him spiritually. Jesus often talked to the Father when he had a problem, and Jesus was always obedient to him.

ACTIVITY

Fill out this certificate of achievement for an adult you love. List three ways in which the person has done much more than meet your material needs.

This Certificate of Achievement for an Outstanding Caregiver

Is Awarded to

____

IN HONOR OF LOVING ACCOMPLISHMENTS, ESPECIALLY

1. _______________________________
2. _______________________________
3. _______________________________

This Award Is Granted with Love on _______________
DATE

Signed _______________________________
YOUR NAME

How did Jesus teach us to pray?

Hear and Believe **Scripture**

Jesus' Ministry

Throughout his ministry, Jesus often spoke to large crowds, teaching about the Kingdom of God.

[Jesus] came to Nazareth, where he had grown up, and went according to his custom into the synagogue on the sabbath day. He stood up to read and was handed a scroll of the prophet Isaiah. He unrolled the scroll and found the passage where it was written:

> **"The Spirit of the Lord is upon me,**
> **because he has anointed me**
> **to bring glad tidings to the poor.**
> **He has sent me to proclaim liberty to captives**
> **and recovery of sight to the blind,**
> **to let the oppressed go free,**
> **and to proclaim a year acceptable to the Lord."**

. . . [T]he eyes of all in the synagogue looked intently at him. He said to them, "Today this scripture passage is fulfilled in your hearing." And all spoke highly of him and were amazed at [his words]. Luke 4:18–22

But soon people in the synagogue became angry. They could not accept Jesus' claims that he fulfilled the prophecies from their Scriptures and that God's saving message was not just for themselves.

Jesus went all around Galilee. He taught in the synagogues, proclaimed the gospel of the kingdom, and cured disease and illness. Many followed him. When he saw how large the crowds were, he went up a mountain, and began to teach the disciples, saying:

. . . "When you pray, do not be like the hypocrites, who love to stand and pray in the synagogues and on street corners so that others may see them. . . . [W]hen you pray, go to your inner room, close the door, and pray to your Father in secret. And your Father who sees in secret will repay you.

"This is how you are to pray:

Our Father in heaven,
hallowed be your name,
your kingdom come,
your will be done,
on earth as in heaven.
Give us today our daily bread;
and forgive us our debts,
as we forgive our debtors;
and do not subject us to the final test,
but deliver us from the evil one."

Matthew 4:23, 25; 5:1-2; 6:5–6, 9–13

Jesus Taught Us How to Pray

The scroll of Isaiah referred to Jesus. Jesus was the one who had come to help the poor, heal people, teach people about God, and free people from sin. People flocked to hear Jesus preach. Jesus announced that God wanted everyone to know his love and forgiveness! Jesus taught people how to pray. In the Lord's Prayer, Jesus called God "Father." He actually used the word *Abba*, which means "Father" in Aramaic. Calling God "Father" would have seemed unusual to people. Jewish people would not even speak God's name. But Jesus taught people that God is a loving Father who looks after his children. Jesus said, ". . . Your Father knows what you need before you ask him" (Matthew 6:8).

Jesus taught that we should pray in secret, or in private. Jesus said it was important to focus on God alone. He said that people who wanted everyone to see how well they prayed and how much they gave to the poor were *hypocrites*, or people who are not sincere.

ACTIVITY

Jesus read a passage from the Old Testament prophet Isaiah. Isaiah's words described Jesus' ministry. In your book, especially in Unit 4, find the words of another Old Testament prophet. Then explain how the words describe Jesus.

____

____

____

____

What did Jesus teach about faith and prayer?

Hear and Believe **Scripture**

The Fruits of Prayer

Old Testament prophets sometimes performed miraculous acts to show people the lessons they were trying to teach. As you learned in Chapter 13, for example, the prophet Elijah called on God to send fire upon the people's sacrifice to teach them about their sinful ways.

Jesus also taught in this manner. In one Gospel passage, a miracle of Jesus illustrates that if we pray to God with very strong faith, there is nothing that God cannot help us with.

> Early in the morning, as they were walking along, they saw the fig tree withered to its roots. Peter remembered and said to [Jesus], "Rabbi, look! The fig tree that you cursed has withered." Jesus said to them in reply, "Have faith in God. Amen, I say to you, whoever says to this mountain, 'Be lifted up and thrown into the sea,' and does not doubt in his heart but believes what he says will happen, it shall be done for him. Therefore I tell you, all that you ask for in prayer, believe that you will receive it and it shall be yours. When you stand to pray, forgive anyone against whom you have a grievance, so that your heavenly Father may in turn forgive you your transgressions." Mark 11:20–25

Jesus used the fruitless tree to teach a lesson. He taught that our minds and hearts should be sincere when we pray to God. We need to have strong faith that will not be overcome by doubt, and we should be making a sincere effort in our daily lives to follow Jesus' example of goodness toward others.

Praying with sincere faith is like being a fig tree that produces lots of fruit. The fruit is all the good that can result.

Our Church Teaches

When Jesus taught the Lord's Prayer, he wanted people to know and understand its meaning. He sent the Holy Spirit to teach us to pray to God as "our Father." In the Lord's Prayer and every prayer, the Holy Spirit, through the Word of God, moves us to pray to God as our Father.

Prayers to God should be sincere. One way to pray quietly and sincerely is through **meditation**. This is a type of prayer in which we are silent and concentrate on our feelings, our imagination, and our thoughts of God.

GO TO page 383 to learn more about prayer.

We Believe

The Lord's Prayer, or the Our Father, comes from Jesus Christ. It is our model prayer.

Faith Words

meditation
Meditation is a type of prayer in which we are silent and concentrate on listening to God through our feelings, imagination, and thoughts. We can meditate by thinking about a Scripture passage, art, and music.

ACTIVITY

Write down five of Jesus' teachings about prayer that you have learned in this chapter.

____

____

____

____

____

____

____

____

How did Jesus pray for help?

Respond

Your Will Be Done, Father

As more people began to follow Jesus, his opponents became angry. Eventually this led to his suffering and Death on the Cross, a death the Son of God endured for the salvation of all people. Before Jesus' died, he called on his Father in prayer. Jesus' final prayers are perfect examples of his loving obedience to the Father.

ACTIVITY

Follow the trail of Jesus' prayers below. On the lines beneath each prayer, write what you think it means.

Jesus stopped to pray in a garden. He knew he was about to be led to his death. . . [H]e said, "Abba, Father, all things are possible to you. Take this cup away from me, but not what I will but what you will." (*Based on* Mark 14:36).

____

____

____

____

After Jesus was condemned to death, he carried the Cross up to the place where he would be crucified. [Then Jesus said, "Father, forgive them, they know not what they do."] (*Based on* Luke 23:34)

____

____

____

____

Women who followed Jesus came to his tomb on the third day after he died. But the tomb was empty. The stone in front of it had been rolled away. [Two men in dazzling garments] said to them, "... He is not here, but he has been raised." (*Based on* Luke 24:5).

As Jesus breathed his last breath, he cried to his Father.... "Father, into your hands I commend my spirit"; ... (*Based on* Luke 23:46)

Even though it was daytime, darkness came over the land. Jesus was dying on the Cross. Jesus cried out in a loud voice, "... My God, my God, why have you forsaken me?" (*Based on* Mark 15:34)

How does the Holy Spirit guide our prayers?

A Meditation Prayer

After Jesus rose from the dead and ascended to Heaven, the Holy Spirit gave Jesus' disciples the strength and wisdom to carry on Jesus' message. The Holy Spirit fills us with the desire to pray to our Father. We can ask the Holy Spirit to give us strength, wisdom, and the ability to pray.

> Come, Holy Spirit, fill the hearts of your faithful.
> And kindle in them the fire of your love.
> Send forth your Spirit, and they shall be created:
> And you will renew the face of the earth.

Meditation:

Look at the painting on this page. It shows the first Pentecost. On that day, the Holy Spirit came to the disciples of Jesus to give them strength to carry out Jesus' mission. How do you think the disciples felt? What symbols for the Holy Spirit are in the painting? What do those symbols tell you about God's power?

The Pentecost by Juan Juanes (1510–1579, Spanish)

Chapter Review 20

A **Match** Column A with Column B by writing the correct number in the space provided.

A Jesus' Words	B Words I Might Say
1. "Father, forgive them, they know not what they do" (Luke 23:34).	____ God, I give myself to you completely.
2. "Take this cup away from me, but not what I will but what you will" (Mark 14:36).	____ Oh, God, why have you allowed me to suffer like this?
3. ". . . My God, my God, why have you forsaken me?" (Mark 15:34)	____ Let me avoid this suffering, but only if it is your will.
4. . . . "Father, into your hands I commend my spirit" (Luke 23:46).	____ Please forgive the people who are persecuting me. They are not aware of their sin.

B **Respond** to the following.

1. In what ways did Jesus fulfill the prophecy that he read from the scroll of the prophet Isaiah?

____

____

____

2. What did Jesus teach the people of Galilee about prayer?

____

____

3. What did Jesus say about people who wanted everyone to see how well they prayed and how much they gave to the poor?

____

20 Chapter Review

C **Complete** the following sentences.

1. ________________ is a type of prayer in which we are silent and concentrate on listening to God.
2. Come, ________________, fill the hearts of your faithful and kindle in them the fire of your love.
3. On ________________, the Holy Spirit came to Jesus' disciples to give them strength to carry out his mission.

D **Describe** what Jesus wanted us to know when he taught the Lord's Prayer.

____

____

____

E **Respond** to the following.

1. What is meditation? ________________________________

   ____

   ____

2. What is one way to meditate? ________________________

   ____

3. Look at the painting on page 350 in your book. What does it show?

   ____

4. Meditate by looking at and thinking about the painting. Write a prayer that asks the Holy Spirit to help you hear what God is saying to you as you pray.

   ____

   ____

   ____

Faith in Action

CONFIRMATION SPONSORS Young people preparing to receive the Sacrament of Confirmation choose a person they know, usually a family member or other relative, to be their Confirmation sponsor. The role of the sponsor is to guide the young person in living a moral life as a committed Catholic and follower of Christ. Confirmation sponsors are examples of what it means to live the Catholic Social Teaching of **Call to Family, Community, and Participation.**

In Everyday Life

ACTIVITY Name two people you know who might be suitable candidates for a Confirmation sponsor for you. Tell what characteristics each person has that would make him or her ideal for this role.

This person...	would be a good Confirmation sponsor because
______________	______________________________
______________	______________________________
______________	______________________________
______________	______________________________

In Your Parish

ACTIVITY Being an involved member of a parish community can help a person be a good Confirmation sponsor. Name a parish ministry (such as being a catechist, being part of a prayer group, and so forth), then tell how being part of this ministry would enrich a person's spiritual life and make him or her a better Confirmation sponsor.

Parish ministry: ______________________________

Benefits: ______________________________

____

Faith in Action

GODPARENTS When Catholic parents bring their child for Baptism, they choose godparents to support the child as he or she grows in faith and understanding of Jesus' love. Godparents share openly about their own faith and help guide new and growing Catholics to be committed to Jesus and to the Catholic Church. As their godchildren grow older and prepare to receive and celebrate other Sacraments, godparents offer prayers and support. God gives godparents special graces to help them make a positive difference in the lives of their godchildren. They demonstrate the Catholic Social Teaching of **Call to Family, Community, and Participation.**

In Everyday Life

ACTIVITY Identify a team that you participate in. In addition to attending practices or meetings, list five important things you can do to show you are committed to meeting your responsibilities on that team.

1. ______________________________
2. ______________________________
3. ______________________________
4. ______________________________
5. ______________________________

In Your Parish

ACTIVITY Write three questions about your personal faith, the Catholic Church, the Sacraments, or the Scriptures. See how your classmates would respond to them. Then discuss your questions with a parent or godparent.

1. ______________________________
2. ______________________________
3. ______________________________

Faith in Action

MINISTRIES OF COMFORT One of the Spiritual Works of Mercy is comforting the sorrowful. A parish's bereavement ministry offers comfort to people who have experienced the death of a loved one. Often, people who have experienced loss offer comfort and support to one another, with the guidance of a counselor trained to help people through these experiences. Other ministries of comfort in a parish might be for cancer patients and for children of divorced parents. People involved in ministries of comfort demonstrate that we are one human family, responsible for one another. This is the Catholic Social Teaching of **Solidarity**.

In Everyday Life

ACTIVITY Before we can offer comfort to others, it helps to stop and think about how we ourselves get through difficult situations and what we have learned from our experiences. Fill in the blanks below so that you can be ready to help someone the next time a need arises.

The hardest thing I ever had to get through was ____________________.

Talking to ____________________ really helped a lot. Other resources I found

helpful were ____________________.

One thing I learned about myself was ____________________.

One thing I learned about God was ____________________.

The most important thing I learned was ____________________.

In Your Parish

ACTIVITY Every parish provides comfort ministries. What are some questions you have about your parish's comfort ministries, such as the bereavement group? Be prepared to discuss your questions with your classmates.

____

____

Faith in Action

PRAYER GROUPS Praying to God for their own intentions and the needs of others is what members of a school prayer group do. By caring for one another through prayer, they demonstrate the Catholic Social Teaching of **Rights and Responsibilities**. These students make themselves available to pray in groups or as individuals during special times of each week. Prayer group members pray for specific prayer requests for those in need. They ask God to intercede in situations they do not even know about. They also organize prayer meetings for other members of the student body.

In Everyday Life

ACTIVITY Sometimes we are afraid to do something because we do not think we can do it perfectly. In the space provided, list one or two things you are good at that you were afraid to try at first. Then describe how good you are at praying and what you can do to be better at it.

I am good at:

____

____

How well I pray:

____

____

____

____

____

____

In Your Parish

ACTIVITY Write some needs or prayer requests that you are aware of from your parish community or elsewhere. Be sure to take some time this week to bring these needs to God in prayer.

____

____

____

____

____

____

____

____

____

____

____

____

Unit Wrap-up 5

On the lines under each chapter title, write three words or phrases that you learned about in the chapter. Use all words and phrases from the box.

resurrection	Maccabees	Spiritual Works of Mercy	Essenes
Pharisees	temple of the Holy Spirit	John the Baptist	meditation
Mary and Joseph	the Lord's Prayer	Communion of Saints	Jesus' prayers

New Life and a Coming Messiah

____

____

____

Baptism and Repentance

____

____

____

Christians and the Reign of God

____

____

____

Hope for the Ages

____

____

____

5 Unit Review

A **Complete** the following sentences, using words from the box.

grave	Jonah	dignity	Holy Spirit	image
temples	John	repent	dove	Old Testament

1. John the Baptist said that to prepare for Jesus' coming people needed to

   ______________________.

2. The story of the Maccabees' praying for the souls of soldiers who were killed is an example of how belief in resurrection is revealed in the

   ______________________.

3. ______________________ or mortal sins must be confessed in the Sacrament of Penance and Reconciliation.

4. God created us in his own ______________________.

5. Because the Spirit of Christ dwells in each one of us, we must respect the

   ______________________ of all God's children.

6. As ______________________ of the Holy Spirit, we are called to respect our bodies and to become saints.

7. We can ask the ______________________ to give us strength, wisdom, and the ability to pray.

8. After ______________________ baptized Jesus, the heavens opened up, and

   the Holy Spirit descended like a ______________________ upon Jesus.

9. The Old Testament story of ______________________, who went reluctantly to preach God's message to the wicked people of Nineveh, teaches us that we are called to respect the dignity of others, no matter what.

Unit Review 5

B **Match** Column A with Column B by writing the correct number in the space provided.

A	B
1. Corporal Works of Mercy	_____ everlasting happiness with God after death
2. Essenes	_____ prayer in which we are silent and concentrate on listening to God
3. Heaven	_____ devout Jewish people who lived simply in the desert
4. hell	_____ each of us, within whom the Holy Spirit dwells
5. meditation	_____ everlasting suffering and separation from God after death
6. Pharisees	_____ Jewish people who accepted both the written law and spoken teachings
7. Purgatory	_____ Jewish people who accepted only the written law of the Old Testament
8. Sadducees	_____ loving deeds to meet the spiritual needs of others
9. Spiritual Works of Mercy	_____ a final purification from sin after death
10. temple of the Holy Spirit	_____ the new life given to us when our bodies reunite with our souls at the end of time
11. resurrection	_____ loving deeds that relieve the physical suffering of others

C **Write** the Come, Holy Spirit prayer. [See page 302.]

____

____

____

____

5 Unit Review

E **Match** column A with column B by writing the correct number in the space provided.

A	B
1. Advent	_____ people who did not worship the God of Israel
2. Saint Lucy	_____ the community of people in the Church on Earth, in Purgatory, and in Heaven
3. the Sacrament of Confirmation	_____ patron saint of people with eye disease
4. Communion of Saints	_____ the person who prepared people for the coming of Jesus by telling them to repent
5. John the Baptist	_____ the season in which we prepare to celebrate the birth of Jesus
6. the Sacrament of Penance and Reconciliation	_____ the Sacrament in which we are anointed with Sacred Chrism, sealed with the Holy Spirit, and given grace to witness to our faith
7. pagans, or Gentiles	_____ the Sacrament that reconciles us with God and the Church

F **Respond** to the following.

1. What did Jesus teach us about how we should pray to God?

____

____

2. Choose one verse from the Lord's Prayer and tell what it means to you.

____

____

Feasts and Seasons

The Liturgical Year

The Church calendar is called the liturgical year. Throughout the liturgical year, the Church leads us through a cycle of specially chosen prayers and readings to help us recall various mysteries of Jesus from his birth to his suffering, Death, Resurrection, and Ascension. We also celebrate feasts honoring Mary and the saints.

Holy Week begins on Palm Sunday of the Passion of the Lord, when we remember Jesus' triumphant entry into Jerusalem, and ends with the celebration of the Triduum. The events we recall during Holy Week are at the center of our lives as Christians.

The **Triduum** begins on Holy Thursday evening and ends on Easter Sunday evening. During these days, we recall the Last Supper when Jesus gave us the Eucharist, Jesus' Death on the Cross to save us from sin, and his Resurrection from the dead.

HOLY WEEK

The liturgical year begins.

ADVENT

Advent is the four-week season that precedes Christmas. During this time, we joyfully await the coming of the Messiah, the long-awaited Savior who will save us from sin and bring us eternal life.

ORDINARY TIME

In the second part of Ordinary Time, we learn more about the life and teachings of Jesus. This is the longest part of the liturgical year.

EASTER

The Easter season begins on Easter Sunday evening and continues until Pentecost Sunday. During the Easter season, we rejoice in the Resurrection of our Savior, Jesus Christ.

LENT

Lent begins on Ash Wednesday and ends on Holy Thursday evening. The Church sets aside these forty days to help us prepare to celebrate Christ's Resurrection. Lent is a season of prayer, almsgiving, and repentance.

ORDINARY TIME

Ordinary Time is celebrated in two segments: between the Baptism of the Lord and Ash Wednesday, and between Pentecost Sunday and the First Sunday of Advent. During Ordinary Time, we reflect on Jesus' life and message.

CHRISTMAS

The Christmas season begins with the Solemnity of the Nativity of the Lord (Christmas), when we celebrate the birth of Jesus, the Son of God. The Christmas season ends with the Feast of the Baptism of the Lord.

Holy Days of Obligation

The Catholic Church guides us in celebrating the great events and people of our faith through the seasons and feasts of the liturgical year. The special feasts of the liturgical year include Sundays and the holy days of obligation. The holy days of obligation are special days when we honor Jesus, Mary, and the saints. Like Sunday, these holy days are so important that the Church requires us to attend Mass.

Sunday

On Sunday, also called the Lord's Day, we celebrate the Resurrection of Jesus. We gather with our family and our parish community to give thanks to God for sending his Son, Jesus, to save us from sin and death and give us eternal life. We are required to attend Mass every Sunday.

Holy Days of Obligation

The holy days of obligation are special days when we honor Jesus, the Blessed Virgin Mary, and the saints. Like Sundays, these holy days are so important that the Church requires us to attend Mass. In the United States, the Church observes the following six holy days of obligation.

Immaculate Conception of the Blessed Virgin Mary December 8	We celebrate that Mary, the Mother of Jesus, was conceived without Original Sin.
Nativity of the Lord (Christmas) December 25	We celebrate the birth of Jesus, our Savior.
Mary, the Holy Mother of God January 1	We celebrate that Mary is the Mother of God's Son, Jesus Christ.
Ascension of the Lord Forty Days after Easter Sunday (or the Seventh Sunday of Easter)	We celebrate the moment when Jesus, in his resurrected body, returned to his Father in Heaven.
Assumption of the Blessed Virgin Mary August 15	We celebrate that Mary was taken body and soul into the glory of Heaven. She uniquely shares in the Resurrection of Jesus.
All Saints November 1	We celebrate all the people who lived holy lives on Earth and who now live with God in Heaven.

Gospel Readings at Mass

At Sunday Mass, we listen to three readings from Sacred Scripture. The First Reading is usually from the Old Testament, the Second Reading is from the New Testament, and the Third Reading is always from the Gospels.

There are two cycles of readings: the Sunday Cycle and the Weekday Cycle. The Sunday Cycle contains readings for Year A, Year B, and Year C. The Gospel readings for Year A are usually from the Gospel of Matthew, Year B from the Gospel of Mark, and Year C from the Gospel of Luke. The Gospel of John is read on certain Sundays and feast days during each year.

ACTIVITY

1. Complete the following chart by telling what year the Church is in (Year A, B, or C) and which Gospel is usually read at Mass. The first year has been identified for you.

Calendar Year	Liturgical Year	Gospel Reading at Sunday Mass
2017	A	Gospel of
2018		Gospel of
2019		Gospel of
2020		Gospel of
2021		Gospel of
2022		Gospel of
2023		Gospel of
2024		Gospel of

2. Read the Gospel readings for Year A, Year B, and Year C for the Second Sunday in Advent. On the lines below, tell what the message of these three Gospels is.

Second Sunday of Advent			
	Year A	Year B	Year C
Gospel	Matthew 3:1–12	Mark 1:1–8	Luke 3:1–6

____

____

____

Blessed be the God and Father of our Lord Jesus Christ, who has blessed us in Christ with every spiritual blessing in the heavens, . . .

Ephesians 1:3

Archangels

Angels are God's messengers. They are spiritual beings who praise God continually. We read about these messengers of God in the Bible. They come to human beings in visions and in dreams, giving them warnings and telling them what God wants. In fact, so many angels are mentioned in the Bible that the tradition has been to group the angels into nine types, or orders: seraphim, cherubim, thrones, dominations, principalities, powers, virtues, archangels, and angels. Arranging the angels into nine orders is a way to describe them according to purposes they serve in the Scriptures. When we discuss angels, we most commonly talk about seraphim, cherubim, archangels, and a category called guardian angels.

The word *archangel* means "chief angel." The Church celebrates the Feast of Saints Michael, Gabriel, and Raphael, Archangels, on September 29.

Michael. Some stories about Michael say that he is the leader of all the angels. He is mentioned by name in the Book of Daniel, an Old Testament book. He is the protector of Israel. In art, he is often shown with a sword and with scales of justice because he is powerful.

Gabriel. The archangel Gabriel is mentioned in the Book of Daniel. In the Gospel of Luke, he appears to Mary to tell her that she will become the mother of Jesus. In art, he is often shown with a white lily in his hand, a symbol of purity. It is said that he presented the Virgin Mary with a bouquet of white lilies.

Raphael. This archangel is mentioned in the Book of Tobit, a book in the Old Testament. Over the centuries, some people have believed that Raphael is the chief of all guardian angels. Raphael is also known as the angel of healing. In the book of Tobit, we read that Raphael used a fish to cure Tobit of blindness so that Tobit would once again see God's light.

Our belief in angels helps us recognize that God loves us and always takes care of us. We do not know very much for certain about angels. Some of what is said about the angels may be legend, but we do know that they bring us closer to God. Believing in angels can help us put our faith in goodness and holiness.

Heavenly Father,
we thank you for
all the good things
you give us.
We thank you especially
for your messengers, in
whatever form or way
they come to us.
They guide us and help
us do your will. Amen.

Messengers of the Lord

The word *angel* means "messenger." In Scripture, we can read how angels like Michael, Raphael, and Gabriel, were messengers of God. Over time art has depicted angels in various ways, but angels are spiritual creatures without bodies like us. Can you recall anyone in the Scriptures who was visited by one of these messengers of the Lord?

ACTIVITY

In the space below, draw or write about times in which a guardian angel can help you in your own choices and decisions.

Advent

... More than sentinels for daybreak,
let Israel hope in the LORD.

Psalm 130:6–7

The Second Coming of Christ

"But of that day and hour no one knows, neither the angels of heaven, nor the Son, but the Father alone. For as it was in the days of Noah, so it will be at the coming of the Son of Man. In [those] days before the flood, they were eating and drinking, marrying and giving in marriage, up to the day that Noah entered the ark. They did not know until the flood came and carried them all away. So will it be [also] at the coming of the Son of Man. Two men will be out in the field; one will be taken, and one will be left. Two women will be grinding at the mill; one will be taken, and one will be left. Therefore, stay awake! For you do not know on which day your Lord will come."

Matthew 24:36–42

During the season of Advent, the Church remembers that Jesus Christ will come again at the end of time. On the First Sunday of Advent, the Church proclaims the Gospel about Christ's Second Coming. In the Gospel of Matthew, read in Year A, we read that Christ's coming will be sudden and unexpected.

To stress the idea that his return would happen when least expected, Jesus used the stories of the flood that completely changed the world, the workers in a field, and the women grinding grain. These stories also tell us that the Lord's return will change everything.

Harvest, Tying the Sheaves
Sir George Clausen, 1902

Getting Ready

Throughout the Gospels, we read that Jesus told his followers that his return would mean the end of everyday life as we know it. So it is important that we live our faith each day, ready and waiting for the risen Christ's return.

Lord, we are waiting for your return. We know that you love us and care for us. May we one day be with you forever in your kingdom. Amen.

The Church always waits in hope and joy for Jesus Christ's return, but especially during Advent. Recalling Jesus' birth at Christmas reminds us that we will see him again at the Second Coming. The Church encourages us to take time to think about our lives and our faith during Advent. By reflecting on what it means to be a Christian and a follower of Jesus, we will await his return with love and hope in our hearts.

In the Gospels we read that Jesus wants his followers to be ready for his return. He wants us to draw close to him through the celebration of the Sacraments and to live as part of his community. This Advent, reflect on what being a Christian means to you.

ACTIVITY

Color the stained-glass shapes marked with an asterisk to discover a hidden message. Then color the rest of the stained glass in contrasting colors.

God Keeps His Promises

In the Bible we read about the many promises God made to his Chosen People. He promised never to destroy the earth again by water, and then he set a rainbow in the sky as a sign of his promise. God promised Abraham and Sarah that he would make of them a mighty nation and that their descendants would be as many as the stars in the sky. Then Sarah, who was childless, became pregnant in her old age. Years later, God promised to deliver his people from slavery in Egypt, and then he led them into a land overflowing with milk and honey. These examples show God's generosity in keeping his promises.

Christians believe that Jesus is the fulfillment of God's promise to us. When the time was right, God sent his only Son to be the **Messiah** and to save all people from sin. Advent is the time in the liturgical year when we recall God's fulfilled promise and wait with joy for Jesus to return in glory at the end of time.

One way the Church recalls and awaits our Lord's Second Coming is by chanting the "O Antiphons" during Advent. During the liturgies of the last days of Advent, beginning on December 17, an antiphon, or short hymn verse, beginning with "O," is prayed and chanted. The O Antiphons come from Old Testament prophecies. Each antiphon calls for the coming of the Messiah. The popular hymn "O Come, O Come, Emmanuel" is based on the O Antiphons.

Here are the first two O Antiphons.

O Wisdom, O holy Word of God,
you govern all creation
with your strong yet tender care.
Come and show your people
the way to salvation.

O sacred Lord of ancient Israel,
who showed yourself to Moses in the burning bush,
who gave him the holy law on Sinai mountain:
come, stretch out your mighty hand
to set us free.

Evening Prayer Antiphons
December 17 and December 18

Preparing for Christmas

The season of Advent consists of the four weeks before Christmas. During this time we prepare to celebrate Jesus' coming anew at Christmas. How do you prepare during the season of Advent?

ACTIVITY

Write your own "O Antiphon" to praise God for his generosity. Remember to start your prayer with the word "O."

____

____

____

____

____

____

____

Lord Jesus,
we wait for your coming. Help
us prepare to welcome you anew
with lives filled with good works
and kindness.
Amen.

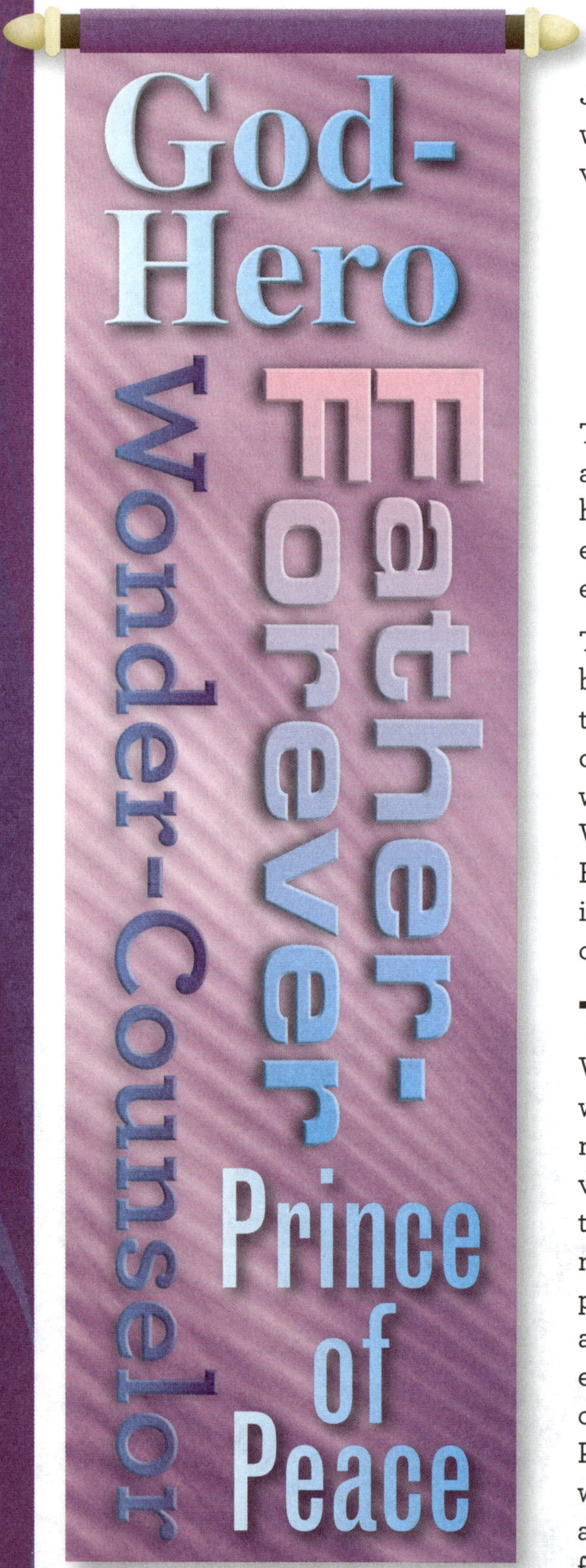

The Prince of Peace

Jesus is often called the Prince of Peace. Do you know why? In the Old Testament Book of Isaiah, there is a verse for prayer for that describes the Savior. It says:

> For a child is born to us, a son is given to us;
> upon his shoulder dominion rests.
> They name him Wonder-Counselor, God-Hero,
> Father-Forever, Prince of Peace.
>
> Isaiah 9:5

The early Christians read the Jewish Scriptures, which are part of our Old Testament today. These Scriptures helped the first Christians understand their faith experience. The Book of Isaiah in particular helped the early Christians understand Jesus and his ministry.

The Book of Isaiah was written several centuries before Jesus was born. Part of the book's message is that a good king for God's people would have special qualities. For example, a just ruler of God's people would bring peace and be known for ruling with peace. When the early Christians read passages from the Book of Isaiah that described this kind of leader, they immediately recognized him as Jesus. This is why we call Jesus the Prince of Peace.

The Kingdom of God

When the Risen Christ comes again in glory, the world will know peace. At the Second Coming of Christ, a new kingdom of peace and justice will begin. All the violence, confusion, misunderstanding, pain, and hurt that human beings experience will be wiped away. For now, Jesus Christ already touches our hearts with his peace whenever we celebrate the Eucharist together, and he guides us in making peace among people. We eagerly await the day when we will know his peace completely and for eternity. Until then, the Lord, our Prince of Peace, wants us to share the gift of peace with others. Whenever we help end an argument, solve a problem, or act generously toward others, we can feel peace within ourselves and bring peace to others. When we do so, we remind others that the Prince of Peace will come in glory, bringing the fullness of the Kingdom of God.

Sharing Peace

From the time of the early Church, Christians have called Jesus the Prince of Peace. They have shared in Jesus' gift of peace. When have you felt the gift of peace in your own life?

ACTIVITY

Suggest peaceful endings to the following situations.

1. Ryan and Carlos are having an argument in the cafeteria. At first, they are just saying mean things to each other. But then Carlos looks as if he is going to knock over Ryan's lunch tray.

   You ____

   ____.

2. Ariel, Jennifer, and Sachiko used to be good friends. Now they don't even want to speak to one another. You are assigned to work with them to complete a class assignment.

   You ____

   ____.

3. Monica's younger brother Stuart goes into her bedroom and steals her MP3 when she isn't home. Sometimes he even hides it to make her angry. She tells you about this.

   You ____

   ____.

O Lord, you bring peace to the world. Bring your peace into our hearts more each day. Help us know you as the Prince of Peace so that we may share your gift of peace with everyone we meet. Amen.

God's Promises

(Gather the class around the Advent wreath, and begin by praying together the Sign of the Cross.)

Leader: Each year during Advent we recall God's promises to his people, the people of Israel. We also recall that he sent his Son, Jesus, to live among us. Now we await Jesus' return in glory. Let us sing together.

(Sing together a verse from "O Come, O Come, Emmanuel" or another familiar Advent hymn or refrain.)

Leader: Let us pray. Lord God, we await the coming of your Son, Jesus Christ. He fills our hearts with love and hope, and brings light to our lives. As we gather around the Advent wreath, we look forward in hope to Jesus' return at the end of time.

All: **Amen.**

Reader 1: A reading from the book of the prophet Isaiah.

(Proclaim Isaiah 9:1–5)

The word of the Lord.

All: **Thanks be to God.**

Leader: Let us offer our petitions for all those in need.

Reader 2: For all the people in the world who live in loneliness, we pray to the Lord.

All: **Lord, hear our prayer.**

Reader 2: For those who are ill and suffering, we pray to the Lord.

All: **Lord, hear our prayer.**

Reader 2: For people who have had arguments with one another, that they may be reconciled, we pray to the Lord.

All: **Lord, hear our prayer.**

Reader 2: For those who have many worries and troubles in their lives, we pray to the Lord.

All: **Lord, hear our prayer.**

Reader 2: For those who are fearful and need courage, we pray to the Lord.

All: **Lord, hear our prayer.**

Reader 2: For people throughout the world who need hope in their lives, we pray to the Lord.

All: **Lord, hear our prayer.**

Leader: Let us pray. Lord, thank you for the gift of your Son, Jesus. He is Emmanuel, the hope of all peoples. He is Wisdom, who teaches and guides us. He is our Savior. Bless us and bless all who are in need of your healing love as we light the candles of our Advent wreath. May they be a sign of your promise to grant us salvation.

(Light the appropriate candles on the Advent wreath, then conclude the prayer as follows.)

May Jesus come quickly and not delay. We ask this in his name.

All: **Amen.**

Leader: Let us reconcile with one another by sharing a sign of Christ's peace.

(All share a sign of peace.)

Based on the Blessing of the Advent Wreath
Book of Blessings

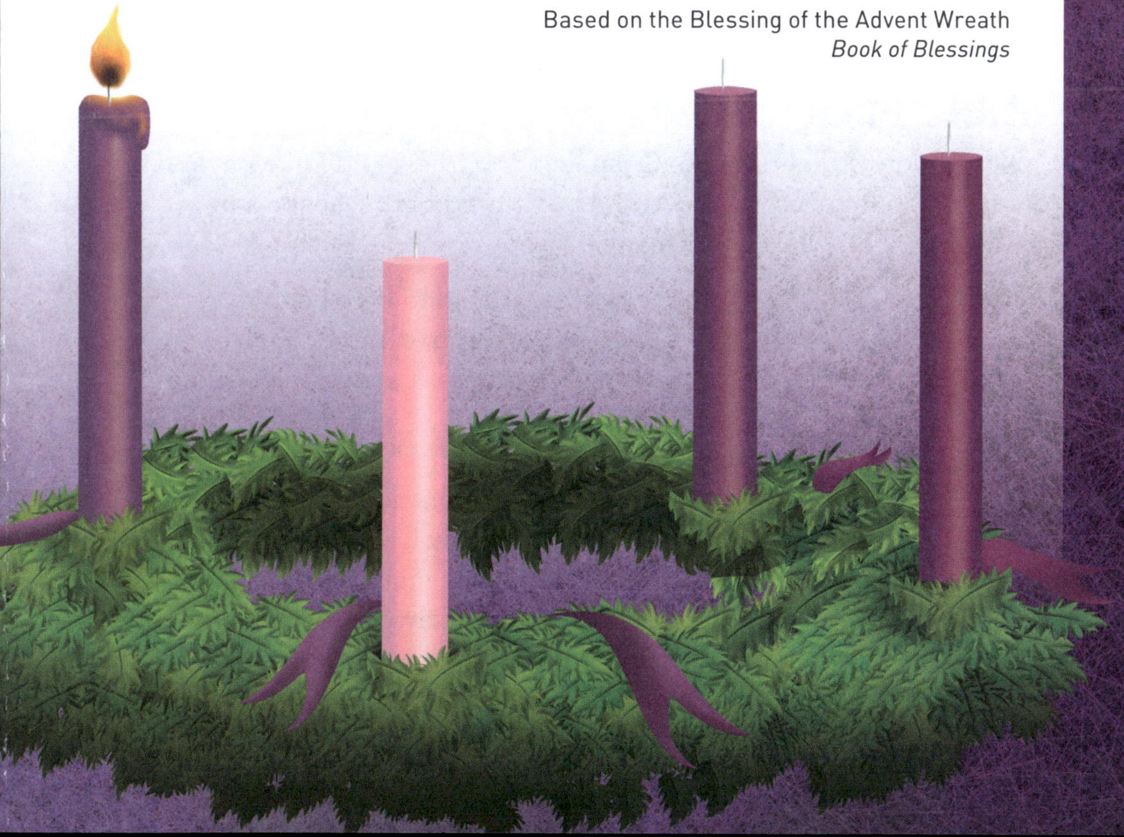

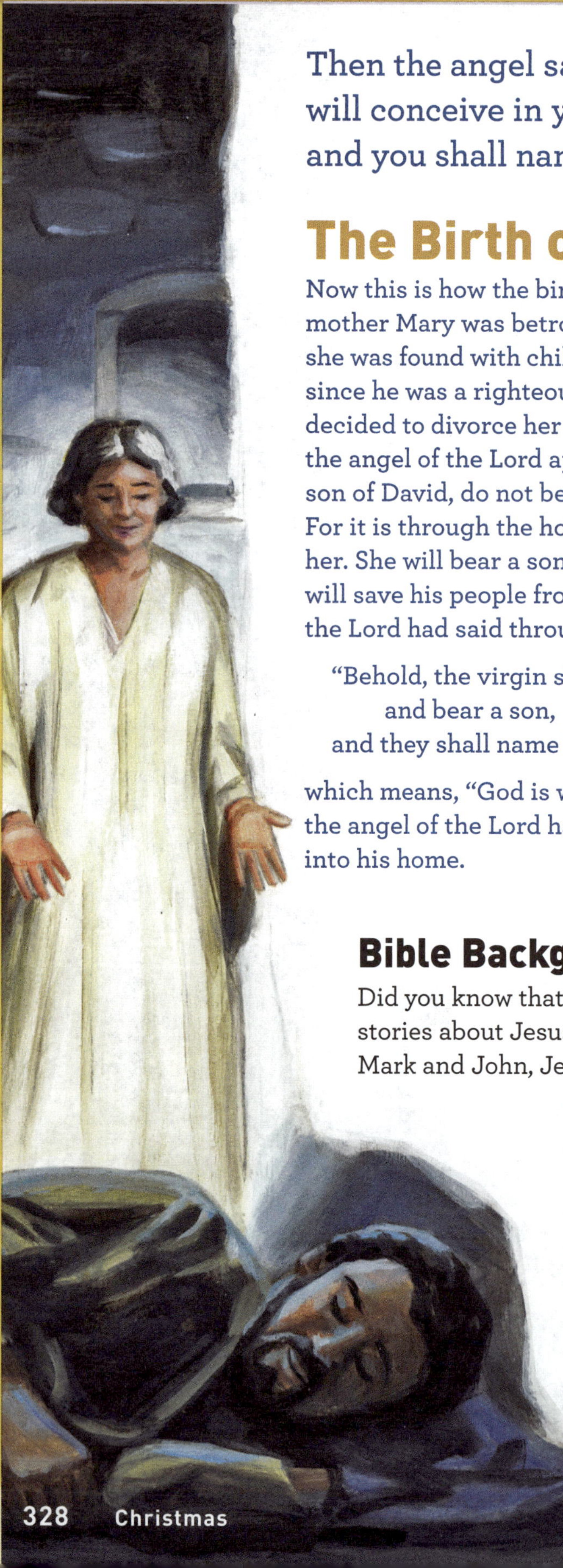

Then the angel said to her, . . . "Behold, you will conceive in your womb and bear a son, and you shall name him Jesus." Luke 1:30–31

The Birth of Jesus

Now this is how the birth of Jesus Christ came about. When his mother Mary was betrothed to Joseph, but before they lived together, she was found with child through the holy Spirit. Joseph her husband, since he was a righteous man, yet unwilling to expose her to shame, decided to divorce her quietly. Such was his intention when, behold, the angel of the Lord appeared to him in a dream and said, "Joseph, son of David, do not be afraid to take Mary your wife into your home. For it is through the holy Spirit that this child has been conceived in her. She will bear a son and you are to name him Jesus, because he will save his people from their sins." All this took place to fulfill what the Lord had said through the prophet:

"Behold, the virgin shall be with child
and bear a son,
and they shall name him Emmanuel,"

which means, "God is with us." When Joseph awoke, he did as the angel of the Lord had commanded him and took his wife into his home.

Matthew 1:18–24

Bible Background

Did you know that only the Gospels of Matthew and Luke have stories about Jesus' birth? At the beginning of the Gospels of Mark and John, Jesus is already grown up.

The Gospels were written to help people believe in Jesus. Sometimes, the Gospel writers focused on different aspects of Jesus' story. According to the Gospel of Matthew, for example, the story of Jesus' birth was anything but ordinary. In this story, angels appeared and spoke in dreams to make sure that God's will was followed. Joseph married Mary even though he didn't completely understand what was happening.

The writer of the Gospel of Matthew reminds us that all these extraordinary events occurred because this birth was special. The writer even reminds us that a prophet had written about this special event long before it happened. The writer's message is that Jesus is no ordinary human being. From the beginning, even before he was born, there were signs that Jesus had a special role to play in the world. In this way, the Gospel explains who Jesus really is: the Savior, the one whom God had promised long ago. The writer of the Gospel of Matthew wanted to make it very clear from the beginning of the Gospel that Jesus is the Son of God, the chosen one, Emmanuel.

Lord, you always keep your promises to your people. From age to age, you have cared about us and loved us. Help us pay more attention to your will for us as we celebrate Jesus' birth at Christmas. Amen.

Angels and Dreams

The writer of the Gospel of Matthew tells us that God sometimes speaks in dreams. When Joseph dreamed that an angel was giving him a message, he discovered how to follow God's will. As described in Chapter 4, Joseph of the Old Testament also discovered God's will through dreams.

Painting of the Nativity
St. Anthony Coptic church
Jerusalem Israel

ACTIVITY

Answer these questions in the spaces provided. Then discuss your answers with your class.

1. In what ways can the stories about Jesus' birth help people believe that Jesus is the Savior?

____

____

____

2. What are some ways that you have discovered God's will for you?

____

____

____

Solemnity of Mary, the Holy Mother of God

Every year on January 1, the Church celebrates the Solemnity of Mary, the Holy Mother of God. This is an important feast day honoring Mary. In the United States, it is a holy day of obligation. On this day U.S. Catholics are required to go to Mass.

Although the Solemnity of Mary, the Holy Mother of God, is one of many holy days that Catholics celebrate to honor Mary, a solemnity is an especially important holy day. This particular solemnity honors the special role Mary plays in the story of human salvation because she is the Mother of God. This holy day is celebrated one week after Christmas because it is only right that we celebrate Mary's motherhood in the season when we honor the birth of Jesus.

Trusting God

On this solemnity of Mary, we remember who Mary is and what she has done for us. Of her own free will, Mary chose to accept the difficult challenge of being the mother of our Savior, Jesus Christ. The angel Gabriel came to her and let her know God's will for her. Mary did not hesitate. Of course, at the time, she did not know everything that God would ask of her. But she loved and trusted God and was eager to do his will for her.

Mary said yes to God and, in this way, showed how much she loved us. By becoming the Mother of God, Mary was giving us the chance to get to know her son. She was making it possible for salvation to enter the world. At a wedding in Cana, as described in John 2:1–12, Mary urged her son to make himself known through the miracle of turning water into wine. She helped encourage him to begin his public ministry.

Throughout her life, Mary continued to support her son. The Gospel of John tells us that she was at the foot of the Cross when Jesus was crucified in Jerusalem. There, according to the Scriptures, Jesus entrusted Mary to the Apostle John's care. In doing so, he was also giving Mary to us to be our Mother.

Through the centuries, Christians of every culture have looked to Mary and thanked her for being the Mother of God. They have prayed to her and devoted their lives to her. Mary is still with the Church today. She wants us to turn to her and ask her for help, strength, guidance, or anything else we need. As Jesus' mother, Mary continues to love us and take care of us.

Mary, the Mother of God, brought hope into the world when she gave birth to Jesus. This is why we celebrate a special holy day in her honor. On January 1, we recall that because Mary chose to say yes to God, we enjoy Jesus' love, peace, and joy in our lives.

Mary, thank you for saying yes to bringing God's Son into the world. May we find the strength and courage to say yes to God in our own lives. Remember us, O Mother of God, and take care of us, for we love you. Amen.

Getting to Know Mary

Mary was probably about twelve years old when she told the angel Gabriel that she would do whatever God wanted. While none of us has such big challenges to face, there are many difficult situations that we face every day. For what kinds of problems can someone turn to Mary for help?

ACTIVITY

Think about everything you have learned about Mary. In the space below, describe how you would explain to someone of a different faith why she is so important to Catholics.

Christmas Prayer

Hark! The Herald Angels Sing

Leader: Some of the Christmas carols we love the most have interesting stories behind them. For example, "Hark! The Herald Angels Sing" came about almost by accident. Charles Wesley is famous for writing the words to more than 3,000 religious hymns, including the lyrics to the hymn we know as "Hark! The Herald Angels Sing." But Wesley didn't write the melody.

Felix Mendelssohn was a famous composer who wrote a melody for a song in honor of Johann Gutenberg, the inventor of the printing press. Mendelssohn wrote the melody to celebrate that the first book Gutenberg printed was the Bible.

In 1855, an English musician named William Cummings took the lyrics written by Charles Wesley and combined them with the melody written by Felix Mendelssohn. Both Wesley and Mendelssohn were dead by the time he did this, so they never knew that they had collaborated on one of the most famous Christmas carols of all time.

Leader: Let us gather together and celebrate the birth of the Savior.

(All gather in the prayer center.)

All Sing:
Hark! The herald angels sing,
"Glory to the newborn King!
Peace on earth and mercy mild,
God and sinners reconciled!"
Joyful, all you nations rise;
Join the triumph of the skies;
With the angelic host proclaim,
"Christ is born in Bethlehem!"
Hark! The herald angels sing,
"Glory to the newborn King!"

The Birth of Jesus

Reader: *(Proclaim Luke 2: 8–14.)*

Now there were shepherds in that region living in the fields and keeping the night watch over their flock. The angel of the Lord appeared to them and the glory of the Lord shone around them, and they were struck with great fear. The angel said to them, "Do not be afraid; for behold, I proclaim to you good news of great joy that will be for all the people. For today in the city of David a Savior has been born for you who is Messiah and Lord. And this will be a sign for you: you will find an infant wrapped in swaddling clothes and lying in a manger." And suddenly there was a multitude of the heavenly host, praising God and saying:

"Glory to God in the highest
and on earth peace to
those on whom his favor rests."

Leader: Let us pray.

Group 1: Sing to the LORD a new song;
sing to the LORD, all the earth.

Group 2: Sing to the LORD, bless his name;
proclaim his salvation day after day.

Group 1: Tell his glory among the nations;
among all peoples, his marvelous deeds.

Group 2: Let the heavens be glad and the earth rejoice;
let the sea and what fills it resound;

Group 1: let the plains be joyful and all that is
in them.

Group 2: Then let all the trees of the forest rejoice
before the LORD who comes,
who comes to govern the earth,

Group 1: To govern the world with justice

Group 2: and the peoples with faithfulness.

Psalm 96: 1–4, 11–13

All Sing: **Hark! The herald angels sing . . .**

Lent

Now the Lord is the Spirit, and where the Spirit of the Lord is, there is freedom.

2 Corinthians 3:17

Jesus knew that one of the gifts we would need most in our lives was the gift of forgiveness. Whenever we sin, either by doing something wrong or by failing to do the right thing, our relationship with God is weakened. Jesus knew that we would need a way to turn back to God and say that we are sorry. We would need a way to show our sorrow and ask for forgiveness.

The Sacrament of Penance and Reconciliation is our celebration of God's forgiveness in our lives. This Sacrament is called a Sacrament of Healing because when we celebrate it, we heal our relationship with God and one another. It also heals us of the pain and guilt caused by our sins. When we confess our sins and express our sorrow, we are *reconciled,* or brought back together, with God and the Church.

God's Gift of Healing

In order to experience God's gift of healing in the Sacrament of Penance and Reconciliation, we need to do several things. We need to feel sorrow for our sins, to want to change the way we are living, and to confess our sins to a priest. In the Sacrament, the priest will pray a prayer of absolution over us, which asks for God's mercy. The priest will also suggest a *penance,* an action or prayer to help us change our lives and avoid sin in the future.

The gift of forgiveness that we receive in the Sacrament of Penance and Reconciliation is so powerful that Catholics have many different ways of describing this Sacrament. It is described as a Sacrament of *conversion,* a word that means "being changed." This name is fitting because this Sacrament helps us change our lives and become united with God again. It is also called the Sacrament of Penance, because in it we admit our wrongdoing and express our wish to make up for what we have done or failed to do. And it is called the Sacrament of forgiveness, because we ask God to pardon us.

The forgiveness we experience in the Sacrament of Penance and Reconciliation flows into the rest of our lives. Because we have been forgiven, we are better able to forgive others. We can forgive friends and family members when they hurt us. We can even learn to forgive our enemies—for if we can forgive them, we can learn to love them, as Jesus commanded us.

During the six weeks before Easter, a season we call Lent, the Church asks us to look at our lives and repent of our sins. Lent is an especially good time to celebrate the Sacrament of Penance and Reconciliation.

Jesus,
thank you for your gifts
of mercy and forgiveness.
Help us forgive others as you
have forgiven us. Guide us in
making good decisions
and avoiding sin.
Amen.

Seeking God's Mercy

Lent is a time of penance and conversion. We are called to repent of our sins and turn back to God. The Sacrament of Penance and Reconciliation is Jesus' special gift to the Church for doing just that. How can God's gift of forgiveness help you?

ACTIVITY

Complete the following sentences.

I think people are most likely to celebrate the Sacrament of Penance and Reconciliation when ____

____.

I think conversion means ____

____.

One new thing I learned about the Sacrament of Penance and Reconciliation is ____

____

____.

To me, forgiveness means ____

____

____.

A Time of Preparation

In ancient times, people used numbers to symbolize, or stand for, important ideas. The Jewish people, for example, used the number forty to symbolize a long period of time. This is because centuries ago, most people only lived about forty years. So "forty" meant a long time. It also came to mean a period of testing, waiting, and change.

The number forty is important in both the Old Testament and the New Testament of the Bible. The Book of Exodus tells us that the Israelites, our ancestors in faith, wandered for forty years in the desert before they arrived in the Promised Land. Having been the slaves of the Egyptians, the Israelites trusted in God to lead them to freedom. They endured many hardships to reach their goal. By the time they finally reached the Promised Land, their faith had become even stronger. They were changed people.

In the Gospels, we read about Jesus and his stay in the desert. For forty days, Jesus remained faithful to the will of the Father by rejecting the temptations of the devil. Jesus' victory over Satan in the desert shows us that he is truly the Messiah, the Son of God. He shows us the way to remain faithful to God in the face of struggles and temptations. Jesus left the desert prepared to help all people know what it means to live as the children of God.

The Church sets aside the forty days of Lent to remind us of our goals as Christians. During Lent, we prepare for Easter. We do this by considering how we can follow the Gospel message better and by reflecting on the challenges we experience in our lives. We try to become better Christians. We may try to follow the example of the heroes of our faith, such as saints or people of the Old Testament. They lived their faith in times of testing, waiting, challenge, and struggle.

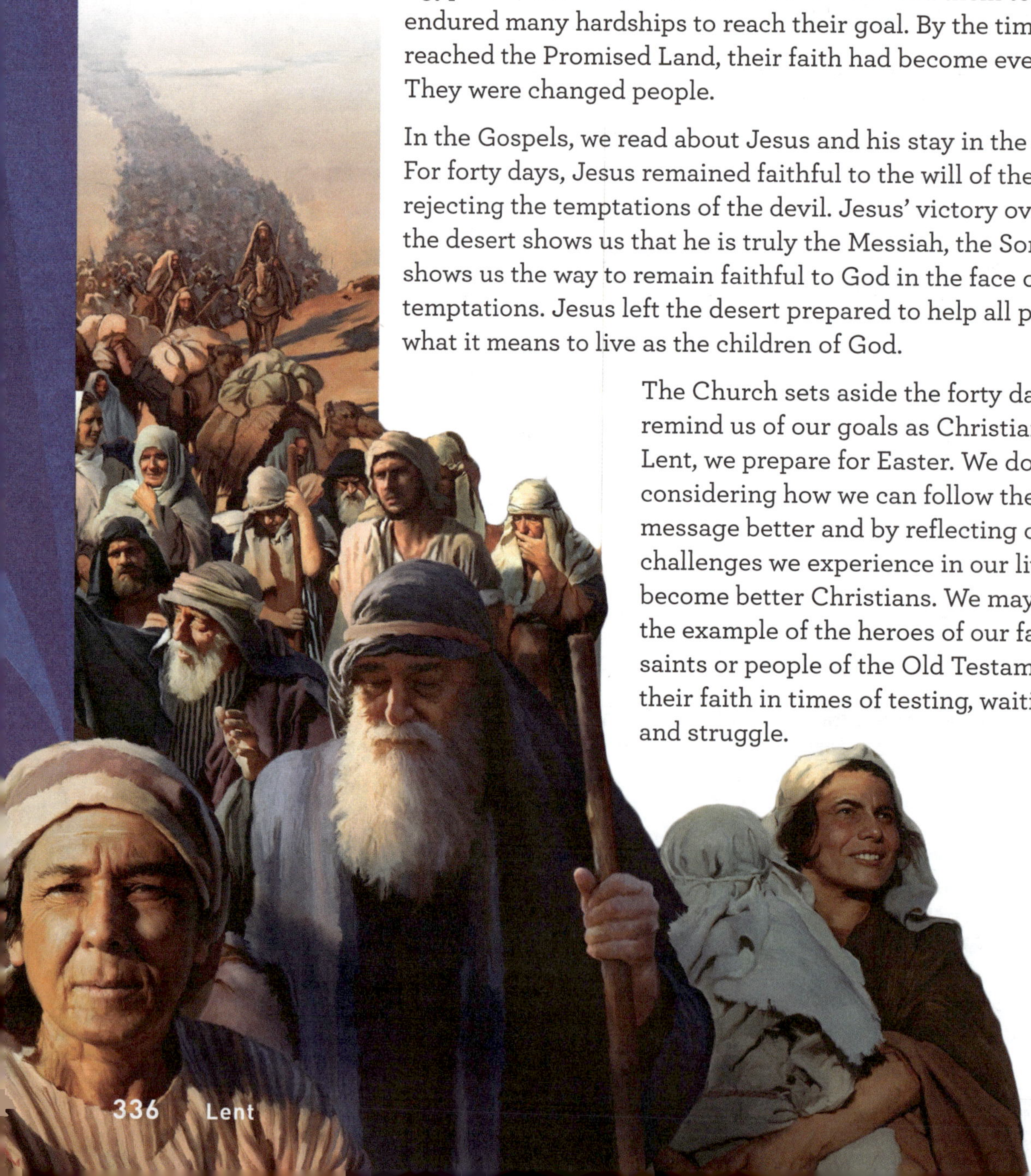

Throughout Lent we will hear Scripture readings at Mass that contain the number forty. These readings remind us that many people have gone through times of struggle and testing for their faith. The readings also inspire us to make good use of our own forty-day period of Lent so that we may grow closer to God and live our faith more completely. We try to become different people—people with new attitudes and a stronger willingness to live the Gospel.

Jesus, be our strength.
Help us spend
the forty days of Lent
preparing for the joy of Easter.
We ask this in your name.
Amen.

Getting Ready

We have all experienced a time when something important is about to happen, such as moving to a new home, entering a new school, taking an exam, or playing in an important sports match. To prepare, we have to concentrate our efforts on our goal. Lent has a goal also. It is to prepare to celebrate Jesus' Resurrection at Easter. How will you prepare to celebrate Jesus' Resurrection?

ACTIVITY

Circle the ways you will use Lent as a time to deepen your faith.

Celebrate the Eucharist each Sunday.

Forgive people who have hurt me.

Be more patient with others.

Give money to charity.

Pray the Rosary once a week.

Examine my conscience.

Spend several minutes in prayer and reflection every day.

Read about the life of a saint.

Celebrate the Sacrament of Penance and Reconciliation.

Choose ways to be generous to friends and family members.

Choose an action to support a charity or a group that helps those who are poor and homeless.

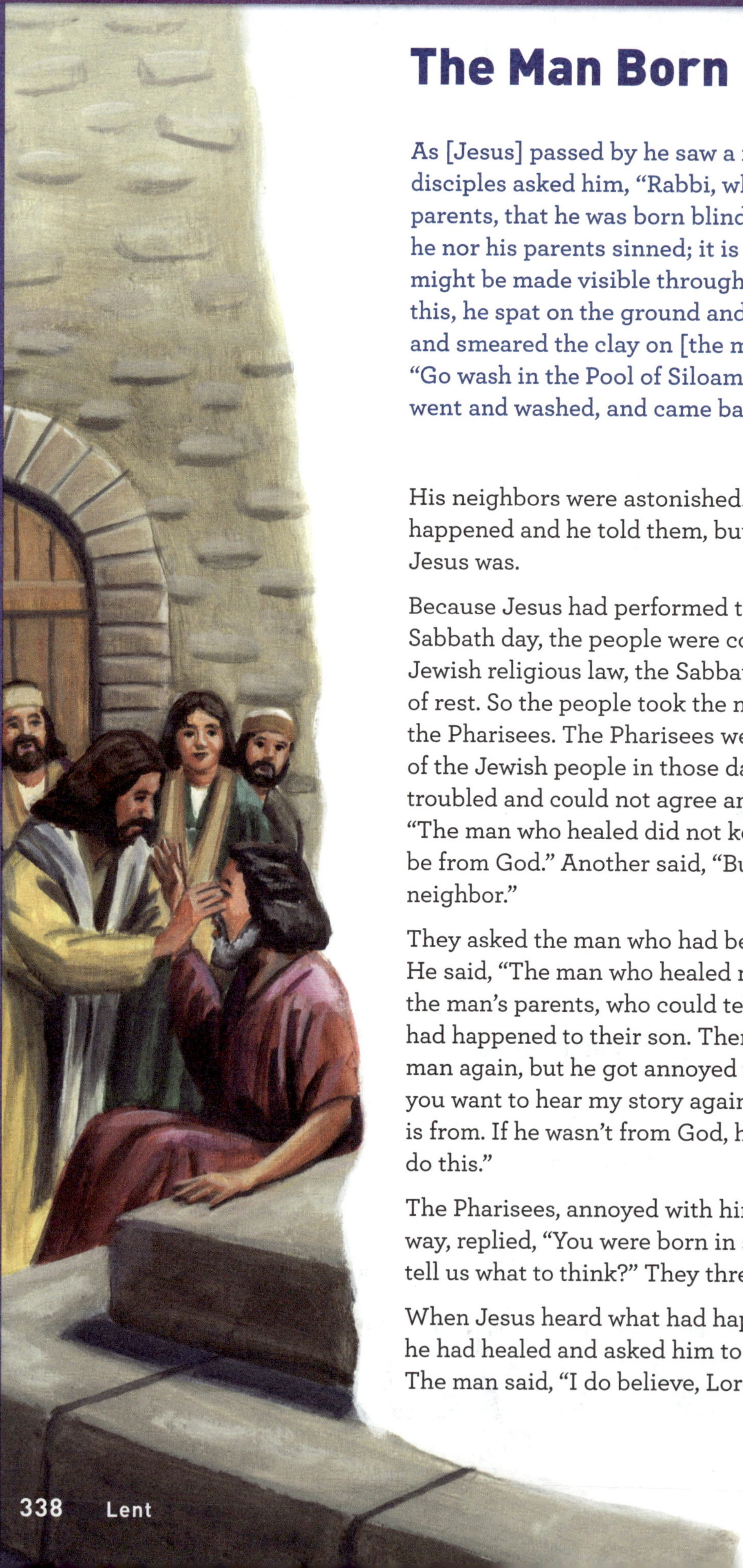

The Man Born Blind

As [Jesus] passed by he saw a man blind from birth. His disciples asked him, "Rabbi, who sinned, this man or his parents, that he was born blind?" Jesus answered, "Neither he nor his parents sinned; it is so that the works of God might be made visible through him."... When he had said this, he spat on the ground and made clay with the saliva, and smeared the clay on [the man's] eyes, and said to him, "Go wash in the Pool of Siloam" (which means Sent). So he went and washed, and came back able to see.

John 9:1–3,6–7

His neighbors were astonished. They asked him what happened and he told them, but he could not tell them who Jesus was.

Because Jesus had performed this healing miracle on a Sabbath day, the people were concerned. According to Jewish religious law, the Sabbath was supposed to be a day of rest. So the people took the man whom Jesus had cured to the Pharisees. The Pharisees were the religious authorities of the Jewish people in those days. The Pharisees were troubled and could not agree among themselves. One said, "The man who healed did not keep the Sabbath, so he can't be from God." Another said, "But he did good in helping his neighbor."

They asked the man who had been healed what he thought. He said, "The man who healed me is a prophet." They asked the man's parents, who could tell them nothing about what had happened to their son. Then they talked to the healed man again, but he got annoyed with them, saying, "Why do you want to hear my story again? I don't know where the man is from. If he wasn't from God, he wouldn't have been able to do this."

The Pharisees, annoyed with him for speaking to them this way, replied, "You were born in sin and now you are trying to tell us what to think?" They threw him out.

When Jesus heard what had happened, he went to the man he had healed and asked him to believe in the Son of Man. The man said, "I do believe, Lord," and worshiped him.

Some of the Pharisees who were with [Jesus] heard this and said to him, "Surely we are not also blind, are we?" Jesus said to them, "If you were blind, you would have no sin; but now you are saying, 'We see,' so your sin remains."

John 9:40–41

Jesus,
you are the Son of Man
sent by God to bring us
into your kingdom.
Help us recognize signs of
your Father's love in our lives.
Amen.

This Gospel narrative is read on the Fourth Sunday of Lent in Year A. It invites us to think about our own attitudes about sin and belief. It also reveals that the people of Jesus' time often thought that the troubles and challenges of life were the result of sin. They did not always recognize a sign from God when they saw it.

Signs from God

Through Jesus' conversations with the man he healed and with the Pharisees, we learn that it is important to have faith when we witness a sign of God's power in our lives. God's generosity touches our lives. What signs from God could you pay more attention to?

ACTIVITY

Email the Pharisees about the man who was healed. Give your opinion about whether or not they should accept the healing as being from God. Give reasons for your opinion.

To Pharisees

From

Subject Healing

Laetare Sunday

The Fourth Sunday of Lent is also called Laetare Sunday. The word *Laetare* is a Latin word that means "rejoice." This Sunday in Lent got its name from part of a prayer said at the beginning of Mass: "Rejoice, Jerusalem, and all who love her" (see Isaiah 66:10). Why is this Sunday a day of joy if it is in the middle of Lent?

Lent can be a difficult time in our lives. If we are seriously reflecting on our actions and beliefs, and if we are spending our time in prayer and acts of penance, by the middle of Lent we need a break. We need some time to remember that God acts in our lives with great love and generosity. On Laetare Sunday, as we hopefully and joyfully continue to prepare for the celebration of Easter, the priest may wear rose-colored vestments at Mass, the sanctuary area may contain a few more plants and flowers than usual, and hymns about rejoicing may be sung.

Laetare Sunday is also known as "Rose Sunday," partly because of the rose-colored vestments, but also because the pope traditionally blesses the "Golden Rose" on this day. The Golden Rose is an award made of solid gold in the shape of a rose. It is occasionally given to a notable Catholic person or group in thanks for special service or loyalty to the pope. This is an ancient custom. As far back as the eleventh century, the pope would carry a rose in his left hand when coming back from Mass on Laetare Sunday. By the fifteenth century, the pope's custom became to bless the rose and send it to someone in thanks for doing good.

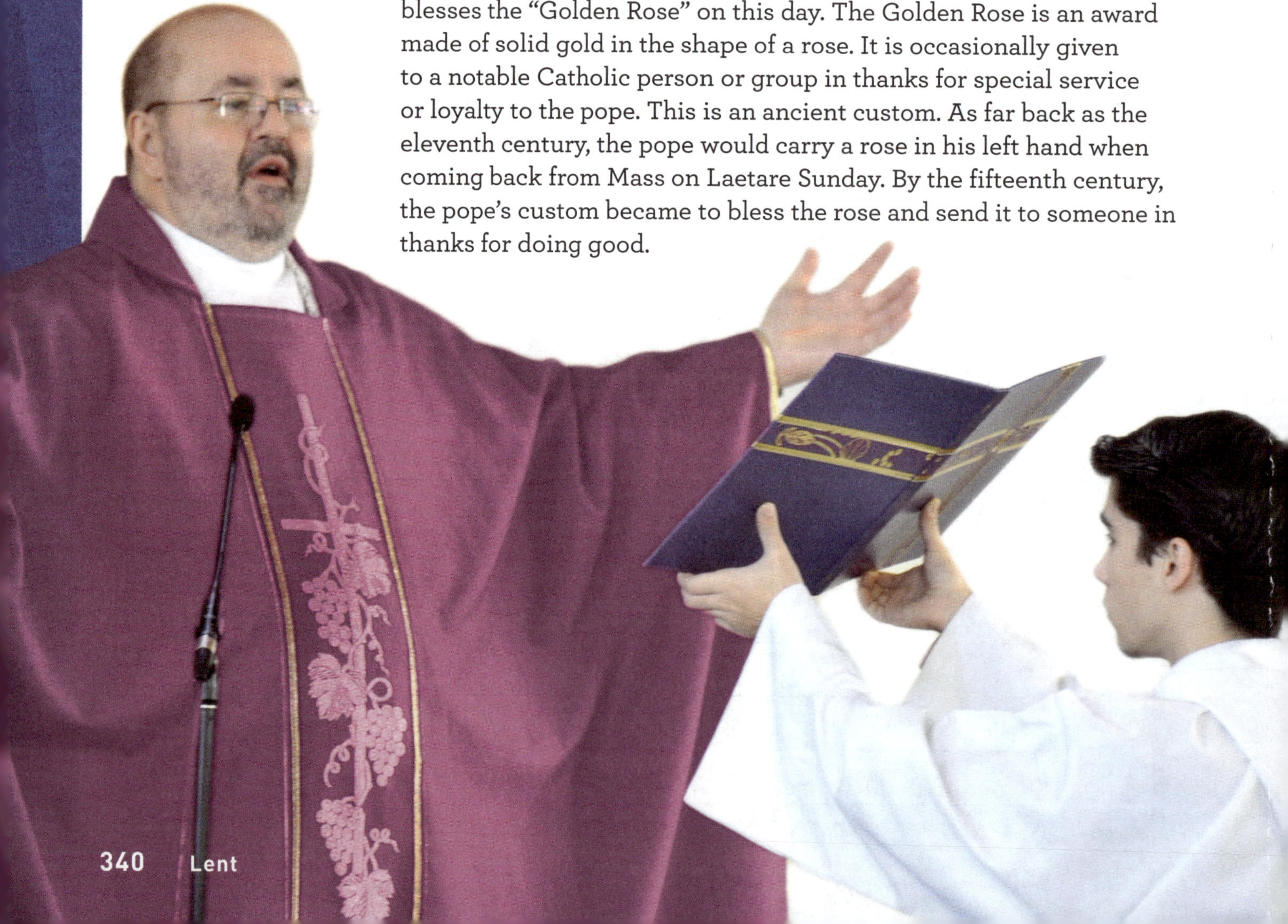

In some European countries, the Fourth Sunday of Lent is celebrated as "Mothering Sunday." Traditionally, on this day people return to their native parishes and cathedrals as well as visit their mothers and spend some time with their family members.

Lord, you bless us so much.
You surprise us with
your kindness and your love.
May we share the joy
you give us with others.
We rejoice and we praise
you for your goodness.
Amen.

A Pause to Rejoice

Lent is halfway finished when we celebrate Laetare Sunday. It is natural at this point during our season of reflection and penance to begin to feel a sense of joyful anticipation. We begin to grow more aware of the coming of Easter and spring. We look forward to the new life that awaits us during the Easter season.

On the Fourth Sunday of Lent we remember that God loves us. He blesses us with his mercy and generosity. What blessings do you enjoy in your life?

ACTIVITY

Create joyful words that relate to the season of Lent using the letters of the word Laetare. The letter may appear anywhere in the word.

_______________ **L** _______________

_______________ **a** _______________

_______________ **e** _______________

_______________ **t** _______________

_______________ **a** _______________

_______________ **r** _______________

_______________ **e** _______________

For Repentance

Leader: The Book of Psalms is a book in the Old Testament. A psalm is a religious song from the Old Testament. Psalms were written centuries ago, some around the time of King David. Tradition says that King David actually wrote some of the psalms. Today the psalms are prayed and sung as a part of Christian worship. There are so many psalms that they are numbered. Some of the psalms are so well known that they also have titles. Psalm 51, for example, is called "The Miserere: Prayer of Repentance." Let us pray together some verses from it now.

All: **Have mercy on me, God, in accord**
with your merciful love;
in your abundant compassion,
blot out my transgressions.
Thoroughly wash away my guilt;
and from my sin cleanse me.
For I know my transgressions;
my sin is always before me.
Against you, you alone have I sinned;
I have done what is evil in your eyes . . .

A clean heart create for me, God;
renew within me a steadfast spirit.
Do not drive me from before your face,
nor take from me your holy spirit.
Restore to me the gladness of
your salvation;
uphold me with a willing spirit.

Psalm 51:3–6,12–14

Leader: Let us call to mind and write down the things that we have done wrong and the things that we have failed to do. When you have spent several moments in reflection, come forward and place your slip of paper in one basket, and take a prayer card from the other basket.

(Leader pauses until all have come forward.)

Leader: We often read the Book of the Prophet Isaiah when we want to remember the promises that God made to his people. Let us do so now.

Reader:

Rejoice with Jerusalem and be glad
because of her,
all you who love her;
Rejoice with her in her joy,
all you mourn over her— . . .

For thus says the LORD,
I will spread prosperity over her
like a river,
like an overflowing torrent,
the wealth of nations. . . .

As a mother comforts her child,
so I will comfort you;
in Jerusalem you shall find your
comfort.

Isaiah 66:10,12,13

All: **O Lord, thank you for taking care of us and being with us always. May we be mindful of your presence every day of our lives. May we always remember your great mercy and generosity. As Lent continues, draw us near to you. Amen.**

Holy Week

In [Christ] we have redemption by his blood, the forgiveness of transgressions, in accord with the riches of his grace that he lavished upon us. Ephesians 1:7–8

Celebrating Our Salvation

The events we recall during Holy Week are at the center of our lives as Christians. We believe that God loves us so much that he sent his only Son to suffer, die, and then rise to new life so that we might be free of sin and live with him forever. This belief is at the heart of Christianity.

Palm Sunday of the Passion of the Lord

Palm Sunday is the first day of Holy Week. On Palm Sunday we recall Jesus' entry into Jerusalem by waving palm branches and singing, "Hosanna!"

Holy Thursday

On Holy Thursday evening we celebrate the Mass of the Lord's Supper. On the night before he died, Jesus gave us the gift of himself in the Eucharist.

Friday of the Passion of the Lord

Most Catholics call this day Good Friday. On this day we recall Jesus' suffering and Death on the Cross. Jesus' suffering and Death brought about God's gift of resurrection and new life.

Holy Saturday and the Easter Vigil

Holy Saturday morning and afternoon are filled with silence and waiting. We recall Jesus' time spent in the tomb, his descent to the realm of the dead, and God's promise of resurrection. Holy Saturday evening, the Easter Vigil, is considered the holiest night of the year. We praise and thank God for raising Jesus from death to new life and we welcome new members into the Church through the Sacraments of Baptism, Confirmation, and Eucharist.

A Walk Through Holy Week

We call Holy Week "holy" because for Christians it is the holiest week of the liturgical year. During Holy Week we recall and celebrate God's great love for us as shown through the Passion, Death, and Resurrection of his Son, Jesus.

Jesus, help us walk by your side through Holy Week. May we keep our eyes and hearts focused on you and recognize you as our King, Messiah, and Lord. Amen.

ACTIVITY

After the name of each day, write something you remember about it that is not included on the previous page.

Palm Sunday of the Passion of the Lord

___

___

___

Holy Thursday

___

___

___

Friday of the Passion of the Lord (Good Friday)

___

___

___

Holy Saturday and the Easter Vigil

___

___

___

Tre Ore

On Good Friday, many Catholics spend the hours between noon and three o'clock in the afternoon in prayer and meditation, recollecting the three hours that Jesus hung on the Cross. This devotion is called *Tre Ore* (tray or ay), which means "three hours" in Italian. During the three hours, Catholics reflect on the seven last statements of Jesus. In between reflecting on these words, people sing hymns and say prayers.

According to the Gospels, when Jesus was hanging on the Cross, he spoke seven times. First, when he was being crucified, he prayed aloud, **"Father, forgive them, they know not what they do"** (Luke 23:34).

When Jesus saw his mother at the foot of the Cross, he was concerned about who would take care of her. Jesus entrusted Mary to the care of "the disciple there whom he loved," saying to Mary, **"Woman, behold your son,"** and to the disciple, **"Behold your mother"** (see John 19:26, 27).

The Crucifixion, a detail from *The Easter Painting*, 1994 by Laura James.

When Jesus said, **"I thirst"** (see John 19:28), he was given a sponge soaked in wine by those standing around him. According to the Gospel of Mark, this wine contained myrrh, which was supposed to help a crucified person die more easily.

When one of the thieves crucified next to Jesus asked for forgiveness, Jesus told him his sins were forgiven. Jesus said, **"Amen, I say to you, today you will be with me in Paradise"** (see Luke 23:43).

Jesus expressed his humanity as well as his trust in God when he cried out in prayer, **"My God, my God, why have you forsaken me?"** (see Matthew 27:46, Mark 15:34). These words are from Psalm 22, a psalm about hope in the midst of persecution.

The Gospel of John tells us that Jesus' last words before he died were **"It is finished"** (see John 19:30). For the writer of this Gospel, Jesus was announcing that his mission was completed and that he died willingly for us.

The Gospel of Luke, however, tells us that Jesus' last words were **"Father, into your hands I commend my spirit"** (see Luke 23:46). For the writer of this Gospel, Jesus died still obeying God's will, faithful to his Father in all things.

Lord, thank you for the writers of the Gospels. Through them and the inspiration of the Holy Spirit, we deepen our understanding of your Crucifixion. Thank you for your great sacrifice. Amen.

ACTIVITY

Every Good Friday we have the chance to deepen our faith by spending the hours between noon and three o'clock in prayer and reflection about Jesus.

On the lines below, write how you will spend the afternoon on Good Friday.

The Redeemer of the World

Leader: Jesus took all our sins upon himself and asked forgiveness for our offenses, placing his trust in God. According to the Scriptures, as Jesus died, he called out to God in the words of Psalm 22. We pray these words in the Good Friday liturgy.

Reader 1: My God, my God, why have you
abandoned me?
Why so far from my call for help,
from my cries of anguish?
My God, I call by day, but you do not
answer;
by night, but I have no relief.
Yet you are enthroned as the Holy One;
you are the glory of Israel.

Reader 2: In you our fathers trusted;
they trusted, and you rescued them.
To you they cried out and they escaped;
in you they trusted, and they were not
disappointed. . . .

All the ends of the earth
will remember and turn to the LORD;
All the families of nations
will bow low before him.

Reader 3: For kingship belongs to the LORD,
the ruler over the nations. . . .

The generation to come will be told
of the Lord,
that they may proclaim to a people
yet unborn
the deliverance you have brought.

Psalm 22:1–4, 5–6, 28–29, 32

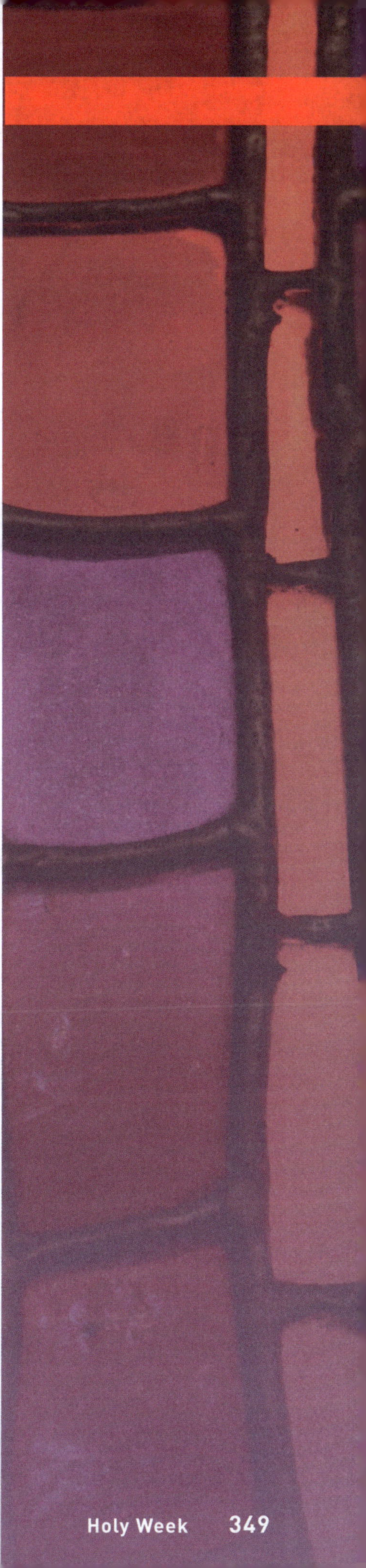

Reader 1: . . .[B]e kind to one another, compassionate, forgiving one another as God has forgiven you in Christ.

So be imitators of God, as beloved children, and live in love, as Christ loved us and handed himself over as a sacrificial offering to God for a fragrant aroma. Ephesians 4:32–5:2

Group 1: We adore your Cross, O Lord,
Group 2: we praise and glorify your holy Resurrection,
Group 1: for behold, because of the wood of a tree
Group 2: joy has come to the whole world.

Chants to Be Sung During the Adoration of the Holy Cross
The Passion of the Lord, *Roman Missal*

Reader 2: The Savior of mankind destroyed death by dying and restored life by rising. Let us humbly ask him:
All: **Make your people holy, Lord.**

Reader 2: Redeemer of the world, may we share in the glory of your Resurrection.
All: **Make your people holy, Lord.**

Reader 2: May we comfort others as you comfort us.
All: **Make your people holy, Lord.**

Reader 3: Reveal your saving power in the lives of your faithful people.
All: **Make your people holy, Lord.**

Reader 3: Give all who serve you the gifts of obedience and patience.
All: **Make your people holy, Lord.**

Reader 3: Bring us at last into the fellowship of the Communion of Saints.
All: **Make your people holy, Lord.**

Leader: Father, in your plan of salvation, your Son, Jesus Christ, trusted you, accepted the Cross, and freed us from the power of evil. May we share in the glory of his Resurrection, for he lives and reigns with you and the Holy Spirit, one God, for ever and ever.

All: **Amen.**

(Share a sign of peace with those nearest you.)

Based on Evening Prayer Intercessions
Thursday of Holy Week, *Liturgy of the Hours*

Easter

"... Blessed are those who have not seen and have believed."

John 20:29

God Raises Jesus to New Life

On Easter Sunday and throughout the Easter season we rejoice in the Resurrection of Jesus. After Jesus died, God the Father glorified him, raising him to new life. Jesus did not return to his old life after the Resurrection. Instead, God saw fit to give him new life that would last forever.

Jesus shares that new life with us. No longer are we our old selves, returning to the same habits and sins of our old lives. We are now alive in Jesus, through his Passion, Death, and Resurrection. We live in him, and he lives in us. Because we share this new life with Jesus, we have the chance to live better lives, open to the Spirit and growing closer to our heavenly Father every day.

Believing in Jesus' Resurrection requires faith. Jesus' first disciples struggled to understand Jesus' Resurrection and what it meant for them. They had locked themselves in a room out of fear, but Jesus came and stood before them. Wishing them the gift of peace, Jesus showed his friends the wounds in his hands and his side so that they would believe that he had risen from the dead. Today we do not have fear about what we believe because the Holy Spirit is with us. In the Spirit, we are free to live our faith and share it with others. Especially during the Easter season, we celebrate our belief in Jesus, and our hearts are filled with joy.

Easter is the time of the Church year when we rejoice that God raised Jesus from death to new life. It is the most important celebration of the liturgical year. In fact, the Easter season lasts for fifty days. During that time we also celebrate Jesus' Ascension into Heaven and the sending of the Holy Spirit on Pentecost. We praise and thank God the Father for giving us his Son and for bringing us to new life in him. Easter is a new beginning for us because we are invited to change our lives. When we celebrate Jesus' gift of new life with the rest of the Church, we are invited to live every day as if it were Easter.

A Fresh Start

Our lives are full of new beginnings. Every birthday can seem like a new beginning, as can every new school year or every summer vacation. We see ourselves growing, changing, and becoming stronger, smarter, and more capable. Easter is a new beginning for us, too. It is a fresh chance to live our new life in Christ.

Risen Jesus,
help us believe that all
who fall asleep in death will
not die forever but will live
with you, the Father,
and the Holy Spirit.
Amen.

ACTIVITY

Piece together the puzzle to discover the message from Saint Paul found in Romans 6:23.

____

____

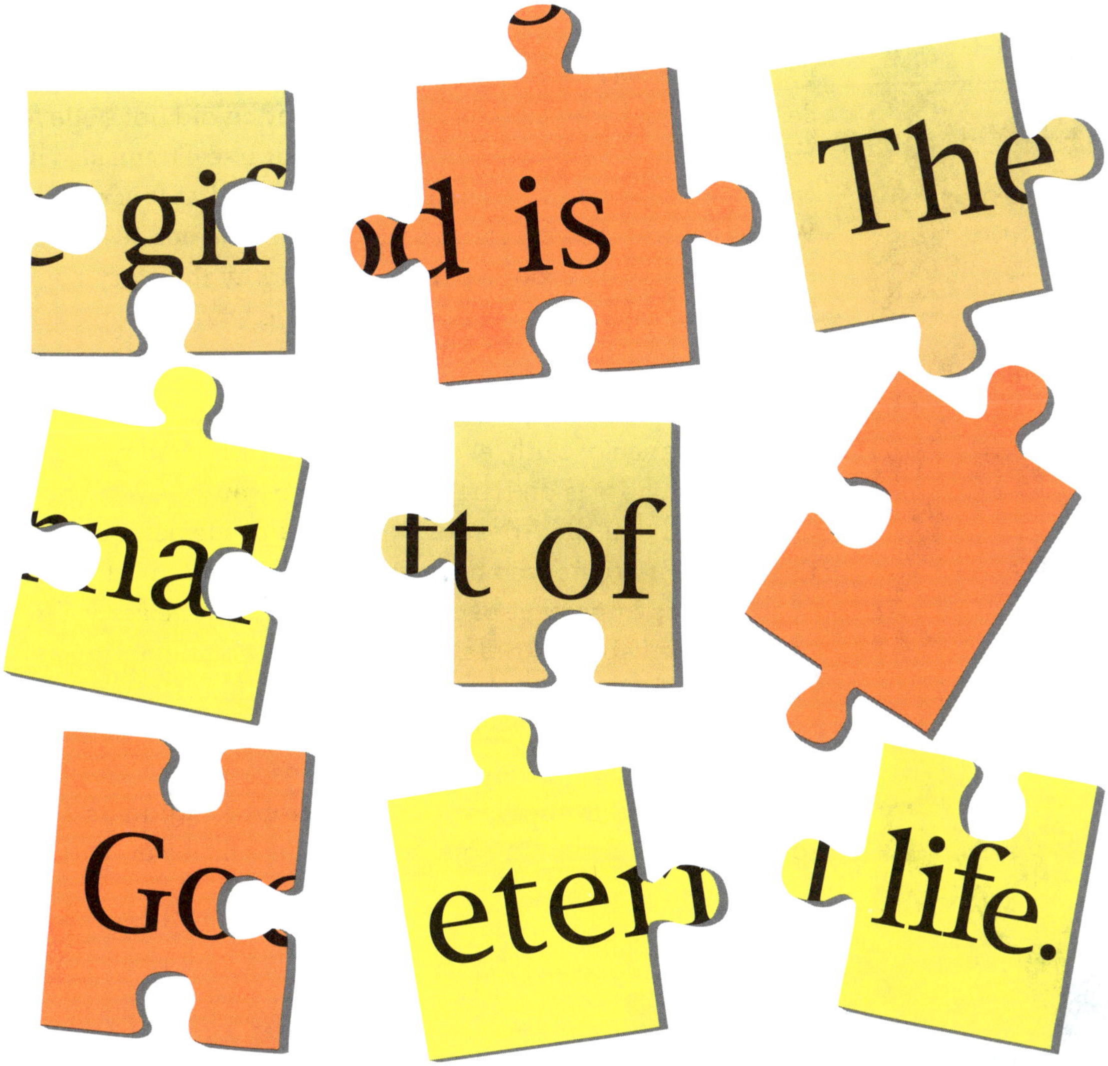

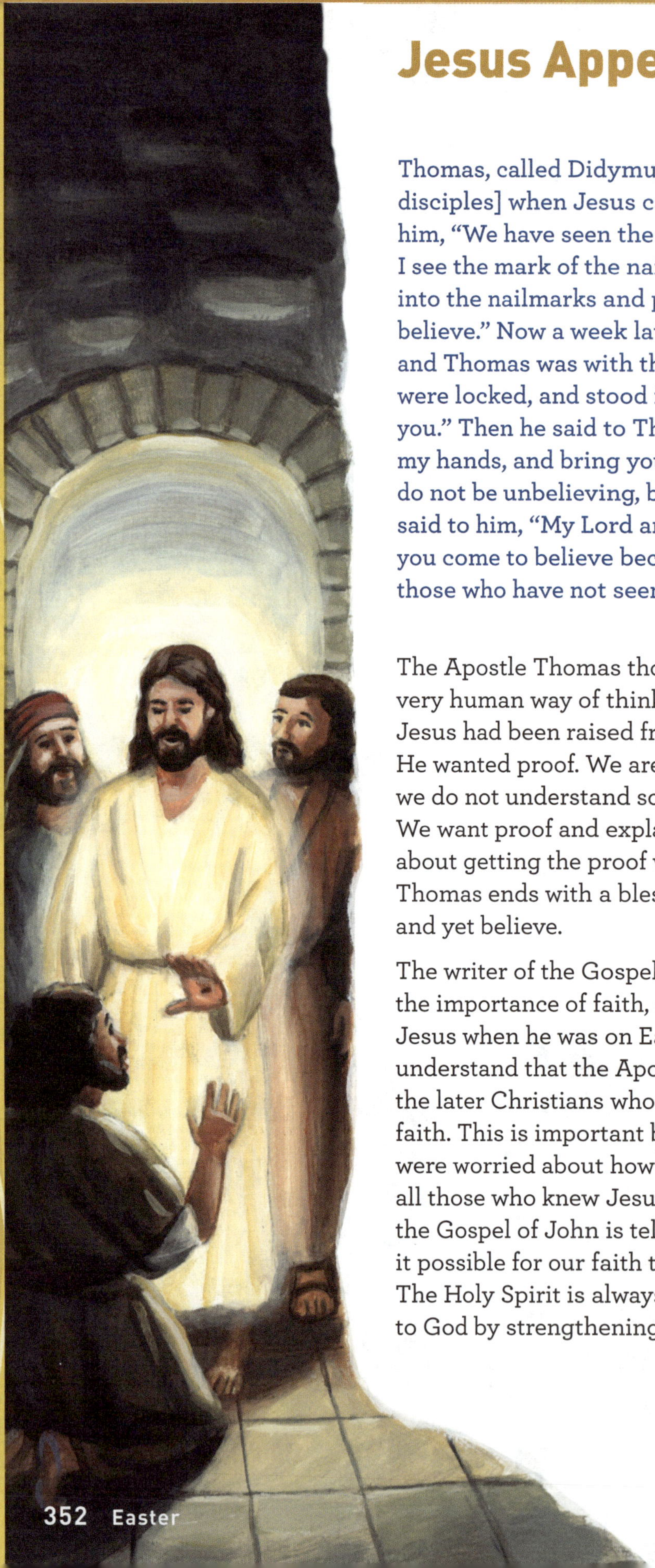

Jesus Appears to the Disciples

Thomas, called Didymus, one of the Twelve, was not with [the disciples] when Jesus came. So the other disciples said to him, "We have seen the Lord." But he said to them, "Unless I see the mark of the nails in his hands and put my finger into the nailmarks and put my hand into his side, I will not believe." Now a week later his disciples were again inside and Thomas was with them. Jesus came, although the doors were locked, and stood in their midst and said, "Peace be with you." Then he said to Thomas, "Put your finger here and see my hands, and bring your hand and put it into my side, and do not be unbelieving, but believe." Thomas answered and said to him, "My Lord and my God!" Jesus said to him, "Have you come to believe because you have seen me? Blessed are those who have not seen and have believed."

John 20:24–29

The Apostle Thomas thought that seeing was believing—a very human way of thinking. He heard the Apostles say that Jesus had been raised from the dead, but he did not believe it. He wanted proof. We are sometimes a lot like Thomas. When we do not understand something, we doubt that it is real. We want proof and explanations. But belief is not always about getting the proof we want. This is why the story about Thomas ends with a blessing for all those who have not seen and yet believe.

The writer of the Gospel of John wanted to teach people about the importance of faith, especially people who had never met Jesus when he was on Earth. This writer wanted everyone to understand that the Apostles, who knew Jesus personally, and the later Christians who had never met Jesus, shared the same faith. This is important because Christians in the early Church were worried about how faith in the Lord would continue after all those who knew Jesus personally had died. The writer of the Gospel of John is telling us that the Holy Spirit has made it possible for our faith to be the same as that of the Apostles. The Holy Spirit is always with the Church, bringing us closer to God by strengthening our faith in his Son, Jesus.

Blessed Are Those Who Believe

The Apostle Thomas is remembered for the story about his doubts. This is why we sometimes refer to a person who is suspicious about things until they are proven as a "Doubting Thomas." Jesus helped Thomas overcome his doubts. Because he regained his faith and worked to spread the Gospel for the rest of his life, the Church honors him today as a saint. Jesus will help us overcome our doubts as well. When do you most need to have your faith strengthened?

Saint Thomas, help us believe in Jesus, our Savior. Pray that we may overcome our doubts. Remind us of all that Jesus has done for us. Amen.

ACTIVITY

Imagine you are a reporter interviewing the Apostle Thomas about his encounter with Jesus after his Resurrection. Write three questions you would ask and how you think Thomas would respond.

Reporter: ______________________________

____

____

Thomas: ______________________________

____

____

Reporter: ______________________________

____

____

Thomas: ______________________________

____

____

Reporter: ______________________________

____

____

Thomas: ______________________________

____

____

Living Our Faith

Easter is a time to strengthen our faith in God. How can we do this? We can receive the Sacraments of Eucharist and Penance and Reconciliation regularly. We can also pray every day and read Scripture by ourselves and with our family. Another thing we can do is practice our faith through the choices we make every day. When we make choices that show our faith, we are making acts of faith. We are living what we say we believe.

What is an act of faith? It is taking a chance and risking doing the right thing, even when there may be difficult consequences. Here are some examples of what sixth-grade students at Our Lady of Mercy School do to strengthen their faith.

Melissa's teacher gave the class a geography test that was very difficult. As Melissa and her classmates were taking the test, their teacher was called out of the room. Melissa knew she could easily look up some of the answers in her textbook, but she decided not to cheat. She believes in honesty. This is part of her faith.

Ethan's parents told him to come home right after school, but he didn't. He stopped at his friend's house for a little while before going home. When Ethan's mother asked him where he was, Ethan told the truth even though he knew he would be grounded. He knew he had done wrong and decided not to do it again. Ethan believes in respecting his parents. This is part of his faith.

Yolanda had some money to buy a treat for herself at lunch in the cafeteria. All morning she looked forward to buying a package of chocolate chip cookies. Then, in the cafeteria line, Morgan did not have enough money to pay for her lunch. Yolanda heard herself saying, "Don't worry. Here's some money." Morgan thanked her gratefully. Yolanda was not able to get her cookies, but she believes in being generous. This is part of her faith.

It can be difficult to make acts of faith, but until you practice your faith every day, you don't show that you truly believe. When you put your beliefs into practice by being generous, patient, kind, and honest, you are living your faith. Then you begin to grow closer to God.

Making Good Choices

Although saints and other holy people are good models for living faithfully, we do not always know how to be faithful in ordinary, everyday situations. What are some examples of situations in which the right thing to do is not obvious?

Jesus, help us to trust our heavenly Father, especially when it is hard to be honest or to do the right thing. May we recall the events of Easter and turn to you as our model and our Savior. Amen.

ACTIVITY

1. You may have heard that practice makes perfect. Here is a dilemma to test your skills. Think about it and then write your response.

   Miguel finds ten dollars outside a convenience store. He first thinks that he could take it inside and spend it on a sports magazine and some snacks. He reasons that it's not as if he knows who the money belongs to. What else could Miguel do? What would you do?

   ____

   ____

   ____

   ____

2. Now help your classmates practice their decision-making faith skills. Write a dilemma that involves a faith choice. Be sure it is not too easy to figure out. After you have written it, share it with your class. Invite your classmates to decide who gave the best response to the dilemma.

   ____

   ____

   ____

   ____

   ____

   ____

   ____

   ____

Easter Prayer

Alleluia!

Leader: Alleluia! Christ is risen!

All: **He has risen as he said. Alleluia!**

Leader: Rejoice and be glad for our Lord is raised to new life. Alleluia.

All: **The Lord has risen indeed. Alleluia.**

Reader 1: The Jewish people call Psalm 136 the Great Hallel and recite it at every Passover Seder. It is a song of praise for God's enduring love for them. His love for them is eternal and endures forever. The word *Alleluia* means "praise God." From ancient times to the present, people have sung "Alleluia" to praise God with joy and thanksgiving.

All: **Alleluia!**

Reader 2: Praise the LORD, for he is good;
All: **for his mercy endures forever;**

Reader 2: Who alone has done great wonders,
All: **for his mercy endures forever;**

Reader 2: Who led the people through the desert,
All: **for his mercy endures forever;**

Reader 2: The Lord remembered us in our low estate,
All: **for his mercy endures forever;**

Reader 2: Freed us from our foes,
All: **for his mercy endures forever;**

Reader 2: And gives bread to all flesh,
All: **for his mercy endures forever.**

Reader 2: Praise the God of heaven,
All: **for his mercy endures forever.**

Psalm 136:1,4,16,23–26

Reader 3: We continue the tradition from our Jewish brothers and sisters of praising God, and now praise him for the glory of the Resurrection of his Son, Jesus Christ.

Reader 4: With joy in our hearts, let us call upon Christ, the Lord.
All: **Christ is risen. Alleluia!**

Reader 4: Lord, send your Spirit to us, for we proclaim your Resurrection.
All: **Christ is risen. Alleluia!**

Reader 4: May the whole earth be filled with the knowledge of your glory.
All: **Christ is risen. Alleluia!**

Reader 4: Jesus, you have triumphed over death. May we live only for you.
All: **Christ is risen. Alleluia!**

Reader 4: You were obedient to your Father, no matter what. Welcome us into your kingdom.
All: **Christ is risen. Alleluia!**

Reader 5: On the evening of that first day of the week, when the doors were locked, . . . Jesus came and stood in their midst and said to them, "Peace be with you" (John 20: 19).

Leader: May the Risen Lord touch our lives with his love
and bring us joy and hope.
May the Risen Lord open our eyes
so that we will follow him in his risen life.
May the Risen Lord deepen our faith
so that we will share the joy of Easter every day.
All: **Amen.**

Leader: This is the day the Lord has made. Alleluia!
All: **Let us rejoice and be glad. Alleluia!**

Based on Morning and Evening Prayer for Easter Sunday *Liturgy of the Hours*

Mary

The Mighty One has done great things for me,
and holy is his name. Luke 1:49

Mary, Our Intercessor

. . . [T]here was a wedding in Cana in Galilee, and the mother of Jesus was there. Jesus and his disciples were also invited to the wedding. When the wine ran short, the mother of Jesus said to him, "They have no wine." [And] Jesus said to her, "Woman, how does your concern affect me? My hour has not yet come." His mother said to the servers, "Do whatever he tells you." Now there were six stone washing jars there . . . each holding twenty to thirty gallons. Jesus told them, "Fill the jars with water." So they filled them to the brim.

John 2:1–7

The headwaiter tasted the water, and found that it had become very good wine. This was one of the first signs Jesus performed, and his disciples began to believe in him.

Based on John 2:9,11

The story of the wedding in Cana, found in the Gospel of John, is one of the Gospel stories that shows Jesus taking care of people by providing them with food or drink. These stories show us how generous God is. They also show us that when the Lord is with us we should celebrate.

In the early Church, Christians began to honor Mary as the Mother of God. They recognized that because she is the Mother of God, Mary has a unique role to play in God's plan for us. She is an intercessor for us. An intercessor is someone who acts on behalf of another.

At the wedding in Cana, Mary saw that the wine was going to run out. So she asked Jesus to help the couple who were being married. In the same way, Mary asks Jesus to help us. Because she is Jesus' mother, Mary is closer to her son than we are. We can turn to her and she will intercede with her son for us. Whenever we are in need, we can depend on Mary to be there for us.

As our intercessor, Mary acts on our behalf to bring us closer to her Son. She helps us understand that we should celebrate and be joyful because God has done many good things for us. Our heavenly Father loves us and takes care of us. We should praise him and give thanks with full hearts.

Catholics understand that there is even more to Mary's role at the wedding in Cana. Mary is Jesus' mother and his closest and best disciple. She believed in her Son, and knew that he was sent by God to bring salvation to his people. The account of the wedding in Cana is important for another reason as well. It is one of the few biblical passages in which Mary is mentioned in the Gospels.

Mary, at the wedding in Cana you asked your Son to show us a sign of God's glory and love for us. Help us recognize the signs of God's love in our lives. May we always depend on you as a child relies on a parent. Amen.

A Sign of the Kingdom

Jesus came to bring the Kingdom of God to us. Mary, his mother, has a special role to play in drawing us closer to her Son. Have you tried to grow closer to Jesus through Mary?

ACTIVITY

You can imagine how the story of what happened at the wedding must have spread through the community. Pretend that you have been asked to write a news story for the Cana Courier, an online news magazine.

Who would you interview to make sure you got the correct facts about the story?

____

____

What are the three most important aspects of the story that you will want to include?

____

____

Now write a headline and lead sentence for your story.

____

____

Our Lady of Fatima

On May 13, 1917, the Blessed Mother appeared to ten-year-old Lucia dos Santos and her two young cousins, Francisco and Jacinta Marto. As the children were busy tending their sheep in their village of Fatima, Portugal, Mary—dressed all in white—appeared to them in a dazzling light. She asked the children to make sacrifices and pray for sinners, and to pray the Rosary every day to obtain peace in the world.

On June 13, Mary appeared to the children again. She was holding a heart with thorns around it. The children realized this was the Immaculate Heart of Mary. The thorns represented sins for which people had to repent. Mary appeared to the children four more times. On the day of Mary's last apparition, October 13, 1917, a crowd of about 70,000 had gathered. When Mary appeared, she told Lucia that people must repent for their sins, ask God for pardon, and change their lives. Then, as Mary ascended into Heaven, the children saw in the sky a number of visions, including Saint Joseph holding the Christ Child. The crowd, however, saw the sun begin to whirl rapidly and move around the sky. As the crowd watched in amazement, able to look directly at the sun unhurt, the sun seemed to fall to the earth before returning to its normal position in the sky. This occurrence became known as the miracle of the sun.

In her appearances at Fatima, Mary called for people to change their lives. She also asked Catholics to attend Mass and receive the Eucharist on the first Saturday of five consecutive months. This is called the Devotion to the Immaculate Heart of Mary. She promised that the whole world would be in peace and that many souls would be saved if her requests were obeyed.

Today, the Fatima shrine in Portugal is one of the most visited Catholic pilgrimage sites in the world. The Church celebrates the Feast of Our Lady of Fatima on May 13.

The Power of Mary

When we wander away from God, he sometimes gives us reminders of how we are to live. Sometimes the Blessed Mother appears in visions, called *apparitions*, to bring us God's message. Marian apparitions, such as the one in Fatima, Portugal, bring many people back to their faith.

Pray for us, O holy
Mother of God,
that we may be made worthy
of the promises of Christ.
Amen.
From The Angelus

ACTIVITY

1. If Mary appeared in a vision today, what might be some specific requests she would make of people about how to live in the modern world? Name at least three requests you think Mary would make.

____

____

____

2. Choose one of those requests and tell how you would fulfill it in your own life.

____

____

____

The Assumption of the Blessed Virgin Mary

On August 15, Catholics celebrate the Solemnity of the Assumption of the Blessed Virgin Mary. This is an important holy day of obligation that honors Mary. On this day we celebrate the Church teaching that at the end of her life, Mary was taken up, body and soul, into Heaven. Although the Bible does not tell us what happened to Mary, Christians have believed throughout the centuries that the end of Mary's earthly life was special because she was without sin.

The Solemnity of the Assumption was celebrated in Syria as early as the fifth century. By the twelfth century, Christians throughout the Mediterranean world—including Spain, Italy, and France—were celebrating it. In 1950, Pope Pius XII declared the dogma of the Assumption in a formal ceremony in St. Peter's Square before 500,000 people. The Assumption recognizes that since Mary was Jesus' mother, she shared, body and soul, in his Resurrection and his glorification at the right hand of his Father.

Saint John Damascene, who lived centuries ago, wrote an interesting story about the Assumption. According to his story, the Eastern Roman Emperor Marcian asked Saint Juvenal, the bishop of Jerusalem, for Mary's body. He wanted to create a magnificent tomb for her. But Saint Juvenal wrote to the emperor explaining that there were no remains of Mary. From the time of the Apostles, it had been known that Mary had been taken up into Heaven.

The Church teaches that human beings die because they sin and are not perfect. But by God's grace Mary was not born into Original Sin and never sinned in her life. She was full of grace and is the Mother of God, so she shared in Jesus' Resurrection in a special way.

The Assumption of the Blessed Virgin Mary
by El Greco

The Assumption of Mary into Heaven gives us hope in our own resurrection at the end of time. Catholics believe that when Jesus comes again, all of us who serve our heavenly Father will be raised to eternal life with him. When we celebrate our belief in Mary's Assumption every year on August 15, we are also celebrating our belief in the resurrection of the dead. Mary went before us to show us how it will be for us when we follow the Lord as completely as she did.

O holy Mother, you gave the world the Savior, Jesus Christ. In your life and Assumption we see that all of God's promises will be fulfilled. Amen.

Honoring Mary

Throughout the liturgical year, there are many solemnities that honor Mary. We celebrate the Assumption of the Blessed Virgin Mary, the Annunciation of the Lord, the Immaculate Conception of the Blessed Virgin Mary, and Mary, the Holy Mother of God, just to name a few. Of the ones listed here, what is your favorite solemnity in Mary's honor?

ACTIVITY

How much do you know about Mary? Would you be able to share it with others? Choose one of the three statements below. On the lines provided, tell how you would explain it to someone who had never heard of it before.

1. Mary was born without Original Sin.
2. Mary intercedes for us with her Son in Heaven.
3. Mary is our model of how to live as a disciple of Jesus.

____

____

____

____

____

____

Feasts and Seasons Wrap-up

What Is Your Liturgical Year IQ?

Circle the letter of the correct answer.

1. Lent begins on ______.
   a. Ash Wednesday
   b. New Year's Day
   c. the First Sunday of Lent
   d. Christmas Day

2. We celebrate ______ during Holy Week.
   a. Christmas Day
   b. The Assumption of the Blessed Virgin Mary
   c. Good Friday
   d. Pentecost Sunday

3. During which liturgical season are the O Antiphons sung?
   a. Lent
   b. Christmas
   c. Triduum
   d. Advent

4. What is the liturgical color for Easter?
   a. white
   b. green
   c. blue
   d. pink

5. How many days make up the season of Lent?
   a. fifty
   b. thirty
   c. forty
   d. twelve

6. What do we celebrate at every Mass?
   a. the Resurrection
   b. the Annunciation
   c. Pentecost
   d. the Assumption

7. Which of the following is a holy day of obligation?
   a. All Souls' Day
   b. The Immaculate Conception of the Blessed Virgin Mary
   c. Thanksgiving Day
   d. Our Lady of Fatima

8. The Triduum begins on the evening of Holy Thursday and ends on ______.
   a. Holy Saturday evening
   b. Palm Sunday of the Passion of the Lord
   c. Good Friday
   d. Easter Sunday evening

9. The Blessed Virgin Mary is honored on which holy day?
   a. The Ascension of the Lord
   b. The Immaculate Conception of the Blessed Virgin Mary
   c. Holy Saturday
   d. Palm Sunday of the Passion of the Lord

10. Which liturgical seasons have the liturgical colors of purple and rose?
    a. Ordinary Time and Lent
    b. Christmas and Easter
    c. Advent and Easter
    d. Advent and Lent

Our Catholic Heritage

What Catholics Believe

How Catholics Worship

How Catholics Live

How Catholics Pray

What Catholics Believe

We share a common faith based on Sacred Scripture as found in the Bible and on the Sacred Tradition of the Church founded by Jesus Christ.

About

The Bible

The Bible is the Word of God. It contains the story of God and his people. God is truly the author of the Bible because the Holy Spirit inspired the people who wrote it.

Although we usually see the Bible as one volume, it is actually a collection, or a library, of seventy-three books. The Bible is divided into two parts. The first is called the Old Testament. There are forty-six books in the Old Testament, which includes songs, laws, history, poetry, and prayers. The Old Testament gives the account of salvation before the birth of Christ. In it we can read the words of the prophets, such as Isaiah and Ezekiel, that foretold a new Covenant and Jesus' birth.

The Old Testament books are usually listed in four sections: the Pentateuch, the Historical Books, the Wisdom Books, and the Prophetic Books. When we see them referenced, their titles are often abbreviated.

The second part of the Bible is the New Testament, which contains twenty-seven books. The New Testament begins with the four Gospels—accounts of Jesus' life and ministry according to Matthew, Mark, Luke, and John. These are followed by the Acts of the Apostles, and then by the letters of Paul, James, Peter, John, and Jude, which were written to the early Christians. After Jesus ascended into Heaven, the Apostles and early Christians naturally talked about him and all that had happened since the start of his ministry. Some of the Apostles and other disciples wrote the Gospels and letters to share many of the important teachings and events of Jesus' life, and to instruct new converts. The New Testament ends with the Book of Revelation.

One way that Jesus is present to us is in God's Word, the Bible. Catholics are encouraged to read the Bible daily. Every chapter in your religion book contains information from the Bible.

You can learn more about the Bible in the section "A Great Bible Expedition" on pages 15–21 of your book.

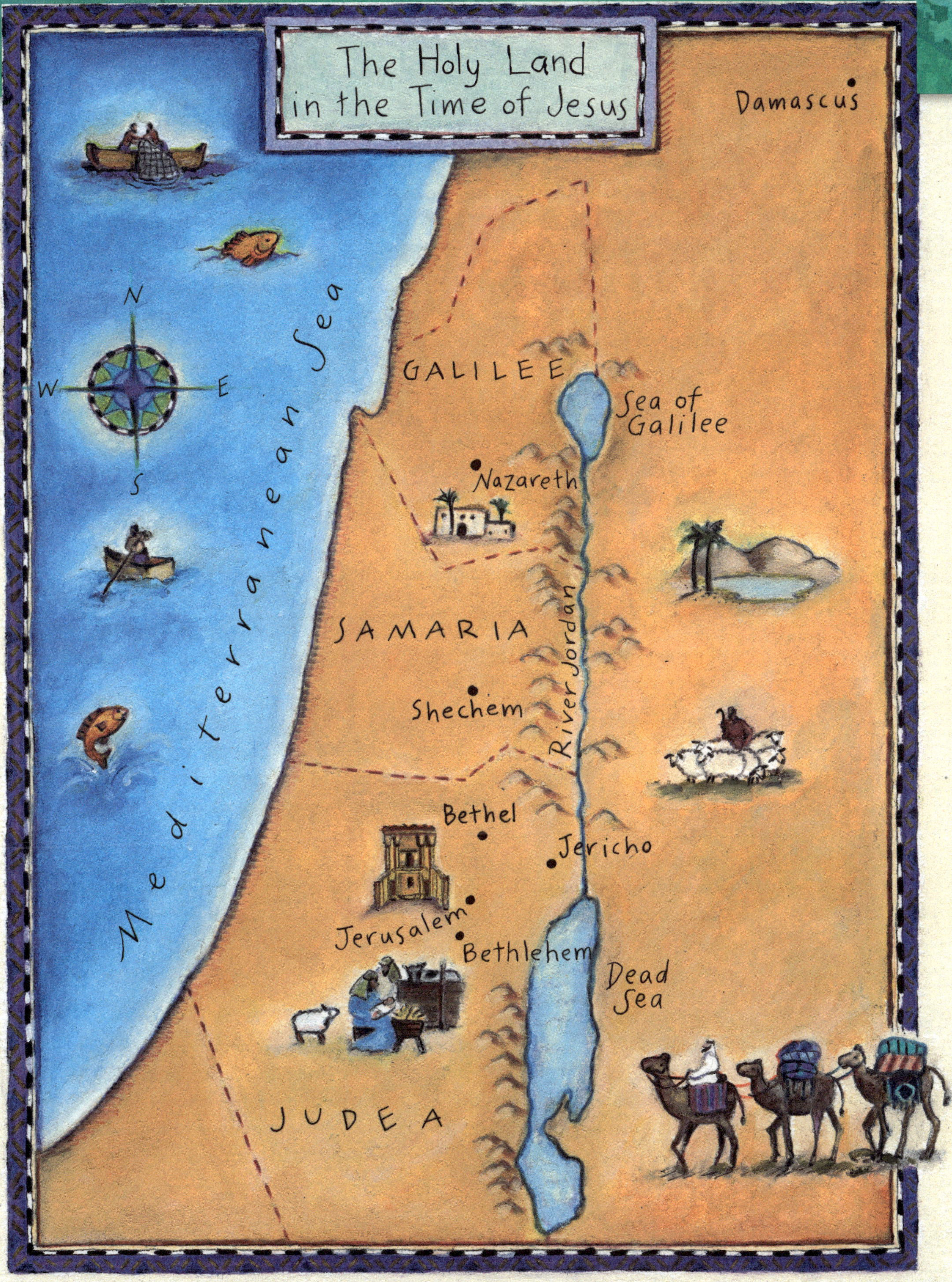
The Holy Land
in the Time of Jesus
Damascus
Mediterranean Sea
N
W
E
S
GALILEE
Sea of Galilee
Nazareth
SAMARIA
Shechem
River Jordan
Bethel
Jericho
Jerusalem
Bethlehem
Dead Sea
JUDEA

About
The Trinity

There is only one God, who is revealed to us to be Three Divine Persons. The Three Persons are God the Father, God the Son, and God the Holy Spirit. We call the Three Divine Persons the Blessed Trinity.

God is the Supreme Being, who always was and always will be. Through the gift of sanctifying grace, we share in God's life. All men and women desire God because they are created by God and for God. Only in God will we find real truth and happiness.

God is all-good, all-holy, and all-knowing. He is always just and merciful. God speaks to us in many ways, especially through his Son Jesus, the Scriptures, and the teachings and life of the Catholic Church.

God the Father

God the Father is the Creator of all things. Jesus taught us to call God "Father" because of the loving care that God has for everyone and everything. Jesus told us to tell our Father our needs in prayer, and that God would always be listening.

God the Son

Jesus Christ is the Father's greatest gift to us. He is the only Son of God. We believe that the Son, without losing his divine nature, took on human nature for our salvation. This belief is called the **Incarnation**. By the power of the Holy Spirit, Jesus was born of the Virgin Mary and became like us in all ways but sin.

Jesus' mission was to announce the Good News. Jesus carried out his mission by teaching, healing, forgiving, and working miracles as signs of God's love. He gathered his followers into a group of disciples who became the Church. Jesus is our Savior. Jesus loved us so much that he died on the Cross for all our sins. He was buried, and on the third day he rose from the dead. The truth of the Resurrection is that death is not an ending but leads to everlasting life. We receive grace when we share in the divine life of the Risen Jesus. Jesus Christ ascended into Heaven, where he lives and reigns with the Father and the Holy Spirit. One day, he will return to judge the living and the dead.

God the Holy Spirit

The Holy Spirit is the love that is shared by the Father and the Son. The Holy Spirit has been at work in the world since creation. Jesus Christ sent the Holy Spirit to guide his Church and the consciences of his people until the end of time. The Holy Spirit comes to us in Baptism and the other Sacraments to help fill us with God's life and lead us to be true followers of Jesus.

How Catholics Worship

We celebrate our faith in worship when we give honor and praise to God. Worship is so important for us that the Church calls it the first "work" of God's people. The official public worship of the Church is called liturgy.

About

The Sacraments

We place the Sacraments into three groups to better understand their purpose. The first group is the Sacraments of Christian Initiation.

About

The Sacraments of Christian Initiation

We become full members of the Catholic Church through the Sacraments of Christian Initiation: Baptism, Confirmation, and Eucharist. These three Sacraments are most often received at different times, as a person grows from infancy to maturity. Before being received into the Catholic Church, older children and adults go through a period of formation called the *catechumenate*.

The Sacrament of Baptism

In the Sacrament of Baptism, we receive the Holy Spirit and are anointed with the sign of the cross. Through the waters of Baptism, which represent life and death, all sin—including Original Sin—is washed away and we rise with Christ to new life. The grace of Baptism prepares us to accept God's call.

The Sacrament of Confirmation

In the Sacrament of Confirmation we stand with a sponsor before the church community and proclaim our faith and our readiness to respond to God's call to discipleship. We should be in a state of grace and old enough to understand the commitment we are making.

When we are confirmed, the bishop or priest says, "Be sealed with the Gift of the Holy Spirit" (*Rite of Confirmation*). The bishop or priest places his hand on our head and anoints our forehead with the consecrated oil of Sacred Chrism. Our baptismal faith is strengthened through the coming of the Holy Spirit.

The grace of Confirmation gives us the courage to live our faith and to be committed to the work of the Catholic Church.

The Sacrament of Eucharist

During the consecration at Mass, the bread and wine become the Body and Blood of Jesus Christ. This change is called **transubstantiation**. When we worship together at Mass, we celebrate the Eucharist. The word *Eucharist* means "thanksgiving." During the Mass we praise and thank God for all our gifts, especially the gift of his Son, Jesus Christ.

At Mass, Jesus is present in the people gathered, in the Word of God proclaimed, and especially in the Eucharist.

About

The Sacraments of Healing

The second group of Sacraments is the Sacraments of Healing. The Sacraments of Healing are Penance and Reconciliation and the Anointing of the Sick.

The Sacrament of Penance and Reconciliation

Penance and Reconciliation is the Sacrament instituted by Christ that celebrates God's loving forgiveness. God always loves us and is ready to forgive our sins. When we sin, we freely choose to turn away from God and one another. The Sacrament of Penance and Reconciliation reunites us with God and the Church. We may celebrate the Sacrament of Penance and Reconciliation whenever we need God's mercy and peace and are sorry for our sins. We may celebrate the Sacrament individually or with others.

We prepare for the celebration of Penance and Reconciliation by examining our consciences.

When we meet the priest, he welcomes us in the name of Jesus and the Church. He may read a passage from the Bible. Then we confess, or tell the priest our sins. The priest may suggest ways we can improve and grow closer to God. He then asks us to do some act of service or to pray a particular prayer or prayers. This is called an act of penance. The priest then asks us to tell God we are sorry for our sins by praying the Act of Contrition.

Then the priest extends his hands over us and prays, "I absolve you from your sins in the name of the Father, and of the Son, and of the Holy Spirit" (*Rite of Penance*). This action is called *absolution*. Then, with the priest, we praise God for his mercy. The priest tells us to go in peace and that our sins are forgiven. We respond, "Amen."

The Sacrament of Anointing of the Sick

In the Sacrament of Anointing of the Sick, the Church prays for the healing and forgiveness of persons who are seriously ill or in danger of death. The priest lays hands on the sick, praying for their physical and spiritual healing. He anoints them with blessed oil.

Through this Sacrament, physical healing may occur if it is beneficial to the salvation of a person's soul. Forgiveness of sins may also be granted if the person was unable to receive forgiveness through the Sacrament of Penance and Reconciliation.

About

The Sacraments at the Service of Communion

The third group of Sacraments is the Sacraments at the Service of Communion. These Sacraments are Holy Orders and Matrimony. Those who receive these Sacraments have a special mission to serve and work for the salvation of others and to build up the People of God.

The Sacrament of Holy Orders

Holy Orders is the Sacrament that celebrates the ordination of bishops, priests, and deacons to serve the Church in the name and Person of Christ. The word *ordain* means "to set aside or to empower a person to carry on the work of the Apostles." Those ordained men receive a permanent character helping them to act as representatives of Christ for the Church. Bishops carry on the work of the Apostles and serve the Church by leading a diocese. Priests are ordained by the bishop to be his coworkers by celebrating the Sacraments, proclaiming God's Word, and guiding the parish community. Deacons, also ordained by the bishop, assist with the work of the parish. They may read the Gospel and give the homily at Mass, baptize, witness marriages, and preside at funerals. Transitional deacons are men who have been ordained deacons as the step before becoming priests. Permanent deacons have the same ministries as those of transitional deacons but can be married.

At the celebration of the Sacrament of Holy Orders the bishop lays his hands on the head of the man being ordained. He prays a special prayer asking God to bless the man being ordained and to help him preach the Gospel, celebrate the Sacraments, and serve others.

The Sacrament of Matrimony

The Sacrament of Matrimony celebrates the commitment of a baptized man and a baptized woman to each other for as long as they live. In the Sacrament of Matrimony, the man and woman's love for each other is a sign of Christ's love for the Church. God gives them special grace to sustain them and to help them grow in their love for each other. Through their physical love and openness to children, they become one and share in God's creative power. Sexual love is reserved for married couples only. Their spousal love is to reflect God's plan for life and love.

Catholic parents accept the responsibility of sharing their faith with their children. The love and care that parents give to their children are a reflection of God's love.

In the celebration of the Sacrament of Matrimony, the man says to the woman, "I take you to be my wife." The woman says to the man, "I take you to be my husband." The couple confer the Sacrament on each other in the presence of a priest or deacon and the church community.

About

The Mass

The greatest and most important prayer of the Catholic Church is the Mass. At Mass, we come together to worship God with our parish community. Jesus is present with us at Mass in the people gathered, in the presider, in the Word of God proclaimed, and especially in the Eucharist.

The Introductory Rites

The Entrance Procession and Opening Hymn
The priest and those assisting him in the Mass enter the church. As the procession begins, we sing the opening hymn.

The Greeting
The procession pauses before the altar to show reverence, and the priest, deacon, and servers move to their places. The priest kisses the altar to show reverence for the table on which the bread and wine will be offered.

As we begin our worship, the priest welcomes us by saying, "The Lord be with you." We answer, "And with your spirit."

The Penitential Act
As a community, we confess that we have sinned. We ask for God's forgiveness and the prayers of the church community. Then we say or sing, "Lord, have mercy."

The Gloria
We sing or pray the Gloria, which is a hymn of praise to God. Then we pray the Collect.

The Collect
The priest prays a prayer that helps us focus on the theme of the Mass for that day.

The Liturgy of the Word

The First Reading
The lector proclaims the First Reading. It is usually from the Old Testament. We sit quietly and listen to God's Word.

The Responsorial Psalm
The cantor leads us in singing the Responsorial Psalm.

The Second Reading
The lector proclaims the Second Reading from the New Testament, other than the Gospels. The Second Reading is usually from one of Saint Paul's letters. We sit quietly and listen to God's Word.

The Gospel Acclamation
Before the Gospel is proclaimed, we praise God by singing "Alleluia" or another acclamation.

The Gospel
We stand in reverence as the priest or deacon proclaims the Gospel.

The Homily
The priest or deacon explains the meaning of the Gospel and the other Scripture readings. We sit quietly and pay attention as the homily is given.

The Profession of Faith
We recite the Nicene Creed or the Apostles' Creed as a community of faith to affirm our belief in what the Catholic Church teaches.

The Prayer of the Faithful (Universal Prayer)
We pray for the Church, our country, and the needs of God's people. We also pray for those who are sick and those who have died.

The Liturgy of the Eucharist

The Preparation of the Altar and the Gifts
As the altar is prepared, members of the community bring the gifts of bread and wine in procession to the priest.

The Eucharistic Prayer
In this prayer of praise and thanksgiving, the priest praises God our Father and invites us to lift up our hearts to the Lord in prayer. We join with the angels and say or sing the "Holy, Holy, Holy."

The priest prays to God the Father, asking him to send the Holy Spirit and change the bread and wine into the Body and Blood of Jesus. Then in the words of Jesus himself at the Last Supper, the priest says the prayers of consecration, and Jesus Christ becomes truly present under the appearances of the bread and wine.

Mystery of Faith
After the consecration, we proclaim the mystery of our faith by singing or saying these or similar words of joy and promise:

> We proclaim your Death, O Lord,
> and profess your Resurrection
> until you come again.

The Great Amen
At the conclusion of the Eucharistic Prayer, we sing or say "Amen."

The Communion Rite

The Lord's Prayer
We pray the prayer that Jesus taught us.

The Sign of Peace
We offer each other the Sign of Peace to show that we wish goodness for our brothers and sisters in Jesus.

The Breaking of the Bread
As the priest and deacon prepare for the distribution of Holy Communion, we say or sing, "Lamb of God, you take away the sins of the world, have mercy on us."

Communion
We reverently walk up to receive the Body and Blood of Jesus in the Eucharist. When we receive the Eucharistic bread, the priest, deacon, or extraordinary minister of Holy Communion says, "The Body of Christ." We respond, "Amen." When we receive the cup, the priest, deacon, or extraordinary minister of Holy Communion says, "The Blood of Christ." We respond, "Amen." We return to our places and spend time in quiet prayer and thanksgiving.

Concluding Rites

Blessing
The priest blesses us in the name of the Father, and of the Son, and of the Holy Spirit. We answer, "Amen." Our celebration ends when the priest or deacon tells us to go in peace. We respond, "Thanks be to God."

Dismissal
The priest, deacon, and altar servers leave the altar in procession as we sing a song of praise and thanksgiving.

How Catholics Live

Living as Jesus taught us is not easy, but God gives us lots of help. Our conscience and other special gifts help us. When we turn away from sin and make good choices, we live as children of God.

About

Conscience

Our conscience is a gift from God. Our conscience helps us know what is right and what is wrong. We must learn ways to form a good conscience. The Beatitudes, the Ten Commandments, the teachings of Jesus, and the guidance of the Church help us develop a good conscience.

One of our greatest blessings is free will. Free will is our freedom to choose to do what is right or what is wrong. We can pray to the Holy Spirit to guide our choices, but we must always take responsibility for our actions.

About

The Theological and Moral Virtues

The Holy Spirit gives us gifts that are so wonderful they help us become more like God. These gifts include the Theological Virtues and the Moral Virtues.

Virtues are often called habits. The more we practice virtues, the more natural they seem to us and the easier they are to live out.

The Theological Virtues are faith, hope, and charity. Faith helps us believe in God. Hope allows us to trust in God's promises. Charity prompts us to show our love for God and others.

The Moral Virtues are prudence, justice, fortitude, and temperance. Prudence is the habit of making good judgments and decisions. Justice is the practice of treating others fairly. Fortitude is the courage to do what is right. Temperance is the habit of living in moderation and controlling desires.

About

Sin and Mercy

The Bible tells us that Jesus came to show mercy to sinners. Before Jesus was born, an angel told Joseph, Mary's husband, "... [Y]ou are to name him Jesus, because he will save his people from their sins" (Matthew 1:21).

Sin

Sin is a free choice to turn away from God's love. We sin by doing what we know is wrong. Sin keeps us from living as Jesus taught us. Sin turns our hearts away from God.

Mortal sin is a very serious refusal to love God. A sin is mortal when:

1. The action is seriously wrong.
2. We know that the action is seriously wrong.
3. We make a free choice to commit the sin.

Less serious sins are called venial sins. Venial sins weaken but do not completely destroy our relationship with God and the Church.

Mortal and venial sins committed by individuals are called personal sins. Our personal sins are always our choices. But some of our personal sins may tempt others to sin. We have a responsibility for the sins committed by others when we cooperate in them.

Social sins are those that reflect the unjust and oppressive wrongs in our society. Some examples of social sins are racism, failure to pay just wages, abortion, unjust wars, sexism, ignoring the poor, and prejudice in any form. As Catholics, we must work to put an end to these sins wherever they exist.

Mercy

Even when we sin seriously, we can remember that God's mercy never leaves us. Mortal sins must be confessed in the Sacrament of Penance and Reconciliation. Through Christ we receive God's forgiveness, and we are reunited with the Church.

God loves us so much and wants to forgive us even more than we want to be forgiven. When we share in God's life of love, we receive the grace to live good and holy lives. The Holy Spirit helps us turn away from sin. The Holy Spirit helps us form our conscience so that we know when something is right or wrong.

About

The Beatitudes

Jesus gave us the Beatitudes to teach us how to love God and others. The Beatitudes are Jesus' way of telling us what life will be like in the Kingdom of Heaven. When we live the Beatitudes, we can be truly happy.

The Beatitudes	Living the Beatitudes
Blessed are the poor in spirit, for theirs is the kingdom of heaven.	We know that we need God more than anything else. We obey God and trust in his goodness.
Blessed are they who mourn, for they will be comforted.	We try to help those who are in sorrow or those who are hurting. In turn, we know the Holy Spirit is with us and will comfort us when we are in sorrow.
Blessed are the meek, for they will inherit the land.	We try to be gentle and patient with others. We try to please God more than anyone else so we will share in his promises.
Blessed are they who hunger and thirst for righteousness, for they will be satisfied.	We try to be fair and just toward others. We share what we have with those in need.
Blessed are the merciful, for they will be shown mercy.	We forgive those who are unkind to us. We accept the forgiveness of others.
Blessed are the clean of heart, for they will see God.	We try to keep God first in our lives. We show our love for God by loving our neighbor. By doing this we will live forever with God.
Blessed are the peacemakers, for they will be called children of God.	We try to bring God's peace to the world. When we live peacefully, we are known as God's children.
Blessed are they who are persecuted for the sake of righteousness, for theirs is the kingdom of heaven.	We try to do what is right even when we are made fun of or insulted. By doing this we will be with God forever.

Based on Matthew 5:3–10

About

The Commandments

The Ten Commandments are God's law. God gave the Ten Commandments as a gift to help people live in peace with one another. The Ten Commandments are a guide to help us live as children of God. Jesus told us that it is important to obey the Commandments.

The Ten Commandments	Living the Ten Commandments
1. I am the Lord your God. You shall not have other gods besides me.	We believe in God. We only worship God. To place anything or anyone above God or to improperly worship God is idolatry. We are to love God above all else.
2. You shall not take the name of the Lord, your God, in vain.	We never use the name of God in an angry way. We use the names of God, Jesus, Mary, and the saints with respect at all times.
3. Remember to keep holy the Lord's Day.	On Sunday we honor God in a special way. We worship him by participating in Mass with our family.
4. Honor your father and mother.	We love, honor, respect, and obey our parents and all adults who care for us.
5. You shall not kill.	God gives us the gift of life. We must protect the lives of children not yet born, the sick, and the elderly. We must respect the life and health of others. We must live peacefully and prevent harm from coming to ourselves and others.
6. You shall not commit adultery.	God created man and woman in his image. He calls us to chaste living. We are to respect our bodies and the bodies of others. We honor the lifelong marriage covenant.
7. You shall not steal.	We share with others the gifts God has given us. We do not waste the earth's resources so others who come after us will have them, too. We do not cheat.
8. You shall not bear false witness against your neighbor.	We must not lie, or mislead others on purpose. We must not hurt others by what we say. If we have misled somebody, then we must correct what we have said.
9. You shall not covet your neighbor's wife.	We respect the promises married people have made to each other. We must always dress and act in a decent way.
10. You shall not covet anything that belongs to your neighbor.	We are satisfied with what we have. We are not jealous, envious, or greedy. We place God first in our lives.

Based on Exodus 20:2–17

The Great Commandment

Jesus told us that all of God's laws can really be summed up in the Great Commandment: "Love God with all your heart, with all your soul, with all your mind, and with all your strength, and love your neighbor as yourself" (based on Mark 12:30–31). The Great Commandment teaches us that God's laws are based on love of God and love of neighbor.

The New Commandment

Jesus told us that besides wanting us to keep the Great Commandment, he also wanted us to keep a New Commandment. The New Commandment Jesus gave us is, "Love one another as I have loved you" (based on John 13:34). We are called to live as followers of Jesus. When we love others and treat them as Jesus taught us, we live in happiness and freedom.

About

The Gifts of the Holy Spirit

The seven Gifts of the Holy Spirit help and guide us. Below is a list of the Gifts of the Holy Spirit and what they do for us.

1. **Wisdom** helps us know how God wants us to live.
2. **Understanding** helps us know what God teaches through Jesus, the Bible, and the Church.
3. **Knowledge** helps us know and appreciate that God is more important than anything else in life.
4. **Counsel** helps us make good decisions in our everyday lives.
5. **Courage** helps us be strong when we face problems.
6. **Piety** helps us love God more than anything else.
7. **Fear of the Lord** helps us to be thankful for all that God creates.

About

The Works of Mercy

Jesus expects us to care for the poor and those who are in need. Jesus wants us to live in peace and to be just. Jesus even wants us to love our enemies. Catholics call these ways to show love for others the Spiritual Works of Mercy and the Corporal Works of Mercy. The Corporal Works of Mercy are described in Matthew 25:31–46.

The Spiritual Works of Mercy
Counsel the doubtful.
Instruct the ignorant.
Admonish sinners.
Comfort the afflicted.
Forgive offenses.
Bear wrongs patiently.
Pray for the living and the dead.

The Corporal Works of Mercy
Feed the hungry.
Give drink to the thirsty.
Clothe the naked.
Shelter the homeless.
Visit the sick.
Visit the imprisoned.
Bury the dead.

About

The Precepts of the Church

The Catholic Church also gives us some very specific duties and responsibilities. These are called the precepts of the Church. They are:

- Celebrate Mass on all Sundays and holy days of obligation.
- Confess your sins at least once a year.
- Receive the Eucharist at least during the Easter season.
- Fast and abstain on the days appointed by the Church.
- Contribute to the Church to provide for its material needs.

About

Vocations

As we get older, we begin to think about what choices we will make in the future. Those choices will include devoting time to service in the Catholic Church. This is called our vocation—what we believe the Gospel message of Jesus calls us to do.

The Church names four special vocations in which God may call us to serve. They include the ordained ministry, serving as a religious brother or sister, and married life. They also include single people who choose the state of consecrated life, making a permanent commitment to celibacy. They give themselves to God and to the service of the Church. Even if you are not called to one of these four vocations, you are still called by your Baptism to live in a way that builds up the Church.

Many Ways of Serving

Many people devote some of their time to service within the Church. They choose a particular ministry in their parish or diocese, such as caring for the poor, teaching, planning and leading the liturgy, helping with parish management, or inviting others to join the Catholic Church.

Some women and men choose to *consecrate*, or devote their lives completely to God and to the work of the Catholic Church. Many decide to join religious communities of sisters or brothers who publicly profess the evangelical counsels of poverty, chastity, and obedience. The vows help them be completely devoted to their ministries. Each religious community chooses to concentrate its efforts on a particular ministry, such as teaching, working with the sick and the poor, preaching, prayer and contemplation, or parish work.

In the Catholic Church there are also ordained ministers—bishops, priests, and deacons. Men who feel that they are called to the priesthood have the special vocation of leading the

community in worship as well as serving in other ways. There are diocesan priests who serve as pastors of parishes, as educators, and as counselors or in other capacities. There are priests who, like sisters and brothers, belong to religious communities. They may also be assigned as pastors or as teachers, or to lead a particular ministry of their community.

There are also men who are ordained as permanent deacons—or deacons who are not going to become priests. They can assist the pastor by leading the celebrations of Baptism and Marriage, giving the homily at Sunday Mass, and helping with parish management. Permanent deacons can be married and live with their families.

Discernment

In what ways are we being called to serve? Answering this question is called *discernment*, which means determining, with God's help, God's will for our lives. We should pray that God will help us understand what the Gospel is calling us to do. We should also try to know more about the possibilities for us in the Catholic Church. Talk to a priest, teacher, parish minister, or religious brother or sister to find out more about how God's invitation can be answered.

How Catholics Pray

When we pray, we are expressing our faith in God. We can pray privately. We can also pray with others in the Church when we gather to worship.

About

Prayer

Prayer is talking and listening to God. We pray to praise the goodness and love of God, to thank him for the many gifts we have received, and to ask him for special blessings for ourselves and others. Sometimes we ask Mary or one of the saints to pray to God for us.

God always hears our prayers and answers them in the way that is best for us.

It is important to set aside a special time or place to pray each day, so that we can form a habit of daily prayer.

About

Kinds of Prayer

Praying is not always asking God for something. Our prayers should include praise and thanksgiving, too.

Quiet Prayer

It is always possible to pray. We can pray without saying words. When we are quiet and think about God, we are praying. In this way, the Holy Spirit speaks to our hearts.

We can pray quietly and think about a passage from the Bible. When beautiful sights in nature remind us of God's wonderful gifts we can pray a quiet prayer of thanks to God.

Prayers with Words

Sometimes we pray by talking to God using our own words.

We also learn and pray the prayers that are part of our Catholic heritage, such as the Lord's Prayer, the Hail Mary, the Glory Be, and the Act of Contrition.

As Catholics, we begin our prayers with the Sign of the Cross, to remind us that we offer our prayers in the name of the Father, the Son, and the Holy Spirit. We end our prayers with *Amen*, which means "I believe."

About

Meditative Prayer

Meditation is praying without words so that God can speak to us in our minds and hearts. Meditative prayer begins with thinking about a single subject. We may begin by reading a passage from the Bible, or by thinking about a holy person whom we admire. All the while we concentrate on God's relationship to this single subject. Another way to meditate is to call upon the Holy Spirit to help us think about whether we are followers of Jesus. We can think about how we can better our relationship with God.

Then, we sort out our thoughts and feelings and think about what God wants us to do. Our prayer leads us to a better understanding of what God wants us to do as followers of Jesus.

About

The Lord's Prayer

Jesus gave us the Lord's Prayer to teach us how God wants us to live, and so that we can honor God and remember his love for us.

The Lord's Prayer

Our Father, who art in heaven, hallowed be thy name;

God is our Father. We praise and thank him for all the wonderful gifts he has given us. We pray that God's name will be spoken with respect and reverence at all times.

thy kingdom come,

Jesus told us about God's kingdom in Heaven. We pray that everyone will live as Jesus teaches us to live. We look forward to the day when God's kingdom will finally come about.

thy will be done on earth as it is in heaven.

We pray that everyone will obey God's law. We know that Jesus has taught us how to live as his followers. We wish to show others how to live as Christians.

Give us this day our daily bread,

God cares for us. We know that we can pray for our needs. We know that we must pray for the needs of the poor. We ask God for the good things we can share with others.

and forgive us our trespasses, as we forgive those who trespass against us;

We ask God for forgiveness when we have done something wrong. We forgive those who have hurt us.

and lead us not into temptation,

We pray that God will help us make good choices and do what is right.

but deliver us from evil.

We pray that God will protect us from what is harmful. We know that we should care for our own health and the well-being of others.

Amen.

When we say "Amen," we say "I believe."

Celebrating Catholic Schools Week

Catholic Schools in America

Mother Frances Cabrini

Teacher of Immigrants

Maria Francesca Cabrini was born on July 15, 1850, in northern Italy. As a child, Maria knew she was destined to help people.

Maria's parents helped her receive an education. She received her teaching certificate as an adult and began her career as a teacher in a neighboring town. Maria wanted to teach people in faraway lands about Jesus. She also wanted to become a Franciscan nun. Her bishop encouraged her to become a religious sister. He also told her to start her own religious order because he was unaware of any nearby Franciscan orders. With seven other women, Maria founded the Missionaries of the Sacred Heart of Jesus. She became known as Mother Frances Xavier Cabrini when she became a nun.

Mother Frances Xavier Cabrini wanted to go to China. However, the pope told her to aid the Italian people arriving in America. On March 31, 1889, Mother Cabrini and six sisters arrived in New York City. Many people, especially poor people, were sick. Many children's parents had died. Mother Cabrini opened a home to take care of these children. Because there was so much sickness, Mother Cabrini also opened a hospital for the poor.

Mother Cabrini believed that the children and their parents needed to learn English. She started schools to teach the children both English and Italian. The sisters in her order held classes to teach the adults English. The sisters also taught the adults how to sew, cook, clean, and perform other tasks that would help them get jobs. All of Mother Cabrini's schools taught people about the love of Jesus.

Mother Cabrini traveled across the United States. In 1909 she became a U.S. citizen. By the time of her death in 1917, she had opened sixty-seven Catholic institutions, including schools, orphanages, and hospitals. She was the first American citizen to become a saint. Her feast day is November 13.

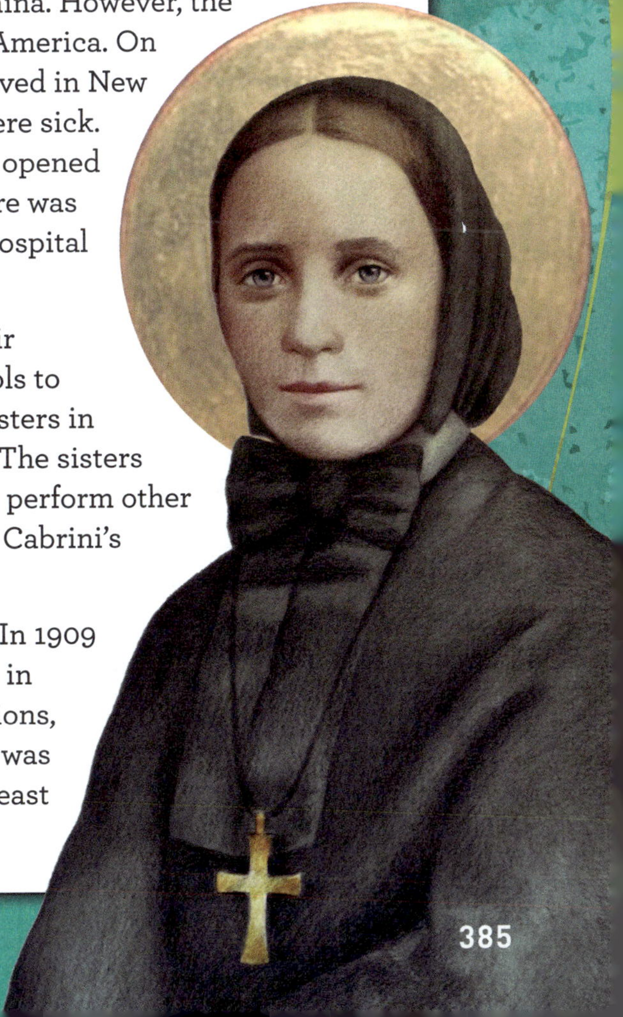

ACTIVITY

Imagine that your class is participating in a poster contest for Catholic Schools Week. The theme of your poster is Mother Frances Cabrini. Design your poster below. Be sure to use both words and images to show why Mother Frances Cabrini's life and work are important to Catholic schools.

Name:____ Date:______________

Catholic Education Today

Catholic Medical Schools

In addition to the hospitals founded by Mother Frances Cabrini, many other Catholic hospitals were opened in the United States by members of religious orders responding to God's call to care for the sick. During times of immigration, war, and other challenges, these hospitals could reach out in a special way to people who needed God's love, compassion, and healing.

Like Catholic hospitals, Catholic medical schools have a unique opportunity to respond to God's call to care for the sick because they train students for healthcare professions. They can educate their students to become physicians, researchers, scientists, or other medical professionals who are compassionate toward those who are ill. There are five Catholic medical schools in the United States: Creighton University Medical School in Omaha, Nebraska; Georgetown University School of Medicine in Washington, D.C.; Loyola University Chicago Strich School of Medicine in Maywood, Illinois; Marian University College of Osteopathic Medicine in Indianapolis, Indiana; and Saint Louis University School of Medicine in St. Louis, Missouri.

Students of all faiths can attend Catholic medical schools. However, these schools can still operate in a way that reflects their Catholic identity and shows the love of Jesus Christ. For example, they can encourage their students to practice medicine or medical research in a morally responsible way.

Saint Louis University School of Medicine encourages its students and faculty to:

- **respect the sanctity of human life**
- **serve those most in need**
- **treat all patients with dignity**
- **have humility about their abilities**
- **practice medicine in a way that honors their relationship with God and the human family.**

In a world where medicine, science, and healthcare may not always serve the needs of the poor or respect the dignity of life, Catholic medical schools have the potential to make a difference.

ACTIVITY

1. Rearrange the letters of the word or the nonsense phrase on the left to form a new word on the right. Hint: Every new word was mentioned in this lesson.

V	E	R	S	E															
M	A	I	N	S	C	O	O	P	S										
N	I	C	E	D	I	M	E												
R	A	C	E																
H	A	I	L	S	P	O	T												
T	I	N	Y	C	A	T	S												
F	I	L	E																
R	O	G	U	E	C	A	N	E											
O	I	L	C	A	T	C	H												

2. Think about the profession you hope to choose as an adult. How could you practice this profession in a way that reflects your Catholic identity and shows the love of Jesus Christ?

____

____

____

____

____

____

An End of the Year Prayer

The Gift of Faith

Begin by singing the program song, "Blest Are We," found on page 22. Then pray together the Sign of the Cross.

Leader: As we come to the end of our year together, we have many reasons to give God thanks. Today we will give thanks for the gift of faith. This gift has grown in us as we have listened together to God's Word and learned about the teachings of the Church.

Let us open our hearts to receive God's Word to us today.

Reader 1: (*Proclaim from the Bible Matthew 21: 21-22.*)

Leader: Let us now offer our prayers of praise and thanks to God.

All: **We praise and thank you, Lord, for the gift of faith.**

Reader 2: Like Abraham, Sarah, Moses, and David, may we be people of faith.

All: **We praise and thank you, Lord, for the gift of faith.**

Reader 3: Like the prophets, may we speak words of truth and justice.

All: **We praise and thank you, Lord, for the gift of faith.**

Reader 4: Like Jesus, may we share your Good News with all we meet.

All: **We praise and thank you, Lord, for the gift of faith.**

(Leader invites all who wish to offer their prayers of petition.)

Leader: God, our Creator, we are grateful to you for the faith journey we shared this year. We learned of your promises to the Israelites, and of your promises to us as followers of your Son, Jesus. Help us to remain faithful followers of Jesus, through the power of the Holy Spirit.

All: **Amen.**

(Conclude by again singing "Blest Are We," or another favorite hymn about faith and discipleship.)

Glossary

altar An altar is a raised place where sacrifices are offered. The altar used for the center of worship during the Mass is also a table, where we gather to share the Eucharistic meal. *(page 43)*

amen Amen is a word we usually say at the end of our prayers. It means "I believe" or "So it is." *(page 183)*

Ark of the Covenant The Ark of the Covenant was a special box that held the stone tablets of the Ten Commandments. *(page 111)*

catholic The word *catholic* means "universal." With a capital C, it describes the Church founded by Christ on the Apostles. *(page 147)*

Chosen People In the Old Testament the Chosen People were Abraham and his descendants, whom God had selected to receive his Word. *(page 123)*

conscience Our conscience is our ability to judge what is right and what is wrong. *(page 171)*

Corporal Works of Mercy The Corporal Works of Mercy are loving deeds that relieve the physical suffering of others. *(page 287)*

covenant A covenant is a sacred agreement or relationship, sometimes sealed by a ritual or ceremony. Isaac honored the covenant the Lord made with his father, Abraham. *(page 53)*

discernment Discernment is discovering, with God's help, God's will for our lives. *(page 125)*

Essenes Essenes were devout Jewish people who lived simply in the desert. *(page 273)*

exile Exile is the forced removal of people from their homeland to another land. The Israelites captured by the Assyrians were living in exile. *(page 215)*

Exodus The Exodus is the Old Testament story of how God freed the Hebrews in Egypt. Exodus is the second book of the Old Testament. *(page 87)*

faith Faith is the assurance of things hoped for, the conviction of things not seen. *(page 29)*

fidelity Fidelity is faithfulness and loyalty to something or someone. Joseph is a model of fidelity to God. *(page 65)*

guidance Guidance is help in making the right choices. God gives us guidance to help us develop our conscience. *(page 171)*

Heaven Heaven is a life of everlasting happiness with God, and with all people who love him. *(page 261)*

hell Hell is everlasting suffering and separation from God after death. *(page 261)*

Incarnation The Incarnation is the belief that the Son of God, without losing his divine nature, took on human nature for our salvation, and became like us in all ways but sin. *(page 368)*

laity The laity are people who are part of the Church and are not clergy or religious brothers and sisters. *(page 145)*

liturgical year The liturgical year is the Church's yearly calendar of celebrations and seasons. *(page 99)*

manna Manna is the bread-like food that God gave the Israelites in the desert. *(page 111)*

meditation Meditation is a type of prayer in which we are silent and concentrate on listening to God through our feelings, imagination, and thoughts. We can meditate by thinking about a Scripture story, art, and music. *(page 299)*

messiah A messiah is a person chosen to save people from a particular fate. The word means "savior." Jesus Christ is the Messiah, chosen by God to free us from sin and death. *(page 215)*

ministry A ministry is a way of serving and caring for others in Christ's name. *(page 145)*

Moral Virtues The Moral Virtues are four spiritual qualities—temperance, prudence, justice, and fortitude—that help us avoid sin. *(page 229)*

Original Sin Original Sin is the sin of Adam and Eve, passed on to all human beings. Because of it, we are weakened in our ability to resist sin and do good. *(page 205)*

Paschal Mystery The Paschal Mystery is the way that Jesus' Passion, Death, Resurrection, and Ascension saved us from sin and gave us life after death. *(page 99)*

Passover Passover is the Jewish celebration of the Israelites' exodus from Egypt. *(page 99)*

patriarch A *patriarch,* a term meaning "father," is a great leader of the Hebrews from early Scripture times. A patriarch is also the male leader of a family or clan. *(page 29)*

persistence Persistence is the act of continually pursuing something in spite of obstacles. Prayer often requires persistence. *(page 239)*

Pharisees Pharisees were Jewish people who accepted both the written law of the Old Testament and spoken teachings and tradition. *(page 273)*

piety Piety is putting God above everything else. *(page 65)*

precepts of the Church The precepts of the Church are the Church's teachings about our obligations as Catholics. *(page 229)*

Promised Land The Promised Land is Canaan, the sacred place God promised to Abraham, Isaac, Jacob, and the Israelites in Egypt. *(page 87)*

prophet A prophet is a person sent by God to speak out against behavior that does not follow God's will. *(page 203)*

psalms Psalms are religious songs and prayers from the Old Testament. The psalms often express praise, thanksgiving, or sorrow. *(page 181)*

Purgatory Purgatory is a final purification from sin after death. *(page 261)*

resurrection Resurrection is the new life given to us when our bodies reunite with our souls at the end of time. *(page 261)*

Revelation Revelation is God's act of revealing himself and inviting us to respond with faith. *(page 31)*

reverence Reverence is honor and respect. We can show reverence for God through our prayers. *(page 183)*

Sacrament A Sacrament is a sacred sign and cause of grace instituted by Christ in the Church to continue his saving action through the Holy Spirit. *(page 159)*

sacramental A sacramental is a symbolic prayer, blessing, object, or action instituted by the Church that can lead us to a fuller participation in the grace of the Sacraments. *(page 159)*

sacramental grace Sacramental grace is the unique gift of God's love that we receive in each Sacrament. *(page 171)*

sacrifice A sacrifice is an act of unselfish giving. It is also a ritual offering made to God by a priest on behalf of the people. *(page 41)*

Sadducees Sadducees were Jewish people who accepted only the written law of the Old Testament and rejected spoken teachings and tradition. *(page 273)*

salvation Salvation is forgiveness of sins and restoration of friendship with God which can be done by God alone. *(page 203)*

Spiritual Works of Mercy The Spiritual Works of Mercy are loving deeds to meet the spiritual needs of others. *(page 287)*

supplication Supplication is humbly and earnestly asking for help. Like Esther, we address prayers of supplication to God. *(page 239)*

Temple The Temple was the Jewish place of worship in Jerusalem that contained the Ark of the Covenant. *(page 157)*

temple of the Holy Spirit Each of us is a temple of the Holy Spirit because the Holy Spirit dwells within us. As temples of the Holy Spirit, we are called to imitate Jesus. *(page 287)*

Theological Virtues The Theological Virtues—faith, hope, and charity—come from God and help us become more holy. They connect us with the Holy Trinity. *(page 229)*

transubstantiation Transubstantiation is the sacred mystery in which bread and wine are changed into the Real Presence of Jesus Christ. *(page 371)*

Yahweh Yahweh is the most sacred name of the God of Israel, revealed to Moses on Mount Sinai. It means "I am who I am." *(page 87)*

Index

Credits

COVER ILLUSTRATION: Richard Johnson/ The Organisation

SCRIPTURE ILLUSTRATION: Craig Orback/ Represented by Liz Sanders Agency; 28, 30, 42, 52, 64, 66, 86, 88, 100, 110, 112, 122, 144, 146, 158, 168-170, 180, 202, 204, 216-217, 230-231, 238-240, 260, 262, 274, 284, 286, 296-297, 328, 338, 352, 358

IMAGE CREDITS
8 (T) ©Tony Arrasmith; 8 (B) ©P Deliss/Getty; 10 ©jarenwicklund/Thinkstock; 11 ©Ewa Mazur/ Thinkstock; 12 ©monkeybusinessimages/ Thinkstock; 14 ©James, Laura (Contemporary Artist)/Private Collection/Bridgeman Images; 23 ©zepperwing/Thinkstock; 25 ©Gene Plaisted, OSC/The Crosiers; 26 ©Gene Plaisted, OSC/The Crosiers; 27 ©Toby Burrows/Getty; 33 ©RCL Benziger; 34 ©Yano Keisuke/Getty; 37 ©Noah Gutierrez/noahpgutierrez@yahoo.com; 38 (T) ©Gene Plaisted, OSC/The Crosiers; 38 (B) ©The Sacrifice of Isaac, 1603 (oil on canvas), Caravaggio, Michelangelo Merisi da (1571-1610)/Galleria degli Uffizi, Florence, Italy/Bridgeman Images; 39 ©akubzak/Thinkstock; 40 ©Bill Wittman; 41 ©Myrleen Pearson ; 44 © Steve Debenport/ Getty; 46 ©Purestock/Thinkstock; 49 ©Gene Plaisted, OSC/The Crosiers; 50 (T) ©Bildagentur-online /Getty; 50 (B) ©Cro Magnon/Alamy Stock Photo; 51 (T) ©David R. Frazier Photolibrary, Inc./Alamy Stock Photo; 51 (B) ©Robin Nelson/ Alamy Stock Photo; 56 ©Christie's Images Ltd./ Christie's Images Ltd./SuperStock; 58 ©mythja/ Thinkstock; 61 ©AFP/Getty; 62 ©Thekla Clark/ Contributor/Corbis Historical/Getty; 67 ©Gabriela Medina/Getty; 68 ©narvikk/Getty; 70 ©Charles Noble/Shutterstock; 73 ©Wavebreakmedia Ltd; 74 ©Bill Wittman; 75 ©Bill Wittman; 76 ©Bill Wittman; 81 ©David Henderson/Thinkstock ; 83 ©Noah Gutierrez/noahpgutierrez@yahoo.com; 84 ©National Maritime Museum, London; 85 ©John Sturrock/Alamy Stock Photo/Alamy; 85 ©KidStock/Getty; 90 ©Private Collection/ Peter Newark American Pictures/Bridgeman Images; 92 ©WitR/Thinkstock; 95 (T) ©Siri Stafford/Thinkstock; 95 (B) ©Noah Gutierrez/ noahpgutierrez@yahoo.com; 96 (T) ©Bill Wittman; 96 (B) ©Bettmann/Getty; 97 (T) ©Lawrence Migdale/Stock Boston; 97 (B) ©Joel S. Fishman/Photo Researchers, Inc.; 97 (B) QBS Learning Illustrations; 98 ©Bill Wittman; 99 QBS Learning Illustrations; 102 ©Franco Origlia/Stringer/Getty; 103 © WENN US/Alamy Stock Photo; 104 ©wayfarerlife/Thinkstock; 107 ©Tracy L. Christianson/portraitsofsaints.com; 108 ©Photononstop/Alamy Stock Photo; 109 ©Images-USA/Alamy Stock Photo; 113 (T) ©Rob Lewine/Getty; 113 (M) ©Christopher Futcher/Getty; 113 (B) ©Myrleen Pearson/Alamy Stock Photo; 114 ©Apic/Contributor/Getty; 115 QBS Learning Illustrations; 116 ©Ron Nickel/ Getty; 119 ©Gene Plaisted, OSC/The Crosiers; 120 (T) ©Bill Aron/PhotoEdit ; 120 (B) ©epa european pressphoto agency b.v./Alamy Stock Photo; 121 QBS Learning Illustrations; 125 ©Queen of the America's Guild; 127 (T) © Fuse/ Getty; 127 (B) ©AnnaPoguliaeva/Thinkstock; 128 ©Andrew_Mayovskyy/Thinkstock; 129 ©Andrew_Mayovskyy/Thinkstock; 132 ©Hero Images Inc./Alamy Stock Photo; 133 ©Marmaduke St. John/Alamy Stock Photo; 134 ©Blend Images/ Alamy Stock Photo; 135 ©RCL Benziger; 140 ©Christopher Futcher/Getty; 141 ©Reproduction by Dottie Mueller/fineartworkoffaith.com; 142 ©Medioimages/Photodisc/Thinkstock; 143 ©Juice Images/Alamy Stock Photo; 148 ©Courtesy of Franciscan Foundation for the Holy Land; 149 QBS Learning Illustrations; 150 ©Design Pics/Kristy-Anne Glubish/Getty; 153 ©Noah Gutierrez/noahpgutierrez@yahoo.com; 154 (T) ©Art Directors & TRIP/Alamy Stock Photo; 154 (B) ©Bill Wittman; 156 ©Bill Wittman; 159 QBS Learning Illustrations; 160 ©Bill Wittman; 161 QBS Learning Illustrations; 162 ©structuresxx/Thinkstock; 165 ©Tracy L. Christianson/portraitsofsaints.com; 166 ©Warner Bros./Kobal Collection/ The Picture Desk; 172 ©ACTIVE MUSEUM/Alamy Stock Photo; 174 ©psynovec/Thinkstock; 177 (T) ©Brand X Pictures/Exactostock-1555/SuperStock; 177 (B) ©Alex Ramsay/Alamy Stock Photo; 178 ©WikiCommons; 179 ©Danita Delimont/Getty; 184 ©1xpert/Thinkstock; 185 QBS Learning Illustrations; 186 ©Sean Pavone/Alamy Stock Photo; 189 ©Bill Wittman; 190 ©Tony Arrasmith; 191 ©Christopher Futcher/Getty; 192 ©Bob Mullen/www.catholicphotographer.com; 193 QBS Learning Illustrations; 197 ©Erich Lessing/Art Resource, NY; 198 ©SerrNovik/Thinkstock; 199 ©Tracy L. Christianson/portraitsofsaints.com; 200 ©dionisvero/Thinkstock; 201 ©Jim Whitmer; 206 ©Gene Plaisted, OSC/The Crosiers; 208 ©Gabriele Maltinti/Thinkstock; 211 (T) ©BC_DS Photo Illustration/Alamy Stock Photo; 211 (B) ©Noah Gutierrez/noahpgutierrez@yahoo.com; 212 ©Helen King/Getty; 213 (T) ©Shestock/ Getty; 213 (M) ©PeopleImages.com/Getty; 213 (B) ©Paul McGee/Getty; 214 ©Bill Wittman; 218 ©Gene Plaisted, OSC/The Crosiers; 219 ©Max Alexander/DK Images; 220 ©Kim Karpeles/ Alamy Stock Photo; 220 ©ESOlex/Thinkstock; 223 (T) ©Ted Foxx/Alamy Stock Photo; 223 (B) ©Mary Wessel; 224 (T) ©Erich Lessing/Art Resource NY; 224 (B) ©Chris Wozniak/Enchanted Realms; 225 ©Buccina Studios/Thinkstock; 228 ©Donald Iain Smith/Getty; 229 QBS Learning Illustrations; 232 ©panaramka/Thinkstock; 235 (B) ©Tracy L. Christianson/portraitsofsaints.com; 235 (T) QBS Learning Illustrations; 236 ©Wikimedia Commons; 242 ©Bill Wittman; 244 ©Sebastien Desarmaux /GODONG/Getty; 247 ©St. Nicholas Academy; 248 ©Bill Wittman; 249 ©Lisa F. Young/Alamy Stock Photo; 250 ©ZUMA Press Inc/Alamy Stock Photo; 251 QBS Learning Illustrations; 255 (T) ©ZoonarRF/ Thinkstock; 255 (B) ©Scala/ArtResource, NY; 257 QBS Learning Illustrations; 258 ©Agencja Fotograficzna Caro/Alamy Stock Photo; 259 ©Ian Shaw/Getty images; 264 ©Joe Viesti/Viesti Collection; 266 ©RubberBall Productions/Getty; 269 (T) ©RCL Benziger; 269 (B) ©Noah Gutierrez/ noahpgutierrez@yahoo.com; 270 ©Courtesty Subiaco Abbey and Academy; 272 ©Bill Wittman; 277 ©Bill Wittman; 278 ©LoweStock/Thinkstock; 281 ©Tracy L. Christianson/portraitsofsaints.com; 282 ©Design Pics Inc/Getty; 283 ©Phil Boorman/Getty; 285 (T) ©Bubbles Photolibrary/ Alamy Stock Photo; 285 (B) ©Radius Images/ Alamy Stock Photo; 288 ©Tim Graham//Getty; 289 QBS Learning Illustrations; 290 ©David Levenson/Getty; 293 (T) ©RCL Benziger; 293 (B) ©Mary Evans Picture Library/Alamy Stock Photo; 294 ©Design Pics/Design Pics CEF/Getty; 298 ©David Young-Wolff/PhotoEdit, Inc.; 299 ©Hanan Isachar/Israeli Images; 300 QBS Learning Illustrations; 301 QBS Learning Illustrations; 302 (T) ©ThinkStock; 302 (B) ©SuperStock; 305 ©Bill Wittman; 306 ©Bill Wittman; 307 ©PeopleImages.com/Getty; 308 ©Christopher Futcher/Getty; 312 QBS Learning Illustrations; 318 (T) ©Noah Gutierrez/noahpgutierrez@yahoo.com; 318 (B) ©Noah Gutierrez/noahpgutierrez@yahoo.com; 319 ©Noah Gutierrez/noahpgutierrez@yahoo.com; 320 ©Christie's Images/Bridgeman Images; 321 (T) ©Radius Images/Alamy Stock Photo; 321 (B) QBS Learning Illustrations; 322 ©shiny7777/Thinkstock; 323 ©Gene Plaisted, OSC/The Crosiers; 325 ©Jamie Kingham/Getty; 326 ©Attitude/Shutterstock; 327 QBS Learning Illustrations; 329 ©robertharding/Alamy Stock Photo; 330 ©Alex Ramsay/Alamy Stock Photo; 330 ©Gene Plaisted, OSC/The Crosiers; 331 ©Dottie Mueller/fineartworkoffaith.com; 332 (T) ©li jingwang/Getty; 332 (B) ©Fleckstone/ Shutterstock; 334 © Jose Luis Pelaez Inc/Getty; 335 ©age fotostock/Alamy Stock Photo; 336 ©Lars Justinen/GoodSalt; 340 ©Bill Wittman; 342 ©Givaga/Thinkstock; 344 ©Al Kancello/Alamy Stock Photo; 345 QBS Learning Illustrations; 346 ©James, Laura (Contemporary Artist)/Private Collection/Bridgeman Images; 347 ©BSIP SA/ Alamy Stock Photo; 348 ©Alena Brozova/Alamy Stock Photo; 356 ©rvika/Thinkstock; 360 (T) ©Chico Sanchez/Alamy Stock Photo; 360 (B) ©GL Archive/Alamy Stock Photo; 361 ©dpa picture alliance/Alamy Stock Photo; 362 ©El Greco; 363 ©Godong/Alamy Stock Photo; 365 ©Karen H. Ilagan/Alamy Stock Photo; 366 ©Myrleen Pearson/Alamy Stock Photo; 369 ©TIZIANA FABI/Stringer/Getty; 370 ©Fred de Noyelle/ Getty; 371 ©Bill Wittman; 372 ©Bill Wittman; 373 ©Gary Roebuck/Alamy Stock Photo; 374 ©Tony Arrasmith; 375 ©Gene Plaisted, OSC/ The Crosiers; 376 (T) ©Adie Bush/Getty; 376 (B) ©Jamie Grill/ Getty; 377 ©Bruce Ayres/Getty; 380 ©Gene Plaisted, OSC/The Crosiers; 381 ©Tim Graham/Getty; 382 ©Marmaduke St. John/ Alamy Stock Photo; 383 ©Wavebreakmedia Ltd/ Thinkstock; 384 ©Hydromet/Thinkstock; 385 ©Tracy L. Christianson/portraitsofsaints.com; 387 ©Wavebreak Media ltd/Alamy Stock Photo; 391 ©Thinkstock;